D0872383

Twenty-five Years
of the
Philadelphia Orchestra

1900-1925

Twenty-five Years

of the

Philadelphia Orchestra

1900-1925

By

FRANCES ANNE WISTER

BOOKS FOR LIBRARIES PRESS

FREEPORT, NEW YORK

First Published 1925

Reprinted 1970

STANDARD BOOK NUMBER:

8369-5492-0

LIBRARY OF CONGRESS CATALOG CARD NUMBER:

70-126265

PRINTED IN THE UNITED STATES OF AMERICA

TO

ALEXANDER VAN RENSSELAER, Esq.

DEVOTED TO
THE CAUSE OF MUSIC IN THIS CITY
AND
FIRST AND ONLY
PRESIDENT
OF
THE PHILADELPHIA ORCHESTRA
ASSOCIATION

FOREWORD

THIS story of the Philadelphia Orchestra has been written during the past few months, for the friends and supporters of the Philadelphia Orchestra Association.

My endeavor has been to give the account in a simple form and to use the Appendix for the statistics which should be recorded at a Twenty-fifth Anniversary.

FRANCES ANNE WISTER

OCTOBER, 1925

ACKNOWLEDGMENTS

With much appreciation of their assistance I desire to thank:

The Board of Directors of the Philadelphia Orchestra Association

and

The Women's Committees for the Philadelphia Orchestra, who have made it possible to publish this book.

Mr. Arthur Judson, Mr. Louis A. Mattson, Miss Ruth O'Neill, Miss E. M. Russell of the Philadelphia Orchestra Office.

Dr. Edward I. Keffer.

FRANCES ANNE WISTER

OCTOBER, 1925

Twenty-five Years

of the

Philadelphia Orchestra

1900-1925

Contents

Part I

APPENDIX

Illustrations

PART I

Twenty-five Years
of the Philadelphia Orchestra

1900-1925

CHAPTER I

A ROAD ONE HUNDRED AND FIFTY YEARS LONG
"Time Was unlocks the riddle of Time Is"

"By PARTICULAR DESIRE

"On Tuesday next, the 25th inst., at the Assembly Room in Lodge Alley will be performed a Concert of Music, under the direction of Mr. John Palma; to begin exactly at six o'clock.

"Tickets to be had at the London Coffee House, at one Dollar each; and no person to be admitted without a ticket."

Such in January, 1757, was the announcement of the first public concert in Philadelphia of which there is record. So began the approaches to the Philadelphia Orchestra, like the approaches to a great bridge which begin hundreds of feet away from the span.

There had been music in private and other entertainments previous to this public concert and in spite of the disapproval of the Society of Friends and of a number of religious sects music found its first refuge in the church. As early as 1701 Justus Falckner, a German Lutheran, wrote as follows:

"I will here take occasion to mention that many others besides myself who know the ways of the land, maintain that music would contribute much toward a good Christian service. It would not only attract and civilize the wild Indians, but it would do much good in spreading the Gospel truths among the sects and others by attracting them. Instrumental music is especially serviceable here. Thus a well-sounding organ would perhaps prove of great profit, to say nothing of the fact that the Indians would come running from far and near to listen to such unknown melody, and upon that account might become willing to accept our language and teaching, and remain with people who had such agreeable things; for they are said to come ever so far to listen to one who plays even a reed-pipe (rohrpfeiffe): such an extra-

*O. G. Sonneck: "Early Concert Life in America."

[3]

ordinary love have they for any melodious and ringing sound. Now as the melancholy, saturnine, stingy Quaker spirit has abolished (relegiert) all such music, it would indeed be a novelty here, and tend to attract many of the young people away from the Quakers and sects to attend services where such music was found, even against the wishes of their parents. This would afford a good opportunity to show them the truth and their error.''*

When Falckner was ordained in Gloria Dei Church in 1703, the Hermits of the Wissahickon played on the viol, hautboy, trumpets and kettledrums (Pauken) and the service was opened with a voluntary on the little organ, all of which he doubtless arranged and enjoyed. Gradually a number of other churches followed suit and installed organs.

In regard to secular music in private houses, letters testify to its existence early in the 18th century; and Whitefield on his arrival was an ally to its opponents. One of his followers printed this information for the public in 1740, although the statement was later denied:

"Since Mr. Whitefield's Preaching here, the Dancing School, Assembly and Concert Room have been shut up, as inconsistent with the Doctrine of the Gospel: and though the Gentlemen concern'd caus'd the Door to be broke open again, we are inform'd that no Company came to the last Assembly night."†

But music was craved by some of the inhabitants or a sensation would not have been made by the Musical Clock:

"The Unparallelled Musical Clock, made by that great Master of Machinery, David Lockwood. It excels all others in the Beauty of its Structure and plays the choicest Airs from the most celebrated Operas with the greatest Nicety and Exactness. It performs with beautiful graces, ingeniously and variously intermixed, the French Horn, Pieces, perform'd upon the Organ, German and Common Flute, Flageolet, etc., Sonata's, Concerto's, Marches, Minuetts, Jiggs and Scots Airs, composed by Corelli, Alberoni, Mr. Handel and other great and eminent Masters of Musick."

It was not until Mr. Palma's concert however, that there seems to have been any music for which the public could buy tickets. This pioneer effort was followed by others. The "Subscription Concerts of Musick" became fashionable in 1764; and later the fortnightly "City Concerts" under John Bentley at the City Tavern. The Amateur and Pro-

---

*J. F. Sachse: "The Missive of Justus Falckner of Germantown, Concerning the Religious Condition of Pennsylvania in the Year 1701."
†Robert R. Drummond: "Early German Music in Philadelphia."

fessional Concerts were a popular series. Groups of men fostered music as the years passed. Francis Hopkinson and his friends both professional and amateur assembled regularly to play "Concerti Grossi." This group of about twelve musicians probably formed Philadelphia's first Orchestra.

The first real musical impetus came undoubtedly from Francis Hopkinson, signer of the Declaration of Independence and later member of Congress. He was besides, a teacher, organist, poet, harpsichordist, essayist, improver of the harpsichord and the first American composer. Among his works are the song, "My Days have been so wondrous free," the earliest American secular composition extant; and "Seven Songs" dedicated to Washington. John Adams described him as:—"One of your pretty, little curious, ingenious men. His head is not bigger than a large apple. I have not met with anything in natural history more amusing and entertaining than his personal appearance, yet he is genteel and well bred, and is very social."**

Other composers were not lacking as is seen by the announcement of John Gualdo, in 1769, of a concert in which five out of thirteen numbers were composed by him. This is the first recorded composers' concert in this country and his name appeared with those of the famous composers of Europe of the day, as Philadelphia was never far behind.

Benjamin Franklin interested himself in the art and constructed an improved Armonica or Musical Glasses. Thus two important public men of the time gave music their sanction and assisted its cause.

As the city grew the people began to feel the need of instruction in music. From early times Philadelphia had its share of music teachers, the first one to publicly advertise, being a woman. Among them were a number of excellent Englishmen who presented at concerts the works of the great masters of Europe; and there were a few Germans. One of these was an accomplished person if the following announcement which appeared in 1755, be true:

*"The subscriber proposes to open a school on Monday next, in the house where the late Mr. Quin formerly dwelt, for the instruction of Gentlemen and Ladies, in the following accomplishments:

**Sonneck: "Francis Hopkinson and James Lyon."

"First, The French, Italian and German languages, in a method concise and easy.

"Secondly, To play on the violin after the Italian manner, with a peculiar method of bowing and shifting in solos or concertos.

"Thirdly, Drawing and miniature painting with colours, flowers, insects, etc. . . . Likewise to draw patterns for embroidery, or any kind of needle work . . . .

"He has a variety of music, composed by the most eminent masters, for the violino solo, concembalo et violoncello, to be disposed of on easy terms.

"JOHN MATTHIAS KRAMER"

Another German was H. B. Victor, who described himself as follows:

"Mr. Victor, Musician to her late Royal Highness the Princess of Wales, and Organist at St. George's in London, lately arrived here, takes this method of acquainting the Musical Gentry in general that he gives instructions on the Harpsichord, or Forte Piano, Violin, German Flute, etc., especially in the thorough Bass both in theory and practice, for that his pupils may soon come to a fundamental knowledge of that fine science.

"N. B. Mr. Victor intended to give a concert, and to perform on his new musical instruments, but is obliged to postpone it for want of able hands; the one he calls Tromba doppia con Tympana, on which he plays the first and second trumpet and a pair of annexed kettle-drums with the feet all at once; the other is called cymbaline de amour, which resembles the musical glasses played by harpsichord keys, never subject to come out of tune, both of his own invention. He is to be met with at his house in Callowhill street near Water street."*

The many quaint advertisements of those times give an idea of the musical activities of the people. Amateurs often assisted professionals.

Joseph Cézar, pupil of Viotti, in 1792, announced that: "Many amateurs of the first eminence being so kind as to honor him with their patronage, will perform," etc. Again we hear of "a young lady who has never before appeared in public and therefore craves protection from all manner of insult." Often the professional was "assisted by a gentleman." Infant prodigies, who were always under ten, were numerous and they had invariably appeared before the crowned heads of Europe.

Organ dealers, spinet, harpsichord and piano makers, as well as dealers in musical merchandise began to appear.

*Drummond: "Early German Music in Philadelphia."

[6]

Michael Hillegas, first Treasurer of the United States and first music dealer in Philadelphia, dealt in organs as early as 1753. His stock of music embraced all the popular and standard compositions of the day, and included those of Tartini, Tessorini, Pepush, Corelli, Handel, Vivaldi, Burney, Stamitz, Barbella, and Scarlatti. Besides sheet music, many other articles were to be had at his shop as we see from this advertisement:

> "To be sold by Michall Hillegas, at his House in Second street, opposite Samuel Morris, Esq., an extraordinary good and neat Harpsichord with four stops; a good Violin-cello, an Assortment of English and Italian Violins, as well as common ones, as double lined, of which some extraordinary; a parcel of good German Flutes, imported here from Italy. Also imported in the last ships from London, a large Assortment of Musick, of the best Masters, viz: Solos, Overtures, Concertos, Sonatas, and Duets, for Violins, German Flutes, Hautboys, French Horns, Violoncellos, and Guitars, Voluntaries, Lessons for Organs and Harpsichords, ruled paper of various Sorts for Musick, and Musick Books, Tutors or Books of Instructions to learn to play on the Violin, German Flute, Hautboy, or Common Flute, without a Master, Song Books, Cantatas, Songs on Sheets, and a Choice Parcel of Violin Strings, etc."* (Penna. Gazette, 1759.)

John Behrent has the honor of being the first piano forte maker in this city. In 1775 his advertisement in the Pennsylvania Packet informed the public that:

> "John Behrent, Joiner and Instrument Maker living in Third street continued in Campington, directly opposite Coate's Burying-ground, Has just finished for Sale, an extraordinary fine instrument, by the name of Piano Forte, of Mahogany, in the manner of an harpsichord, with hammers, and several changes: He intends to dispose of it on very reasonable terms: and being a master of such sort of work, and a new beginner in this country, he requests all lovers of music to favour him with their custom, and they shall not only be honestly served, but their favours gratefully acknowledged, by their humble servant, John Behrent."*

Familiar professional names in the early days were James Bremner, teacher of Hopkinson, John Gualdo, Stephen Forrage, George d'Eissenburg, Philip Roth, Philip Phile, John Bentley, Henri Capron, A. Juhan, Andrew Adgate, and Victor Pelissier, nearly all of whom were teachers as well as performers and were strong influences in the musical life of Philadelphia and in the training of the young who were early taught to crave the best musically.

*Drummond: "Early German Music in Philadelphia."

The American Revolution caused concerts and other entertainments to be almost entirely abandoned, with the exception of the Mischianza and other affairs in which the British were the leading spirits. Little occurred during this period to advance musical art.

With the country again at peace and with the dawn of a new century, interest in music revived and early in 1820 eighty-five men organized the Musical Fund Society, so far Philadelphia's greatest musical achievement. The officers and directors chosen on January 29th, 1820, were:

Dr. William P. De Wees, *President*
Dr. Robert Patterson, *Vice-president*
Daniel Lammot, *Treasurer*
John K. Kane, *Secretary*

Managers of the Fund: James W. Barker, Thomas Artley, Francis G. Smith, Edward Hudson, Benjamin Carr, William Strickland, Henry P. Barrekens, William Hawkins, Charles A. Poulson, Benjamin Say, George Schetky and Andrew Farrouihl.

The Charter states "That the essential objects of the said corporation shall be the relief of decayed musicians and their families and the cultivation of skill and diffusion of taste in music." Four years later Musical Fund Hall was built at Eighth and Locust streets. For over thirty years this building was the centre of all music in Philadelphia, except opera. The Society maintained an orchestra and a chorus, and conducted an Academy of Music, which was the first school in Philadelphia permitted by Charter to confer Academic degrees in music. The orchestra of the Musical Fund Society was composed of its members, professional and amateur, and there were strict regulations as to rehearsals. They were players of no mean attainments for their time, and it is to be regretted that the influx of dazzling foreign performers was permitted to quench the ardor of the audiences and finally their own. The quality of the music performed was of a high order and compared favorably with that of Europe and of other American cities of that period. The "Creation" was chosen for the first concert, but the music could not be procured in Baltimore, New York or Boston, or even in Europe, so the plan was abandoned. When it was first produced trombone players were engaged to come from Bethlehem, as there were none in this town. Indeed, the instrument itself was unknown and aroused much curiosity. Later at these concerts (1845), Beethoven's Symphony No. 1 was given in full. It was announced as "The Entire Grand Symphony of Beethoven," and between the movements were vocal numbers serious and comic. During the next season the Second Symphony was given in the same way, and two years later came the "Eroica," the Overture to Oberon, and the Midsummer Night's Dream.

When the period of the great visiting virtuosi, Jenny Lind, Henriette Sontag, Vieuxtemps, Wilhelmj, Ole Bull, Sivori, Malibran, Lagrange, Alboni, Hensler, Gottschalk and others arrived, the excitement over their first appearances caused a decrease in interest in home talent and achievements, and the activities of the Musical Fund Society were maintained with less and less enthusiasm, until finally the Academy and then the orchestra were abandoned. Another reason for this decline was the growing popularity of opera, to the detriment of personal musical effort by Philadelphians.

During the early years of the nineteenth century, as in the preceding one, Philadelphia was the abiding place of a number of excellent and hard working musicians. These carried on the labors of their predecessors by teaching the young, leading choirs and guiding the musical opinion of the city. Little recognition has been given these men, who included among their number, Alexander Reinagle, George Shetky, Benjamin Carr, Benjamin Cross, Raynor Taylor, Thomas Loud, Charles P. Hupfeldt, and later Charles Jarvis and his son, Charles J. Jarvis.

In our own time among the many musicians who have fostered music here by their own example and by training others, four should be particularly mentioned:

Dr. Hugh A. Clarke, for fifty years Professor of Music at the University of Pennsylvania, whose sway has been felt through the many students who have studied under him; Wm. W. Gilchrist, his pupil; Michael H. Cross, and Richard Zeckwer. These men wielded so potent an influence over music students and music lovers, that Philadelphians owe them a heavy debt. They received the musical laying on of hands and transmitted the traditions that have existed here for two hundred years.

The important undertaking of the middle of the century was the building of the American Academy of Music.

With the growth of population and the increasing number of visiting opera companies, a demand arose for an opera house of adequate size and equipment. In 1852 the project was launched and a Charter obtained, but the amount of money needed, $400,000, was difficult to procure, and it was not until January 26th, 1857, that the Academy was opened with a grand ball. This eclipsed in size and brilliance any assemblage hitherto seen in Philadelphia, and was followed on February 25th, by the first performance of opera in the new house. "Il Trovatore" was presented with Gazzaniga, Aldini, Brignoli and Amodio, and this marked the beginning of the splendid career of the Academy of Music. Gradually other musical events were transferred to the Academy, which became, and still remains, the musical centre of the city.

Now the days of modern orchestral development are at hand. The first visiting orchestra of note was the Steiermärkisches Orchestra, of twenty musicians, under the leadership of Henri Riha, which came from Germany in 1838.

Ten years later the Germania Musical Society, from Berlin, appeared under the leadership of Carl Lenshow. Pecuniary losses caused it to disband and the members scattered. Later the Society was reorganized under Carl Bergmann. It had the honor of appearing at Sontag's concert, in 1852.

The Germania Orchestra, instituted in 1856 and incorporated in 1860, succeeded this Society and for over forty years was an important part of Philadelphia's musical life. Carl Sentz, the drummer of the Steiermärkisches Orchestra, became the first leader. Its concerts were given on Friday afternoons at Musical Fund Hall, at the price of two concerts for twenty-five cents, and packages of eight tickets for a dollar, which price was later raised to twenty-five cents per concert. Sentz was succeeded by Charles M. Schmitz, the 'cellist, who in turn was followed by William Stoll, Jr. Unlike the custom of today the Germania was governed by a conductor and officers chosen by its members. The performances were not confined to classical concerts, but it played engagements for private dances, balls, festivals, oratorios, fairs, commencements, and other miscellaneous entertainments. Besides the performances at Musical Fund Hall, concerts were given on Thursday afternoons at the Pennsylvania Academy of the Fine Arts, from 1879 until 1895, inclusive. It was then customary to play one movement of a symphony each week for four weeks and at the fifth concert to play the whole. Charles M. Schmitz, who so long gave Philadelphians the satisfaction of hearing symphonic music which was their own, was the son of Adolph Schmitz, of Düsseldorf, player of the French horn. He taught woodwind and brass instruments in the Academy of the Musical Fund Society, and had the distinction of being the first musician brought to America for the purpose of teaching.

The Germania Orchestra finally disbanded and orchestral ventures were undertaken at Musical Fund Hall, Witherspoon Hall and the Academy of Music. Mr. Henry Gordon Thunder and Mr. Wm. Stoll, Jr., were active in these efforts, but lack of money hampered the results. Tickets were sold at five for one dollar and twenty for four dollars. The programmes included one or two movements of a symphony or concerto and miscellaneous selections now no longer played.

An interesting enterprise in the musical world was the Philadelphia May Festival, in 1883, of which Mr. S. Decatur Smith was President, Mr. F. T. Sully Darley, Vice-president, and Mr. George Burnham, Jr. and Mr. Hartman Kuhn among the directors. Wm. W. Gilchrist and Charles M. Schmitz were the musical directors. Aside from the advantages derived from this series of concerts, it is worthy of record that Mr. Darley was the first Vice-president of the Philadelphia Orchestra Association and Mr. Burnham and Mr. Kuhn were charter members, while Mr. Smith was one of the original guarantors.

The Philadelphia Symphony Society 1893–1900.

The need of more orchestral concerts was evidently felt, for in 1893 the Philadelphia Symphony Society was organized by amateurs and incorporated for the purpose of "the cultivation of the higher order of Orchestral Work and the fostering of all matters tending to promote the cause of music."

The Society was fortunate in procuring as its first leader, Dr. Wm. Wallace Gilchrist, founder of the Mendelssohn Club in 1875, and its conductor for forty years. Members paid no fees or dues and the three concerts given each year in the Academy of Music were supported by the Associate membership. The two upper galleries were reserved for music students in the public schools and conservatories, and about fifteen hundred such tickets were distributed for each performance. The Society possessed a musical Library and a Reading Room. Rehearsals were open to accredited music students, much to the benefit of those who were studying orchestration. It also fostered chamber music by bringing the Kneisel Quartette to Philadelphia during sixteen seasons.

After the resignation of Dr. Gilchrist, Fritz Scheel became the conductor. The list of works performed under both leaders was of the highest standard and would do credit to any professional orchestra. The place of this amateur orchestra in the symphonic succession is a noble one and one of immense influence in this community. The incentive that it gave to young players was worth all the expense and effort involved. Scheel had hesitated when asked to become leader of an amateur organization for fear of endangering his reputation. Therefore, when the Philippine Concerts were arranged, a separate committee was formed having no connection with the Philadelphia Symphony Society.

In 1900 the Society disbanded and sold to the Executive Committee of the Philadelphia Orchestra its library, a set of kettledrums and its music desks, and issued the following circular to its members:

"The Society, always active in promoting the musical interests of Philadelphia, gave its earnest and hearty assistance to the organizing of the Philadelphia Orchestra, which, now established on a firm basis and fortunate in its splendid personnel of professional musicians, is in a position to continue orchestral work in Philadelphia and carry it to a point beyond the possibilities of amateurs. For this new orchestra, which aims to do and can do so much for music in Philadelphia, the Society asks from its associate members the same generous support that heretofore has been given to our amateur organization."

Thus ended the only connection that ever existed between the Philadelphia Symphony Society and the Philadelphia Orchestra, which was that Fritz Scheel led this amateur orchestra for one season before the formation of the Philadelphia Orchestra, composed entirely of professional Philadelphia musicians.

Besides the impetus given to music in Philadelphia by the Musical Fund Society, the Germania Orchestra, and the Philadelphia Symphony Society, another group of musicians has been important in this community since 1893. The Manuscript Music Society founded by Dr. Gilchrist for the encouragement of native composers, continues to have a far-reaching effect on our musical life and is of fundamental value.

Years passed and the fact became more and more accentuated in the minds of musicians that Philadelphia, a city of 1,500,000 people, was dependent on visiting orchestras for the performance of great orchestral works. But while they were despairing of ever seeing in this city an orchestra akin to the modern ones in Europe and in other American cities, a seed was germinating. Philadelphia had had a taste of what a modern orchestra was, as far back as 1876, when Theodore Thomas played at the Centennial Exhibition, under the auspices of a Women's Committee, headed by Mrs. E. D. Gillespie. The concerts were given up for lack of support, but a sip of ambrosia can never be forgotten. It is to Mr. Thomas and to Mrs. Gillespie, pioneers in the modern orchestral world, that we owe the Philadelphia Orchestra today. Mrs. Gillespie made another effort in 1881, on her return from a sojourn in Germany, for she realized that there were no musical advantages for students in Philadelphia to compare with those in Germany or in Boston, where Mr. Higginson had lately founded the Boston Symphony Orchestra. She invited Theodore Thomas to come to Philadelphia, give a series of symphony concerts, and share the profits. A few musicians supported this enterprise, but for the majority the programmes were severe and boring, and when after four seasons the profits were found to be $28.00, the attempt to establish a large modern orchestra in this city was abandoned. Thomas was lost to Philadelphia because the time was not ripe. This be said to our regret, not to our shame. As Mrs. Cornelius Stevenson remarked many years afterwards, one cannot feed meat to babes. Even twenty years later the majority of Philadelphia citizens felt that the season was being forced,

[13]

when after a number of unsuccessful attempts the Philadelphia Orchestra was founded.

However, memories of Theodore Thomas, father of American orchestras, lingered in the minds of a few music-lovers, and their longing was increased by regular visits from the Boston Symphony Orchestra, which gave five and later ten concerts each season. Many people can bear witness to the joy that they felt when Gericke and Nickisch brought that orchestra here. Soon the jealousy of Philadelphia was aroused at hearing that Theodore Thomas was to settle in Chicago. The West had seized the pioneer leader whom we might have had. Philadelphia's eyes also turned to New York City, where Dr. Leopold Damrosch and his son, Walter, and Anton Seidl led orchestras; and where the Philharmonic Society had long had an honorable career. Still Philadelphia made no move. Then, in January, 1899, it occurred to a group of women to raise a fund of $100,000 and bring to Philadelphia as a nucleus the New York Symphony Society under Mr. Walter Damrosch; fill it out with the best available musicians and call it the Philadelphia Orchestra. A circular to this effect was issued with the result that a storm of protest arose headed by another group of women, during which much newspaper publicity was given to the subject of an orchestra for this city. Finally the matter was adjusted and a committee of women issued a prospectus for a Philadelphia Orchestra of which the principal points are quoted :*

Prospectus of Philadelphia Permanent Orchestra

* * * * *

"In order to establish an orchestra such as would be a distinct credit to the city, it is necessary to have a paid-up fund of not less than $250,000.

* * * * *

"1. Subscribers shall not be bound by their subscriptions unless the sum of $200,000 shall have been subscribed.

"2. The fund shall be used only for the purpose of establishing and maintaining a Permanent Philadelphia Orchestra, and it shall be applied for that purpose by the following Trustees:

C. William Bergner	Chas. C. Harrison
John H. Converse	C. Hartman Kuhn
Samuel A. Crozer	Simon A. Stern
Geo. W. Childs Drexel	James F. Sullivan
Thos. B. Wanamaker	

*For full text of Prospectus, see Appendix M.

[14]

The Trustees shall invest $200,000 of the fund, using only the interest thereof and the additional $50,000 shall be used for current expenses of the first few years, when the expenses will be heavier and the deficit greater.

"3. The orchestra shall be composed, first, of the best musicians resident in Philadelphia; then, of the best musicians obtainable either in this country or abroad.

* * * * *

"4. The Board of Trustees, when it considers that the completion of the fund is assured, shall select the leader upon the careful and unbiased consideration of the merits and records of all candidates submitted to it."

* * * * *

Subscriptions towards this immense sum of money — $250,000*—did not come in fast, and finally the proposition was abandoned under the prospect of a Philadelphia Orchestra formed on a very different and much more modest plan. There are two ways of embarking on an enterprise, one is to procure the funds in advance on faith; the other is to start the undertaking on faith and hope for the best to pay the bills. The first plan failed, the second succeeded; and after twenty years of effort, an orchestra was financially established in Philadelphia.

---

*After a year of work the total sum promised was $50,000.

Chapter II

The Last Turn of the Road

The last turn of the road was a long one.   It led from Germany to New York, to the World's Fair in Chicago, to San Francisco, back to New York and to Woodside Park, Philadelphia. The turn was made by Fritz Scheel.

The beginning of the Philadelphia Orchestra was the moment in July, 1899, when Mrs. Innes, wife of Bandmaster Frederic N. Innes, showed some programmes to Dr. Edward I. Keffer and asked whether he had heard Fritz Scheel and his orchestra at Woodside Park. At that moment the man for whom Philadelphia had been waiting was found; and when the place and the man come together the hour has come. Was it chance or was it fate that caused that question to be asked? Who shall determine?

Dr. Keffer speedily went to Woodside Park* and was so pleased with what he heard that he recommended his friends to go to hear Scheel's masterly leading and fine concerts, besides mailing several hundred programmes to the musicians of his acquaintance. He found to his surprise that in one week a Wagner Night, a Beethoven Night and a Symphony Night were included. Many of the listeners were convinced that Scheel was the man to organize an orchestra in Philadelphia. He was competent to do it, he had no permanent position and he saw the opportunity. Mr. John Fasshauer, an active member in Mr. Thunder's orchestra, succeeded in arranging a meeting of professional musicians, who consented to enter into a liberal agreement as to salaries and services. Still a guarantee fund seemed to be a necessity. The plan proposed was to continue the Friday afternoon concerts, long a feature here, under Fritz Scheel at the Academy of Music. A conference was held at the University Club with Mr. John H. Converse, Mr. George Burnham, Jr., and Mr. Thomas a'Becket. The question of a fund was discussed and Mr. Converse, a trustee of the proposed Permanent Orchestra, suggested that the Women's Committee

---

*At this time Willow Grove Park, fifteen miles out of Philadelphia, was the foremost summer musical center.

ALEXANDER VAN RENSSELAER, ESQ.

for that orchestra should co-operate. This plan did not succeed, however, and the idea of a Friday afternoon series was abandoned.

Finally, after much effort, terms were agreed to by which Mr. Scheel consented to remain in Philadelphia. He was to conduct three different enterprises during the winter:

1. The Philadelphia Symphony Society, a well-established amateur orchestra organization (with weekly rehearsals and three public performances).

2. The Opera Class (an amateur chorus meeting weekly at Mrs. Alexander J. Cassatt's house).

3. A week's series of Popular Concerts during October at the National Export Exposition at the Commercial Museum in West Philadelphia.

He was to receive $1000 from each of these associations. He accepted with the provision that at the end of the season he should be given the opportunity to conduct two concerts with an orchestra of professional musicians.

The winter passed and in the early spring Scheel asked to have this part of the contract fulfilled. Like the ogre in the fairy tale, who always claims the beautiful princess, it must have seemed to the men, who had no idea how they were going to keep that promise. Scheel had given this as his only reason for staying, for he wanted a chance to show what he could do with professionals. However, having given their word, a committee was formed consisting of Mr. John H. Ingham, Mr. Oliver Boyce Judson, Dr. Edward I. Keffer, Mr. Edward G. McCollin and Mr. Oscar A. Knipe. Scheel selected his players by visiting the theatres and making notes each evening about the various musicians in the orchestras. At this point his task was easy compared to that of the Executive Committee who were responsible for the financial side of the concerts. Various benefits were contemplated and finally a decision was arrived at through the presence in Philadelphia of Lillie Langtry, who was acting for the benefit of the families of soldiers fallen in the Boer War. Why should not this undertaking be a patriotic one likewise? Why not assist the families of soldiers and sailors fallen and disabled in the Philippines? No sooner said than done. Mrs. Alexander J. Cassatt had a son in the army, and was speedily interested in a plan to raise money for the families of our own men in the service. She embraced the idea with enthusiasm, formed a committee of prominent women and carried the concerts through brilliantly and efficiently. The Executive Committee managed the musical end, and Mrs. Cassatt's Committee of Women advertised the concerts, procured the support of musical and social organizations, secured the patronesses, and filled the house. The tickets were sold at auction with much profit.

The concerts were advertised as follows:

"Our Soldiers and Sailors.
Academy of Music
Thursday, March 29th and April 5th, 3.30 P. M.

Two Orchestral Concerts under the direction of Mr. Fritz Scheel will be given for the Relief of the Families of the Nation's Heroes killed in the Philippines.

Soloist for the first concert: M. VLADIMIR DEPACHMANN
PROGRAMME

Weber..Overture "Euryanthe"
GOLDMARK......................Symphony, "A Rustic Wedding"
CHOPIN....................................Concerto in F minor
SCHUMANN..."Abendlied"
BIZET.....................................Scherzo, Suite Roma
LISZT.............................Rhapsodie Ongroise, No. 2

Soloist for second concert: M. EDOUARD DE RESZKE

Contributions to the Cause may be sent to Mrs. F. A. Packard, Treasurer, No. 110 S. Eighteenth Street."

"Our Soldiers and Sailors
On April 5th, at 3.30 P. M.
Second Concert by an Orchestra of Eighty
Philadelphia Musicians
Under the Direction of MR. FRITZ SCHEEL

For the Relief of the Families of men killed in the Philippines. MR. EDOUARD DE RESZKE, the famous Basso, will sing."

PROGRAMME

BEETHOVEN..................................Symphony "Eroica"
MEYERBEER.....Aria, "O Jours Heureux" (from L'Etoile du Nord)
WAGNER...............................Vorspiel, "Lohengrin"
HOFMANN.."Im Sonnenschein"
VERDI.............................Aria, "Infelice" (Ernani)
LISZT.............................First Hungarian Rhapsody

"THE PHILIPPINE CONCERTS*
MARCH 29, 1900–APRIL 5
UNDER THE PATRONAGE OF
800 PHILADELPHIA MEN AND WOMEN

*Programme of March 27th and 28th, 1925.

[18]

"Philadelphians generally do not know that The Philadelphia Orchestra first appeared in this City of Brotherly Love in disguise, a patriotic one, but none-the-less, a disguise. Had it tried to stalk boldly through the city gates, it would have been riddled by the guns of a critical public which disagreed at every point when a permanent orchestra was discussed.

"The fact was not made public that these concerts for the benefit of the families of American soldiers and sailors fallen in the Philippines were a preliminary experiment, but on November 16, 1900, as a result of their success, the first concert of The Philadelphia Orchestra took place.

"The Committee of Women which launched the concerts, hardly realized that through their efforts a new era in Philadelphia music was being inaugurated. The Executive Committee of men behind the project had such an end in view, but they preferred to remain unknown.

"The concerts were devoted to a popular benefit. They were also the means of carrying out with Fritz Scheel, leader of the amateur Philadelphia Symphony Society, a contract that he should have a public appearance with an orchestra of professional musicians.

"The concerts were brilliantly successful and realized a net profit of $10,252.73. The musicians played at less than Union rates for thirty-six rehearsals and two performances, and Mr. Scheel gave his services.

"The attitude of the public during these years is revealed in the fact that it seemed natural for a group of women to sponsor concerts for war heroes; but in 1904 it seemed an unheard of innovation that women should organize to further the interests of a permanent orchestra.

"Many people who prize The Philadelphia Orchestra as the greatest treasure we possess, remember only too well the days when Philadelphia was dependent on visiting orchestras. Young people today have the good fortune to live in a town where an orchestra of the highest artistic standards under a leader of world-wide reputation is now firmly established. Music lovers and citizens generally, are grateful to the men and women of courage, who gave Fritz Scheel his first opportunity in Philadelphia."

"COMMITTEE OF WOMEN

Mrs. Alexander J. Cassatt, Chairman; Miss Harriet Buchanan, Secretary; Mrs. Frederick A. Packard, Treasurer; Mrs. C. William Bergner, Mrs. Henry C. Boyer, Mrs. Edward Coles, Mrs. Joseph G. Darlington, Mrs. Frank H. Rosengarten, Mrs. Barclay H. Warburton, Mrs. Charles S. Whelen, Mrs. J. B. Sands, wife of Captain Sands, of the Naval Home; and Miss Meade, daughter of the late General George Gordon Meade.

"EXECUTIVE COMMITTEE

MR. JOHN H. INGHAM, of the Melody Club
MR. OLIVER BOYCE JUDSON, of the Operatic Society
MR. EDWARD I. KEFFER, of the Philadelphia Symphony Society
MR. EDWARD G. McCOLLIN, of the Orpheus Club
MR. OSCAR A. KNIPE

The *Philadelphia Times*, March 30, 1900:

"When Johnny comes marching home again from the Philippines he will find that the girl he left behind him has had a place in the hearts of Philadelphia matrons at least. That interest was evidenced in the first of the two widely heralded concerts in the soldiers' and sailors' aid, which took place at the Academy yesterday afternoon. Society turned out bravely and filled the whole of the auditorium and the balcony, but there, unfortunately, it stopped, and the upper part of the house, though the labors of the ladies interested have been unflagging and strenuous, had plenty of room.

"Pacing up and down the corridors were privates from the Arsenal and tars from the Navy Yard. In braided dress uniforms of brilliant blue, shining helmets and buttons that glistened like molten gold, the soldiers stalked to and fro, their belted waists giving pointers to the masculine followers of the latest fad, and their shoulders putting to shame the well cottoned ones of the 'swells' standing near. The tars in their flapping breeches and spreading collars, were a picturesque element among so many landsmen, and they, too, sold programmes, and made good salesmen. On the stage guns were stacked at the sides and colors dipped from the stacks."

It is well to reiterate here that the Philadelphia Orchestra is not and never was a continuation of the amateur Philadelphia Symphony Society. Only one member of that organization played at the Philippine Concerts.

These concerts were so successful and so warmly received, that steps were taken to organize a committee to continue concerts by Philadelphia musicians. Later in the spring of 1900, a meeting was called in the Orpheus Club Rooms by Dr. Richard J. Dunglison, President of the Musical Fund Society. Officers of various musical organizations, representatives of the press and prominent men in civic affairs were present. A plan for organization was discussed and the necessity for a Guarantee Fund was emphasized. The same committee of gentlemen was appointed, with the addition of Mr. John C. Sims, as Treasurer. Within four weeks of the second Philippine concert, the first circular announcing the plan for forming a Philadelphia Orchestra was mailed by this Committee:

"A Plan to Develop the Orchestral
Resources of Philadelphia

"The plan briefly outlined herein is addressed to all those people who are interested in good music and have at heart a desire to propagate musical culture in Philadelphia.

"Much interest has been aroused by the successful result attained in the symphony concerts recently given for the benefit of the sufferers through the Philippine War. It is thought that these concerts proved the availability of many of our resident players, and that the experiment might well be followed by a series of concerts during the season of 1900–1901, conducted upon the same general plan.

"The project of a permanent Philadelphia Orchestra is at present not sufficiently advanced to permit of the hope that such a body can be organized in time to be heard next season; therefore, the series of concerts herein proposed will not conflict with, but will further that movement, because it will provide the resident players with a season's training in symphonic work and thus enable them better to fill positions in the permanent orchestra when it shall need their services.

"The proposed plan embraces a series of about six evening and possibly two afternoon concerts, to be given in the Academy of Music, at customary concert prices. It has been ascertained that each concert with its rehearsals will cost about $2000, an expense that will be covered by a sale of two-thirds of the house.

"Hitherto it has been impracticable, when concerts have been given by local orchestral players, to arrange for a sufficient number of rehearsals. As a rule it has been impossible to obtain more than a single rehearsal. The present scheme contemplates at least five or six rehearsals for each concert.

"Mr. Scheel's reputation abroad, where he was a colleague of von Bülow, Brahms, Joachim, Sarasate, D'Albert and Wilhelmj, and conductor of orchestras in Schwerin, Chemnitz and Hamburg, was a guarantee of what was to have been expected of him here. The professional musicians of Philadelphia are virtually unanimous in expressing hearty admiration for his rare ability as a leader; they acknowledge that his work among them this winter has been a real stimulus to the advancement of their art, and they therefore desire to secure the advantage of his services next season.

"In order to insure the financial success of the proposed concerts, it has been deemed advisable to raise a guarantors' fund of at least $10,000. No payment of money is asked for at the present time; but all who are willing to become guarantors are requested to send in their names and addresses to the Secretary of the Committee, Mr. John H. Ingham, 505 Chestnut Street, stating the amount of their subscription, which, however, shall not be binding until the total sum of at least $10,000 shall be reached.

"As the Committee wishes particularly to obtain a large number of subscribers to the fund, it will be glad to accept contributions of any amount not less than five dollars.

* * * * *

"Committee:

Henry Whelen, Jr.
John C. Sims
Edward G. McCollin
Oscar A. Knipe
Dr. Edward I. Keffer
Oliver Boyce Judson

April 30, 1900   John H. Ingham"

A Guarantee Fund of $15,000 was raised from one hundred and twenty people*, a difficult task in those days, for an untried plan; and six evening concerts were given during the winter of 1900–1901.

The Committee invited four thousand women to be patronesses, and issued many circulars. It was the personal work, however, that accomplished the result in 1900, and that has continued to accomplish results during twenty-five years. Guarantors and patronesses were accorded the privilege of securing seats, for which there was no demand, in advance.

PHILADELPHIA ORCHESTRA**
Mr. Fritz Scheel, *Conductor*
First Concert
Friday, November 16th, 1900, at 8.15 P. M.
PROGRAMME

Carl Goldmark....................Overture "In Spring," Op. 36
Ludwig von Beethoven........Symphony No. 5, C minor, Op. 67
    I. Allegro con brio............................2–4
    II. Andante con moto.........................3–8
    III. Allegro....................................3–4
    IV. Allegro....................................4–4
Peter Ilitsch Tschaikowsky........Concerto for Pianoforte No. 1,
B-flat minor, Op. 23
    I. Allegro non troppo e molto maestoso........3–4
    II. Andantino simplice.......................6–8
    III. Allegro con fuoco.........................3–4
Karl Maria von Weber........"Invitation to the Dance," Op. 65
Orchestration by Felix Weingartner
Richard Wagner..............Entry of the Gods in "Walhalla,"
from "Das Rheingold."
Soloist
Mr. Ossip Gabrilowitsch

This concert was herald as a musical and social event and the newspapers were highly commendatory and friendly in tone.

---
*See Appendix D.
**For remaining programmes see Appendix J.

"Orchestra Concerts Open Auspiciously
"Philadelphia Getting in Line With Boston, Chicago and New York in having Home Organization.
"Ossip Gabrilowitsch,

"The Russian pianist made his Philadelphia début last night.

"The series of concerts by the Philadelphia Orchestra opened under notably happy auspices in the Academy of Music last evening. The musical and social interests engaged constituted the occasion an exceptional one.

"From the results evinced in the performance of the programme under Mr. Scheel's direction it must be regarded as well as marking a distinct period in the musical advancement of the city. Not the least interesting evidences of general sympathy with the movement to place Philadelphia in line with Boston, Chicago, and other cities in the possession of an established orchestra was the fact that Mr. William Stoll, Jr., and Mr. Henry Gordon Thunder, both identified with the endeavor to advance this branch of work in the past, figure in the present movement, the one as a violinist in the organization, the other as a guarantor.

"The Philadelphia Orchestra, as it exists, is, with slight exception, what its name purports, engaging practically all the best orchestral performers in the city. A portion of this material was under disadvantage, both as to individual training and the fact that a few men, fulfilling the demands of an orchestra in a theatre, are mainly required to play as loud as possible, with corresponding absence of any approach to phrasing.

"Considering these facts and in view of the works accomplished in last evening's programme, the results must be regarded as little short of notable, not only as to the outcome of a training by a man of exceptional thoroughness in this direction, but in the aspect of an enthusiastic response on the part of the performers. It is only in case of entire sympathy, between those engaged that an outcome corresponding with that demonstrated in the first programme can be attained."

"The Orchestra at the Academy
"Philadelphia's New Organization Under Herr Scheel Makes Its Début
"Gabrilowitsch the Soloist

"The Young Russian Heard in Tschaikowsky's Concerto in B. Flat Minor. A Brilliant Audience Greets Orchestra and Enjoys an Interesting Program.

"With unequal forces at his command in the orchestral choirs, Herr Fritz Scheel, by the sheer effect of personality, was able to carry artistic conviction home to the brilliant audience at the Academy of Music last evening, when the Philadelphia Orchestra made its first appeal. By wise choice of program, by the happy selection of a soloist and by the spirit which pervaded the interpretation of the numbers read, the leader made a deep impression and the orchestra, when at its best achieved a decided success. It has in it the promise of a new era musically, and its work of last evening is an earnest of better things to come. Certain readjustments are inevitable. The strings show up finely. There is high finish and excellent tonal quality in all they do. They are, indeed, the backbone of the orchestra. The brasses, on the whole, met the demands of the leader and music, but the horns need as keen a concern for time as for tone, and while these choirs in no wise seriously interfered with an adequate realization of the beauty of the work so interpreted, the same cannot be said for the wood-wind which was not up to the standard in several particulars, though the bassoons were notably efficient and in fine trim.

"Herr Scheel's Good Work

"All this was, however, to be expected. Every one present who is in and of the new movement, which started off with such flying colors, knew the limitations and accepted them in the right spirit. With this said and understood one can speak enthusiastically of the really amazing results obtained by Herr Scheel in so short a time. There were moments when the orchestra played with a brilliancy and dash and with a finish that was completely satisfying. Herr Scheel's dynamic range is extensive, his palette of color is rich and his contrasts are striking and yet fully in the spirit of the work. The orchestra was particularly effective in the Goldmark overture, in the "Entry of the gods into Walhalla" and in the Weber music. Weingartner, instead of paraphrasing the famous "Invitation to the Dance" rondo for the ballet, as Berlioz did, has written what is really a brilliant open-air concert version which taxes the full orchestra, and which Herr Scheel carried out in splendid spirit, giving a chance for all the choirs to do their best, the harp coming in for some crisp work that was very brilliantly done. All these three highly colored numbers were set off against the more trying classical demands of the Fifth Symphony. If the reading it received revealed the individual weaknesses of the orchestra as now made up, it was at least a revelation of the great advance the band has made. There was decision and emphasis and grace in phrasing and a keen discrimination in the shading. If Herr Scheel had his view of the traditional tempi the final effect was to reveal the work in its noble proportions and to make every one feel the true import of this great masterpiece.

"Audience Enthusiastic

* * * * *

"The enthusiasm of the audience was most unrestrained and generous. It was marked at the close of the symphony and fairly overwhelmed Gabrilowitsch, and this, with the splendid turnout from top to bottom, was a tribute to the committee and the guarantors who made the concert possible.

The first venture having been successfully concluded, business matters were attended to by issuing the first call of the Philadelphia Orchestra to the guarantors, combined with which was the announcement of the formation of the Philadelphia Orchestra Association, on May 17th, 1901, with the following officers and directors:

President
ALEXANDER VAN RENSSELAER
Vice-president
F. T. SULLY DARLEY
Secretary
JOHN H. INGHAM
Treasurer
HENRY WHELEN, JR.

Board of Directors

A. J. CASSATT
JOHN H. CONVERSE
ECKLEY B. COXE, JR.
F. T. SULLY DARLEY
WILLIAM L. ELKINS
MISS MARY K. GIBSON
CLEMENT A. GRISCOM
MRS. A. C. HARRISON
JOHN H. INGHAM
OLIVER B. JUDSON
EDWARD I. KEFFER
OSCAR A. KNIPE

C. HARTMAN KUHN
EDWARD G. McCOLLIN
THOMAS McKEAN, JR.
CLEMENT B. NEWBOLD
JAMES W. PAUL, JR.
MRS. F. H. ROSENGARTEN
EDGAR SCOTT
SIMON A. STERN
MISS ANNE THOMPSON
HENRY WHELEN, JR.
A. VAN RENSSELAER
P. A. B. WIDENER

Executive Committee

JOHN H. INGHAM
OLIVER B. JUDSON
EDWARD I. KEFFER
OSCAR A. KNIPE

EDWARD G. McCOLLIN
A. VAN RENSSELAER
HENRY WHELEN, JR.

Who was the conductor of this new orchestra, who until eighteen months before was unknown in Philadelphia?

Fritz Scheel was born in Lübeck, Germany, in 1852. His father and grandfather were orchestral conductors and his mother was a highly talented singer, from whom he inherited his remarkable memory and fine ear.

Fritz was the oldest of a large family and worked for his own and his family's support from an early age. He received his education from the city, in return for playing in orchestras and at concerts and operas. As a boy he often had to fill sudden vacancies, and he was also able to play the horn, trumpet, trombone and tuba. He was the principal teacher of his four brothers, all musicians. As his father was a practical musician, Scheel had had from his childhood an inti-

[25]

mate experience with the details of orchestral instruments. As a boy he conducted an orchestra of his own formation, giving subscription concerts in nearby towns which were well attended. At fifteen he appeared as a violin soloist.

Scheel's first appearance as a conductor was when he was the youthful trumpeter in the town band of Chemnitz. Like other municipal bands of Germany, this one furnished the music for all occasions and happened to be playing for the circus. The leader was taken ill, and one of the men was selected as a substitute. When the ring master heard of it, he said, "No, let that boy conduct. It is he who watches the horses' feet, when they dance, and it is he who sets the time for the music." Scheel became the leader of the band, and later on was employed by the town as instructor of all the band and orchestral instruments. This experience gave him an expert knowledge of technique, which proved valuable later.

In an interview given during the first season here, Scheel described conducting his first opera, shortly after receiving a life appointment as first violin in the Court Orchestra at Schwerin.

"Do I recall the first performance that I conducted?" said Mr. Scheel. "Yes, and it was an opera. Meyerbeer's 'Robert Le Diable.' I was exactly nineteen and a half years old, and a lost orchestra score led to it. I was the concertmaster then in the Chemnitz Orchestra, which in summer played for the opera performances in Bremerhafen at the Court Theatre. The opera of 'Robert Le Diable' was announced, and when the morning of the first rehearsal came it was discovered that the entire second act of the conductor's score had been lost. Herr Pohl, the conductor, a young man of thirty-three, refused to go on with the opera. It was too late to think of getting another score in time for the rehearsals necessary for the performance. The only way out of it seemed to be the withdrawal of the opera. Some of the singers, who had noticed the cue for their phrases that I had given them on the violin, asked whether I would not conduct. 'If the conductor invites me I will,' I said. When this was repeated to the conductor he promptly gave the invitation, and it was a pressing one, for they wished to give the opera and keep faith with the public. That entire second act I had to conduct from the first violin part, memory supplying the rest. The performance went without a break. That settled my career. Three days later I conducted Gounod's 'Faust,' and immediately afterward 'L'Africaine,' of Meyerbeer, Herr Pohl himself supplying the harp part on a piano. In the years that followed many were the performances that I conducted, including the entire 'Niebelungen Ring' of Wagner. But I never hear a fragment of Meyerbeer's

'Robert Le Diable' without smiling to myself at the recollection of the time when I conducted the second act from the first violin part."

After nine years at Schwerin, Scheel went to Chemnitz as Kappelmeister, winning the appointment over thirty-five competitors, as successor to Hans Sitt. There he also played weekly solos and conducted for the most famous virtuosi, such as Hans von Bülow, Sarasate, Wilhelmj and Joachim. He once prepared the orchestra for a Beethoven Concert under Von Bülow's direction in an hour and a half, the programme being the Leonore Overture No. 3, the Eroica Symphony and a Concerto. The Chemnitz Orchestra was often called to different cities in Saxony, such as Dresden, Leipzig, etc., to play before crowded houses. Scheel was also elected leader of the Sitt Chor Gesangverein, a Chorus of 400 mixed voices. With this Chorus and the excellent City Orchestra he obtained marvelous results, and produced among other great works, Bach's "Mattheus Passion" and "Trauer Ode"; Beethoven's Ninth Symphony and his Missa Solemnis; Schumann's "Faust Scenes," Liszt's "Christus" and Händel's "Samson." The Choral works of Mendelssohn, Schumann, and Gade were also performed, as well as many small choruses. In 1885 a Music Festival lasting three days was given to celebrate the two hundredth anniversary of Bach's birth, and he kept in the vanguard of musical events in Germany.

During this period, Scheel spent four summers in conducting opera at a Russian watering place. Four different operas were given each week, and the repertoire included: "Tannhauser," "Lohengrin," "The Flying Dutchman," "Rienzi," "Euryanthe," "Der Freischütz," "Faust," the standard Italian operas of Verdi, Rossini, etc., for which he also trained the chorus.

After nine years at Chemnitz, Scheel was called by von Bülow to Hamburg to drill the orchestra for concerts which he and the pianist alternated in conducting. He was a devoted admirer of von Bülow and the great pianist showed his appreciation in many ways. Years later, after von Bülow had retired, he offered to play at a concert given in honor of Scheel. "I do it once more," he said, "as gratitude for a true colleague and friend." He played the piano Concerto in E flat major, by Beethoven, and the Hungarian Fantasie, dedicated to him by his father-in-law, Franz Liszt. This was one year before his death and was his last public appearance as a pianist. Scheel also knew well Brahms, Tschaikowsky and Rubinstein.

In 1892 Dr. Ziegfeld engaged Scheel to go to Chicago the next year and give historical concerts at the World's Fair. The enterprise failed. He then took an orchestra to the Mid-winter Fair in San Francisco, under the name of the "Vienna Prater Orchestra," in the winter of 1893. Later he gave daily concerts, and, during two seasons, cycles of Afternoon Symphony Concerts. For a season he was engaged by Oscar Hammerstein and then he became the first leader of the San Francisco Orchestra. He introduced the great classical and modern works to the people of that city, who still speak admiringly of him and remember his success. After five years in San Francisco, Scheel came to Philadelphia, and was discovered at Woodside Park, conducting his "New York Orchestra." The newspaper criticisms were most flattering.

The following pen picture of Mr. Scheel has been given by a man who played under his leadership and saw him under many conditions.

"A tall man, robust, large-framed, something more than spare, a little less than stout; a back and broad shoulders in strikingly good proportion, and a head poised upon them in easy dignity. The large hands are full of character, delicately formed, refined, noticeably plastic and adaptable.

"A dark-brown military moustache and a prominent nose stand out clearly under a typical, high, German forehead and coiffure.

"In his brown eyes an infinite variety of expressions are lurking. From humorous twinkles that are irresistible, to flashes of fire and scorn that never miss the mark, they assume new and rapidly fleeting phases with every phase of music or speech."

Many stories are told of Fritz Scheel's early efforts with amateurs and with a group of musicians, strange to him, for in those days the requirements for orchestral players were not the present ones, and there were many obstacles to overcome. His ear was absolutely correct, and he often told the players when tuning was needed. He was on occasion obliged to use mechanical strategies to insure the proper intonation. A close friend of his tells the following anecdotes:

"At the first rehearsal for the Philippine concerts, one of the numbers contained a difficult trumpet part, which seemed impossible for the first trumpet player, to play. Scheel postponed the rehearsal of this number until the next day, to allow him time to practice, but next day he could do no better. So the part was given to the second trumpet very much to the humiliation of the first player. But though very stern, Scheel was also very sympathetic with his musicians, and he realized what the feelings of the man must be. He therefore addressed the orchestra, in his usual formal way, and called for the attention of the players. Then turning to the first trumpet player, he remarked: 'I have been listening to your playing for the last two days, and I feel sure it is not your fault that you could not play that one part in the composition. I notice that whenever you play a note in which the middle valve of your instrument is used, you have no difficulty in playing the part which you were unable to do before.' This incident was told by the player, who took his trumpet to his instrument-maker and had one-sixteenth of an inch taken off the middle valve; with the result that, he could play parts that he never could play before. He then remarked, 'It matters not what happens between Scheel and me; I will always take off my hat to him, and say 'Master'.'

"On another occasion the tympanum was not in tune. Scheel stopped the orchestra and asked the tympanist to tune his instrument. When the man started to turn the keys, Scheel said, 'No, it is not on that side; it is on the right-hand side of the drum,' showing that he, at the distance of a great many feet, could tell that the false vibrations were coming from the right side of the drum.

"At one of the rehearsals the harp player had trouble with her part. Scheel said, 'Skip that one chord and you will only have to change your pedals twice in place of five times.'

"He also had the peculiar faculty of being able to get the effect of instruments that were not in the orchestra by the combination of other instruments that would give the same tone. The writer remembers very distinctly Scheel's using the French horn and the 'cello together to play the third bassoon part."

This brief account of the first leader of the Philadelphia Orchestra explains why the Executive Committee pinned its faith to Fritz Scheel.

As the beginnings of the orchestra are recorded, how delightful it is to music lovers to know that the Musical Fund Society, itself a bold pioneer eighty years before, sponsored this most daring enterprise of our musical history. Dr. Dunglison, its president, presiding in the Orpheus Rooms on a spring afternoon in 1900, gave the blessing of the first Philadelphia Orchestra to the present Philadelphia Orchestra. Like Brünnhilde, herself shorn of godly powers, sending forth her hero to do great deeds, so the Musical Fund Society, no longer composed of active musicians, sent forth the young orchestra to conquer the musical world. No magic rings, or swords, or helmets were given to aid it in surmounting difficulties. The only magic formulas known to all the people interested were hard work and an invincible spirit.

FRITZ SCHEEL

Chapter III
Early Years

With the first steps safely passed and the Philadelphia Orchestra organized, the period of financial difficulty began. In 1901–1902 fourteen pairs of concerts in the regular series, and a total of fifty-two concerts for the season were given. The deficit jumped from $14,000 to $72,000. Everything was quadrupled except the audience. That remained almost stationary. Twenty years after Theodore Thomas's time Philadelphia was still not ready to attend symphony concerts or support an orchestra at any general sacrifice to its own purse. The general attitude was that such a project must be supported by a few persons who had time and money to spend. Indifference was widespread.

Scheel early saw the need of traveling to make the orchestra known, especially in New York and Boston, as he realized that the saying about the prophet held good for orchestras as well as for persons. He was faced with the fact that the Association could not see its way to send the orchestra to large cities. Appearances out of town were undertaken as early as 1901–02, in cities in Pennsylvania and New Jersey. During the next season New York, Baltimore and Washington were visited.

He well knew, however, that his work with soloists would bring the orchestra fame, and much effort was expended in preparing accompaniments. A case in point was the time that Ysaye was the soloist and was playing a Bach Concerto. At the end the violinist stood like a statue until the orchestra had finished. When Scheel went off the stage, Ysaye kissed him on both cheeks and said that the accompaniment was the finest he had ever had. Shortly after this a member of the Boston Orchestra told one of our violinists that Ysaye had been booked to play the Bach Concerto with his orchestra; but after starting it he stopped the rehearsal and said: "Not after the Philadelphia Orchestra will I play the Bach Concerto," and another concerto was substituted.

With artistic ambitions ever growing, it was discovered that some of the needed instruments were not to be found in the city and in addition to this a number of players would not accept the terms of the contract. The situation became acute, so in the summer of 1901, and again in 1902, the conductor was commissioned to seek musicians in Europe.

When it became evident that the Philadelphia Orchestra was going to be permanent, application was made in 1902 for a Charter* for the Association, which was granted on January 5th, 1903, to the following persons, only nine of whom are now living:

GEORGE BURNHAM, JR.	EDWARD G. MCCOLLIN
A. J. CASSATT	THOMAS MCKEAN
JOHN H. CONVERSE	CLEMENT B. NEWBOLD
ECKLEY B. COXE, JR.	JAMES W. PAUL, JR.
WILLIAM L. ELKINS	MRS. FRANK H. ROSENGARTEN
MARY K. GIBSON	RICHARD ROSSMÄSSLER
CLEMENT A. GRISCOM	EDGAR SCOTT
MRS. ALFRED C. HARRISON	SIMON A. STERN
JOHN H. INGHAM	ANNE THOMSON
OLIVER B. JUDSON	ALEXANDER VAN RENSSELAER
EDWARD I. KEFFER	HENRY WHELEN, JR.
C. HARTMAN KUHN	P. A. B. WIDENER

From the beginning Scheel inaugurated the policy continued ever since, of putting the orchestra in the lead artistically. "First," performances began almost immediately. Three years after the formation of the orchestra he gave the first complete Beethoven Cycle ever presented in Philadelphia. Five successive concerts were devoted to this, ending with the Ninth Symphony, in which the Mendelssohn Club participated. This event was preceded by a series of five Young People's Educational Concerts with lectures, by William J. Henderson, William F. Apthorp, Louis C. Elson, Hugh A. Clarke and Henry E. Krehbiel, whose subject was "Beethoven." Other lectures were given on the same subject on the days of the concerts.

PROGRAMMES OF THE BEETHOVEN CYCLE
First Concert, Friday, March 20th, 1903

1. Overture......................"Egmont," E major, Opus 84
2. Symphony No. 8............................F major, Opus 93
3. Symphony No. 3...............E flat major (Eroica), Opus 55

*For Charter see Appendix A.

[32]

Second Concert, Saturday, March 21st, 1903

1. Overture....................."Coriolanus," C minor, Opus 62
2. Symphony No. 1...........................C major, Opus 21
3. Symphony No. 6.................F major (Pastorale), Opus 68
   Preceding lecture by Hugh A. Clarke, Mus. Doc., at 3 o'clock,
   Saturday afternoon, at the Broad Street Conservatory,
   1329 South Broad Street, Gilbert R. Combs, *Director*

Third Concert, Tuesday, March 24th, 1903

1. Overture......................."Fidelio," C major, Opus 72
2. Symphony No. 2...........................D major, Opus 36
3. Symphony No. 5...........................C minor, Opus 67
   Preceding lecture by Philip H. Goepp, at 3 o'clock,
   Tuesday afternoon, at the Assembly Hall of the
   Sternberg School of Music, 10 South 18th Street

Fourth Concert, Wednesday, March 25th, 1903

1. Overture................."Leonore" No. 2, C major, Opus 72
2. Symphony No. 4.......................B flat major, Opus 60
3. Symphony No. 7...........................A major, Opus 92
   Preceding lecture by Hugh A. Clarke, Mus. Doc., at 3 o'clock,
   Wednesday afternoon, at the Broad Street Conservatory.

Fifth Concert, Thursday, March 26th, 1903

1. Overture................."Leonore" No. 3, C major, Opus 72
2. Concerto for Piano and Orchestra...............E flat, Opus 73
   Constantin von Sternberg
3. Symphony No. 9...........................D minor, Opus 125
   Preceding lecture by Philip H. Goepp, at 3 o'clock,
   Thursday afternoon, at the Sternberg School of Music

Musical Courier, New York, March 25th, 1903:

* * * * *

"The cycle was to crown the third season of the Philadelphia Orchestra's successful existence, and for many months, the leader, the orchestra, the manager and the committees have been busy in the endeavor to make these five concerts matchless in performance and memorable in historical significance.

"The cycle was projected as an art undertaking pure and simple. Profit was a secondary consideration. Flamboyant advertisement was eschewed. There were announcements dignified and to the point. The prices were put within the reach of the student and the poor lover of music. Society was asked to patronize at the box office, but not on the programme. It is thus apparent that never in the musical life of America has there been conceived a project more ideal, more artistic and more utilitarian than this Beethoven Cycle in the City of Brotherly Love. Fritz Scheel is not overshadowed even by the great Joseph Joachim, who together with three famous fellow musicians, proposes next summer to play all of Beethoven's string quartets at a musical festival in Germany.''

* * * * *

"Beethoven's 'Coriolanus' overture was played by the New York Philharmonic Orchestra this season. The Filharmonic Fathers should have been provided with free transportation to Philadelphia in order to learn how one conductor can mar and another make the same composition. This Philadelphia Coriolanus was a hero indeed, who walked with erect head and proud chest. There was no rheumatism in his knees and there was no crick in his back. When his mother pleaded she spoke in accents human and loving. Her voice was softly attuned. It sang a song that Coriolanus did well to heed. Scheel's graphic characterization made the Philharmonic performance appear in the memory like almost a travesty.''

* * * * *

Musical Courier, April 1, 1903:

* * * * *

"At the end, when the composer abandons absolute music and turns to song, Philadelphia's own distinguished choral body, the Mendelssohn Club, came to the support of the musicians, and the beautiful 'Hymn of Joy' was brilliantly sung. As a quartet for the solo part, Mrs. Marie Kunkel-Zimmerman, Mrs. Osborne, Nicholas Douty and Mr. Schurig did brilliant work. Altogether the playing of this Ninth Symphony formed a fitting climax to this memorable week devoted to the great master's own musical history.''

* * * * *

"After the performance of the overture, Scheel was presented with a floral wreath, lyre and harp, and John H. Converse on behalf of the Directors of the orchestra, bestowed upon him a bronze bust of Beethoven, in well chosen words of compliment and congratulations.''

Scheel's one thought was the artistic development of the orchestra. The story is told of a time when new members of the Board found that the concerts were being given at a tremendous loss. They at once criticised the quality of the music, and said, "The programme must be changed; you are giving too high-class music for the people, and they won't stand it." The Executive Committee therefore decided that Mr. Scheel should put waltzes on his symphony programmes; and a meeting was arranged with him. This was in the early days when his English was less fluent than later, and his understanding of the language less keen. It took him some minutes to find out the real purpose of the Committee. Then he expressed himself in a very formal way—somewhat in this wise: "Gentlemen, I am the head of the department of music of this association. I am elected by you. You represent the business end of this association; I stand for art. I cannot allow any one to interfere with my programme. If my programme and my management of the musical side of the association does not meet with your approval, you may get another conductor; but as long as I am conductor of the Philadelphia Orchestra, waltzes will not be played on a symphony programme." He spoke so emphatically that there was no recourse and the subject of waltzes at the regular series was dropped.

After this decision, however, Mr. Scheel suggested giving popular concerts. The committee immediately accepted this offer, and plans were made for five. At the last minute, when the sale at the box office was found to be exceedingly small, it was considered necessary to call upon outside organizations to make the concerts a financial success, so they were given for the benefit of various charitable organizations, such as the University Hospital, Hahnemann Hospital, St. Christopher's Hospital for Children, and others.

The first Popular Benefit Concert for the Men's Medical Ward of the University Hospital was put in charge of the "Benevolent Aid Society" of that ward. This committee, with Mrs. William W. Arnett, as Chairman, and Mrs. S. Naudain Duer, as Vice-chairman, at ten days' notice secured one thousand patronesses and sold out the house, David Bispham having been secured as soloist, and a popular programme having been announced. This was the first time people representing a so-called "Opera Audience" had heard the Orchestra. In 1905 this same Committee secured the orchestra and gave an afternoon of Music in the Horticultural Hall. Tea was served at tables, and two programmes, with an intermission, were given. In each of these events about one thousand dollars each was cleared by the orchestra and the Men's Ward. While these efforts were not entirely consistent with the dignity of a great orchestra, the financial situation in which the management found itself made such overtures for money making and advertising advantageous.

The Press, November 12th, 1902:
"PHILADELPHIA ORCHESTRA
"First Popular Concert a Great Success—Bispham the Soloist
"The first popular concert of the Philadelphia Orchestra at the Academy of Music last evening was a great success, not only from the financial point of view—the proceeds being for the benefit of the University Hospital—but from the artistic, the soloist, Mr. David Bispham, coming in for a special word by reason of his familiar finesse as an interpreter of aria and song."

Programme
Carl Goldmark............................Overture "In Spring"
Wagner...................Pilgrim's Chorus from "Tannhäuser"
(a) Wagner...................."Evening Star" from Tannhäuser
(b) Verdi.............................Page Song from "Falstaff"
Johann Strauss......................"Danube Maiden's Waltz"
Brahms ....Hungarian Dances Nos. 1 and 2
Beethoven...................Overture "Leonore" No. 3, Op. 72
(a) Schumann............................"The Two Grenadiers"
(b) Schubert.........................."Hark, Hark, the Lark"
Grieg........................"Ase's Death," "Anitra's Dance"
(*For String Orchestra*)
(a) Gounod................. "Oh That We Two Were Maying"
(b) H. H. Weizler.............................."Killiekrankie"
(c) Damrosch...................................."Danny Dever"
Liszt..........................."Hungarian Rhapsody" No. 2
Mr. David Bispham, Soloist

In the early days rehearsals were held in the banquet room of Musical Fund Hall, and in the room of the Commercial Museum, through the courtesy of those organizations. Later Odd Fellows Hall was rented, but since 1912 the rehearsals have been held at the Academy of Music, by a special arrangement with the management, which has always co-operated to the fullest extent with the Association.

The Strauss Concerts
During the fourth season of the orchestra's existence, the Executive Committee took the bold step of engaging Richard Strauss to appear with it in Philadelphia. Later, two appearances in Boston with the Philadelphia Orchestra were added, as it was learned that no guest conductor was permitted to conduct the Boston Symphony Orchestra.

Strauss's first American concert was in New York, where the practice of sending substitutes to rehearsals was common. In the middle of "Don Juan" the orchestra broke down and they had to stop and begin again. Therefore, when Dr. Strauss reached Philadelphia, he was prepared for another such occurrence. He arrived for rehearsal in a perturbed state of mind, and proceeded brusquely to the conductor's stand. Mr. Scheel, however, had spared no pains in preparation for the great event. The rehearsal was held at Odd Fellows Temple, in a small room, where the reverberations in the fortissimo passages were tremendous. After simply bowing to Mr. Scheel, Dr. Strauss began to lead. He had played but a few measures before he discovered an orchestra thoroughly proficient and well-rehearsed in his numbers. After playing a few bars he dropped his arms and allowed the orchestra to play on. There was an entire change in his manner. He turned to Scheel, and, throwing both arms in the air, exclaimed, "Famos!" Every few moments he cried, "Wunderschön!" "Ausgezeichnet!" After making one or two corrections in the parts, he stopped the rehearsal and became highly enthusiastic over the playing of the orchestra.

THE PHILADELPHIA ORCHESTRA

FRITZ SCHEEL, *Conductor*
Increased to 100 Performers for these Occasions
DR. RICHARD STRAUSS
Conducting his own Compositions, and
FRAU STRAUSS-DE AHNA
Dramatic Soprano, accompanied by DR. STRAUSS

PROGRAMMES
Friday Afternoon, March 4, 1904

1. FRANZ LISZT..A Faust Symphony in Three Pictures (after Goethe)
      I. Faust (Allegro)
      II. Gretchen (Andante)
      III. Mephistopheles (Scherzo, Finale)

2. RICHARD STRAUSS
    Songs with Orchestra:
        a. "Das Rosenband"
        b. "Liebes-Hymnus"
        c. "Morgen"
        d. "Cäcilie"
      FRAU STRAUSS-DE AHNA
      Conducted by the Composer

3. RICHARD STRAUSS...."Tod und Verklärung," Tone Poem, Op. 24
      Conducted by the Composer

Saturday Evening, March 5th, 1904

1. JOHANNES BRAHMS..........Symphony No. 2, D. major, Op. 73

      I. Allegro non troppo
      II. Adagio non troppo
      III. Allegro grazioso (Quasi Andantino)
      IV. Allegro con spirito

2. RICHARD STRAUSS

    Songs with Orchestra:
    Three Mother-Songs

        a. "Meinem Kinde"
        b. "Muttertändelei"
        c. "Wiegenlied"

FRAU STRAUSS-DE AHNA
Conducted by the Composer

3. RICHARD STRAUSS...."Till Eulenspiegel and his Merry Pranks,"
Op. 28

Conducted by the Composer

Great preparations were made for this event and much money was spent, for Strauss not only received a large fee, but much had to be used for advertising.

Philadelphia Inquirer, March 5th, 1904:

"RICHARD STRAUSS AT THE ACADEMY

"FIRST APPEARANCE OF THE FAMOUS COMPOSER MADE YESTERDAY
AFTERNOON. HE CONDUCTS A FINE PERFORMANCE OF HIS OWN
"DEATH AND TRANSFIGURATION," AND HIS WIFE SINGS FOUR SONGS

"There was a very large audience at the Academy of Music yesterday afternoon, when the Philadelphia Orchestra gave its last Friday afternoon performance for the current season. The occasion was made notable by the first appearance in this city of the famous composer, Richard Strauss, who had arranged to guide the orchestra through the mazes of the tone poem entitled, "Death and Transfiguration," one of his best and most characteristic works; and it was rendered additionally interesting and important by the Philadelphia début of Mme. Strauss-de Ahna, who has the reputation of being an exceptionally skillful and sympathetic interpreter of her distinguished husband's songs."

* * * * *

"After his wife had finished her group of songs, and the enthusiastic and long continued applause which her work had elicited had died away, Mr. Richard Strauss returned to the platform to conduct his own "Tod und Verklaerung." He is a singularly modest and unobtrusive looking man, with an appearance more suggestive of a school teacher than of a musician, and with nothing about him to

[38]

betray any large estimate of his own consequence, but there can be no question as to his ability as a conductor. That had already been indicated in the manner he played the accompaniments to his wife's singing, but it was conclusively demonstrated by the way in which he conducted the orchestral feature of the programme. In its lucidity and balance, in its delicate sense of proportion; in its wide and pregnant variations of light and shade; in the splendor of its climaxes and the salient force with which each detail was projected and each nuance given its proper value, his performance of "Death and Transfiguration" has certainly never been equalled in this city. It was a very great achievement and the audience rightly recognized it as such."

* * * * *

hiladelphia Ledger, March 5th, 1904:

"STRAUSS CONCERT A GREAT SUCCESS

"WARM GREETING FOR THE COMPOSER AND HIS WIFE

* * * * *

"Strauss has a very precise beat, ordinarily quiet and undemonstrative and making very little use of his left hand; but when he wants a big climax for the brasses—and he is not afraid of noise—he conducts with his whole person. The orchestra knew the music perfectly and was absolutely responsive to every nuance."

ity and State, March 10th, 1904:

"The highest point, not only of the winter, but in a certain sense of all previous musical seasons was reached last week.
    "To have the most eminent musician—we use the word advisedly in the strictest sense—interpret his compositions with our own orchestra in two concerts, certainly marks Philadelphia as one of the self-dependent musical centers of the world. But it was much more significant to hear the unstinted praise which Mr. Strauss bestowed on the orchestra after the concerts. On Friday, after the exalting performance of "Death and Transfiguration," the composer seemed to forget his audience in the heartiness of his acknowledgments to the orchestra. Indeed, we see no impropriety whatever in publishing the fact that Mr. Strauss was immeasurably better pleased with the work of our orchestra than with that of the New York orchestra, which he conducted last Thursday evening. On Tuesday he declared himself entirely contented with the single rehearsal for the Friday concert. It seems almost a pity that we Philadelphians cannot discover for ourselves this excellence of our own enterprise—that we must have the most distinguished musician of the day come from Berlin to tell us that we have a splendid orchestra, and, it may be added, splendid conductor. At any rate, the fact ought not only to be taken to heart by all of us, but we ought not to hesitate to boast bravely of this advantage of ours over New York."

These concerts were repeated in Boston on March 7th and 8th, where they had been well advertised and both houses sold out. But when the programmes were announced there was a cry of protest from the critics and musicians of that city. "Why should Boston have to listen to Fritz Scheel conduct a symphony on each programme?" The Executive Committee replied firmly that Boston had refused to have Dr. Strauss lead the Boston Symphony Orchestra, and now the Philadelphia Orchestra Association was giving Boston an opportunity to hear Dr. Strauss conduct as guest conductor of the Philadelphia Orchestra. The programme was not changed, but Philadelphia had to explain the stand she had taken even after the orchestra had reached Boston.

Then a real contretemps occurred, trying enough to shake the strongest nerves. In those days, either moving orchestras was more difficult, or the Philadelphia Orchestra was still too inexperienced a traveler to do so efficiently. When the hour for rehearsal in Symphony Hall arrived, there was no music and there were no instruments. They had been lost en route. The explanation arrived at after much telegraphing was that these valuable possessions had been placed in a car too high to pass under the bridges on the regular route, so it had been re-routed and would probably not arrive until evening. This was a predicament for a young orchestra, none too easy in its mind at the prospect of playing in the city of the Boston Symphony Orchestra; and now deprived of rehearsal in a hall new to the conductor, as well as to every player. The day passed, evening came, the audience assembled, and still no instruments Twenty minutes after the concert hour, heavy teams were heard outside. The day was saved, the instruments were hurriedly put in place, the men went on, and the symphony, Brahms' No. 2, began. The Philadelphians present say that the orchestra never played so well, and at the end of the symphony Scheel was recalled six times. Mr. Elson, a most friendly critic, who had given a dinner for our conductor the night before, rushed behind, saying, "Scheel, you have conquered Boston." At a reception given for the two conductors after the concert, Mr. Philip Hale said of Scheel: "He has the right arm of Thomas and the left arm of Nikisch."

[40]

Boston Herald, March 8th, 1904 (Philip Hale):

"The performance of the orchestra under Mr. Scheel was admirable.
. . . .Here is a conductor to be respected for many qualities, for his
mastery of mechanism and for his genuine and poetic feeling . . . .
There is no doubt that Mr. Scheel is an accomplished drill master.
His patience and intelligence in rehearsal were shown by the fine
performance of the supple orchestra under his direction."

Boston Evening Transcript:

"Mr. Scheel is unquestionably a conductor of parts, whom one would
gladly know better . . . . The wonderful beauties in the scoring of
Liszt's symphony were all made the most of, and under the hands of
Mr. Scheel the dull passages became less hopeless than usual. Of the
dramatic points Mr. Scheel took full advantage and with the advent
of the Gretchen theme in the third movement he made an electri-
fying effect."

Boston Daily Advertiser (Louis C. Elson):

"Musical Boston was waked up last night! Those who braved the
elements were rewarded by a concert which for novelty, for excitement and for educational value has seldom been equaled even in our
symphonic city.
"The Philadelphia Orchestra proved itself to be the best that has
visited Boston since Theodore Thomas brought his band here.
"Its conductor, Fritz Scheel, is an orchestral genius. He evidently
knows his Brahms thoroughly, and by the time he had finished the
first movement of the D major symphony, he was clasped to the
Bostonian heart. To win a triumph in Brahms in a city where all our
conductors are Brahms scholars (and our auditors too, for the matter
of that), means very much. Mr. Scheel was recalled with enthusiasm
. . . . The Philadelphia Orchestra has proved itself one of the important orchestras of the United States."

A delightful anecdote is told about this visit to Boston.
After the success of the evening concert, Dr. Strauss, full
of enthusiasm, told Mr. Scheel that he must play the
Domestica Symphony at its first performance in New York,
and they arranged to play it together on the piano from the
orchestral score in Symphony Hall the next morning. Scheel
took the score home with him and the next morning the
first playing of the Domestica in America began, Dr. Strauss
taking the treble and Scheel the bass. In Strauss's excitement he knocked the music off the rack just as the fugue
started in the bassoons, but Scheel continued to play. Strauss
turned to watch him, but still he played. The music was
replaced and they finished the symphony. Dr. Strauss then

[41]

discovered that Scheel had spread the score on a trunk and studied it all night, only closing the book at daylight.

Shortly after this Dr. Keffer received the following letter:

"Esteemed Doctor Keffer:

"You wish from me a leaf for your Album. I could not give same a more beautiful contents than to give again expression of my greatest pleasure over the splendid performance of the Philadelphia Orchestra, with which I was so fortunate to obtain such extraordinary successes in Philadelphia and in Boston.

"But the greatest merit of this success belongs to your excellent Kapellmeister Fritz Scheel, who had trained his young and music-loving orchestra so eminently, and who had prepared so well for my concerts, that I was able to give the performance, satisfying my strongest wishes, of my difficult works, after *only one* repetition. Therefore, to Mr. Scheel, my special thanks and felicitation to which I join my heartiest wishes for further flourishing and prospering of the Philadelphia Orchestra under his energetic guidance.

"With especial esteem and best greetings also from my Wife,

"Yours sincerely devoted,

"(Signed) DR. RICHARD STRAUSS

"New York, the 28th of March, 1904."

The next event out of the ordinary in which the orchestra took part was the Special Concert conducted by Felix Weingartner, about a year later.

THE PHILADELPHIA ORCHESTRA

FRITZ SCHEEL, *Conductor*

Special Concert, February 16th, 1905

FELIX WEINGARTNER, *Guest Conductor*

LISZT............Symphonic Poem "Triumph and Death of Tasso"
WEINGARTNER....................Symphony No. 2, E flat major
GLÜCK....................................Overture "Iphigenia"
MOZART........... ....Overture "Zauberflöte"
WEBER......................................Overture "Oberon"

He was well received by the audience and by the critics, one of whom wrote thus:

Public Ledger, February 17th, 1905:

"WEINGARTNER CONCERT"

"GERMAN COURT CONDUCTOR'S FIRST APPEARANCE HERE

"DIRECTS PHILADELPHIA ORCHESTRA IN HIS OWN

"SECOND SYMPHONY" AND OTHER WORKS

"One of the incidental advantages of a permanent concert orchestra is the opportunity afforded from time to time to invite distinguished musicians to conduct performances of their own compositions, or of other works for which they may have a particular penchant. We had an interesting example of this last season in the concerts of the Philadelphia Orchestra at which Richard Strauss directed that expert band of executants in his own interpretation of some of his tone poems. Last evening in the Academy of Music, Felix Weingartner—less widely known as a composer than as a chief orchestral authority in Germany at the present day—similarly conducted the orchestra in a performance of his latest symphony, with an accompanying programme of his own choice, representing classic, romantic and modern music.

"In the remarkable organization of accomplished and enthusiastic musicians which has grown up within a few seasons under Fritz Scheel's masterful direction, the leader of the Berlin Court Orchestra found a perfect instrument of expression ready to his hand. It is not, of course so large an orchestra as that to which he is accustomed, but there could be no doubt that it played the music exactly as the conductor wished it played. While last evening's concert was thus in one sense a glorification of the Philadelphia Orchestra and its distinguished leader, the interest of the occasion was centered entirely in the guest and what he might have personally to express.

"Herr Weingartner is a tall, slim man, erect and precise, but with a winning personality that puts him at once in harmony both with the orchestra and his audience. His manner in conducting is usually quiet and firm, but he employs a great variety of detailed gesture that is expressive and obtains its results. He plays everything with a strongly marked accent, with more care for clarity and precision than for suavity, and makes very strong and abrupt contrasts with tremendous climaxes and with sharp periods. There is not a great deal of attention to grace of phrasing or delicacy of nuance, but evidently the strong effects he gets are what he thinks important."

* * * * *

"Weingartner owes much to Liszt and the Weimar days and it is natural that he should give a fine performance of the "Tasso" with which the concert opened. This symphonic poem is one of so great dignity and beauty as to deserve more frequent hearing. The illness of Saal, the first 'cellist, left a note lacking in the beauty of the performance, though the intrinsic worth of the music made it a pleasure to hear."

* * * * *

"After the concert a reception was given to the guest conductor at the home of Mrs. Spencer Ervin."

During this season Mr. Scheel presented his first programme of House Music at a reception held in his honor, and the next winter he gave six such concerts at the residence of Mrs. Spencer Ervin, as a compliment to the Women's Committee. These concerts much resembled the concerts given by Francis Hopkinson and his friends in the early

[43]

days of Philadelphia, but were a complete and delightful novelty in 1905.

The most important evening of this kind was the concert given by Mr. Scheel and Philadelphia Orchestra musicians for Mrs. Roosevelt and her guests.

PROGRAMME

House Music Concert

THE WHITE HOUSE, WASHINGTON, D. C.

Monday Evening, January 29th, 1906

VOLKMANN.....Serenade No. 3, D minor, Opus 67. Violoncello Solo: Alfred Saal

BEETHOVEN.....Rondino for two Oboes, two Clarinets, two Horns and two Bassoons

MOZART........From the Quintet, Opus 108. For Clarinet and String Quartet

SVENDSEN.......From the Octet, Opus 3, for four Violins, two Violas and two Violoncellos

STRAUSS........Serenade (E flat major) Opus 7, for two Flutes, two Oboes, two Clarinets, four Horns, two Bassoons, and Contra-Bass or Bass Tuba

"DIRECTOR SCHEEL AND THIRTY-TWO MEMBERS OF PHILADELPHIA ORCHESTRA DELIGHT MR. AND MRS. ROOSEVELT AND GUESTS AT WHITE HOUSE CHARM PRESIDENT BY THEIR MUSIC

"Thirty-two members of the Philadelphia Orchestra, and Director Fritz Scheel, made a big impression on administrative, diplomatic and social Washington last Monday evening, when they gave one of their house-music concerts in the White House, and if you ask anyone of those thirty-three men what they think of President Roosevelt you will hear enough compliments to fill several bulky volumes.

"They had a delightful time, did these Quaker City symphony players, and so favorably were they received, that it is probable that they will be heard in the White House several times before the big orchestra disbands for the summer and the members scurry away to all parts of the earth.

"The full orchestra was not taken to the White House. Instead Director Scheel took his baby orchestra, consisting of six first violins, four violas, four cellos, two double basses, two flutes, two oboes, two clarinets, one bass clarinet, three bassoons and the horn quartet, and in that party there was but one American. Most of the players were Germans. The horn players were Frenchmen.

"President and Mrs. Roosevelt gave a small dinner party and afterwards a musicale. The dinner guests numbered about twenty, while over four hundred came for the musicale, including many of the most

[44]

prominent men and women in Washington. It was a gay scene with all the army and naval officers, and the members of the various Diplomatic Corps in their gaudy full evening dress. The only Philadelphians there were Mrs. A. J. Dallas Dixon and Miss Frances A. Wister.

"The orchestra men drove to the White House at 9.30 P. M. and at 10.15 they entered the East Room,where all the guests were assembled. President Roosevelt and Mrs. Roosevelt sat in the front row and listened with the gravest attention.

* * * * *

"Then Mr. Scheel played his rat-a-tat-tat baton solo on his stand, and the thirty-two men broke into harmony as easily and gracefully as a flock of sea gulls lights upon the ocean.

"The concert was to last one hour—no more and no less—and during that hour the audience was treated to Volkmann, Mozart, Svendsen, Beethoven and Strauss in solos, quintets, octets, sextets and altogethers. Alfred Saal was the soloist—he with the long blonde hair and the marvelous cello. He played as only Saal can play and his serenade in D minor by Volkmann was one of the most delightful numbers of the evening.

* * * * *

"Immediately after the closing number, President Roosevelt expressed the wish to meet the musicians, and so one by one the men marched up and shook hands with the greatest American of the day. Each man received some kind word from the President, especially Director Scheel, and to the latter he expressed his deepest thanks and congratulations for having furnished such a delightful concert."

* * * * *

"The next afternoon the full orchestra played a concert in Columbia Theatre before an audience that crowded the house and again won decided success. Just before the concert, Director Scheel received a huge box of roses and carnations from President and Mrs. Roosevelt."

All was not smooth sailing during the early years or for years to come. Scheel had enemies, so did the orchestra. Many people were not pleased when plans other than their own succeeded, and there was unpleasant comment from time to time. This was gradually overcome by the sincere attitude and the industry of the conductor and the improvement in the playing of the orchestra. The Beethoven Cycle, the Strauss concerts and the appearance of Weingartner were helps to popularity, not a sudden popularity, but one achieved by real worth. Scheel was fast making a place for himself in the musical life of the city, and in 1905 he was engaged as leader of the Orpheus Club and of the Eurydice Chorus to succeed Dr. Frank Damrosch. This put added burdens onto him, but it was not understood then that the strain of leading an orchestra is enough for one man.

Recognition also came from outside of Philadelphia. Scheel had the compliment paid him of being invited to lead two concerts in New York in place of Theodore Thomas, who had recently died, which concerts were to mark the semi-centennial of Thomas's connection with the Philharmonic Orchestra. Unfortunately, conflicting dates made acceptance impossible. He was even spoken of as a possible successor to Thomas by Mr. Louis Elson, of Boston, who said:

> "There is a most thorough and progressive musician, who is perfectly fitted for the Chicago position—Mr. Fritz Scheel of Philadelphia. This conductor, although he has been in America but a short time, has already won his spurs and proved his right to the highest orchestral position. He is not too conservative, an essential point with an orchestral conductor of the present."

In the meantime the concerts in Philadelphia were constantly improving, and the number had increased from six single concerts to eighteen pairs in six years. Out-of-town concerts in nearby places had been attempted with varying financial results. The Board of Directors, the Executive Committee and various Sub-committees worked hard to advance the interests of the orchestra.

The standard of excellence was kept at a high point. Fritz Scheel, ever ambitious for this venture in America, and possessing a keen artistic sense, produced programmes of excellence, which equalled and sometimes surpassed those of older American orchestras.

CHAPTER IV

THE WOMEN'S COMMITTEES FOR THE PHILADELPHIA ORCHESTRA

To the Philadelphia Orchestra Association belongs the distinction of first having promulgated the idea of procuring assistance from Women's Committees.

These were formed to promote out-of-town concerts in Harrisburg, Lancaster, Allentown and Trenton. In 1902–03, during the second season of concerts in those cities, it became evident that help was needed to increase interest in the concerts and procure a larger audience. Miss Mary Sergeant, sister of Mrs. A. J. Dallas Dixon, of Philadelphia, undertook this work in Harrisburg; Miss Hall became the Chairman in Trenton; Mrs. A. J. Steinman, in Lancaster; and Mrs. Robert E. Wright, in Allentown. These committees worked hard to make the Philadelphia Orchestra concerts successful.

No help of this kind seems to have been thought of for Philadelphia until the financial situation became so acute in 1904, as to endanger the life of the orchestra.

THE WOMEN'S COMMITTEE FOR THE PHILADELPHIA ORCHESTRA AND THE FIRST TEN THOUSAND

Each year had become more difficult financially and while the orchestra was learning many tunes the Board of Directors could remember but one. They constantly repeated the same question: "Where shall we get the money?" with variations. The Academy was not sold out; if it had been it would not have paid expenses. Nobody wanted to hear the Philadelphia Orchestra. The general attitude was that there were too many concerts, that even the Boston Symphony Orchestra gave only five in a series, and that only a few extreme musical enthusiasts went to the two Boston series, a total of ten. The Executive Committee and the Board of Directors spent hours discussing means of procuring more guarantors to meet the increasing deficit. Every improvement in players or special soloists meant money.

The Guarantee Fund for a three-year term expired in the

spring of 1904, and there would be an extra deficit of $16,000. The Association was facing a crisis. No contracts could be made without some financial background.

Just at this moment an idea occurred to Mrs. Edward G. McCollin, wife of a member of the Executive Committee. After approaching several friends on this subject and failing to interest them, Mrs. McCollin one day spoke to Mrs. A. J. Dallas Dixon, who persuaded Mrs. C. Stuart Patterson to call a meeting. The result was that a number of women met at Mrs. Dixon's house, 709 Pine Street, to discuss plans to assist the orchestra, on March 11th, 1904. Mrs. Dixon was elected president and on March 13th, a Women's Committee of twenty was formally organized. The officers and directors were:*

MRS. A. J. DALLAS DIXON, *President*
MRS. SPENCER ERVIN, *First Vice-president*
MRS. THOMAS S. HARRISON, *Second Vice-president*
MRS. E. G. MCCOLLIN, *Corresponding Secretary*
MRS. E. COLEMAN LEWIS, *Recording Secretary*
MRS. ALFRED REGINALD ALLEN, *Treasurer*

Directors

MRS. S. NAUDAIN DUER	MRS. GEORGE A. HUHN
MRS. THEODORE N. ELY	MRS. EDWARD I. KEFFER
MRS. SAMUEL S. FELS	MRS. W. L. MCLEAN
MRS. SIMON B. FLEISHER	MRS. JOHN B. MILES
MRS. J. M. GAZZAM	MRS. N. DUBOIS MILLER
MISS BEULAH HACKER	MRS. MORRIS PFAELZER
MRS. WALTER HORSTMANN	MRS. GEORGE D. WIDENER

MISS FRANCES A. WISTER

Later the following Honorary Vice-presidents accepted:

Mrs. Wm. W. Arnett, Mrs. George F. Baer, Mrs. Alexander W. Biddle, Mrs. John Cadwalader, Mrs. Alexander J. Cassatt, Mrs. Charles B. Coxe, Miss Mary K. Gibson, Mrs. Austin S. Heckscher, Mrs. Charles Edward Ingersoll, Mrs. Thomas McKean, Jr., Mrs. C. Stuart Patterson, Mrs. Frank Rosengarten, Mrs. Cornelius Stevenson, Miss Anne Thomson, Mrs. Alexander Van Rensselaer, Mrs. Henry Whelen, Jr.

The original of this letter is preserved in the archives of the Committee:

---
*For present membership see Appendix K.

MRS. ALEXANDER J. DALLAS DIXON

"Mrs. McCollin

"Dear Madam:

"I wish to say on behalf of the Executive Committee of the Philadelphia Orchestra that our Committee is in hearty sympathy with the effort to form a Women's Committee, and fully appreciates the kindness of the ladies who propose to form such a Committee in coming to the assistance of the Association, at a rather critical time. We fully endorse any measures you see fit to take in carrying out your plans.

Yours very truly,

John H. Ingham, Secretary
333 South 16th Street

"March 13, 1904."

Committees on Guarantors, Boxes and General Subscriptions were formed and their labors began.

The first work which the women undertook at the request of the Executive Committee was to secure $10,000, in new guarantees within the first month of its existence; the Executive Committee feeling that the best indication of a desire to continue the orchestra would be shown by an increase in the Guarantee Fund.

The Committee at once went to the musical critics of the various Philadelphia newspapers and secured their hearty co-operation in the work of rousing the public to an appreciation of the musical and civic importance of the orchestra. Within the allotted time the Committee had not only secured more than $10,000 in new guarantees, but had received new orders for $5,000 worth of seats and boxes for the next season. The Association thereupon decided to continue the orchestra for one more year, hoping that public interest would continue to increase.

The Guarantee Committee appointed by Mrs. Dixon to raise this sum was composed of Mrs. Spencer Ervin, now Mrs. Harold E. Yarnall, Chairman; Mrs. Morris Pfaelzer, Mrs. Edward I. Keffer, Mrs. George D. Widener and Miss Frances A. Wister, Secretary. A careful plan was made for this attack upon the public purse and all the members of the Committee threw themselves into the task of raising this large sum for a little known and unpopular cause.

Lists of prospective guarantors were compiled and each woman was assigned her quota of people to approach. The time was short, the pace was quick and the excitement was great. To at least one member it was a first experience at raising a large amount, but the novelty quickly wore off in the face of the continuous needs of the Association.

The Committee on Seats and Boxes became active at once, and Mrs. McCollin as Chairman of the Press Committee attended most ably to the publicity. Numberless articles appeared describing the Committee and its activities, and the help of the papers was very valuable.

Another way of making the orchestra and the Committee known was the parlor meetings. These were held in various places, with speakers of influence in the community. The first of these took place at the residence of Mrs. Thomas S. Harrison. Addresses were made by Dr. Alfred C. Lambdin, Mr. Constantin von Sternberg, Miss Esther Kelly and Miss Wister. No money was asked for at these meetings which were held in all sections of Philadelphia and vicinity during many seasons. The fact that Philadelphia had an orchestra was the point emphasized, as there was general ignorance of its existence. Then its importance to the musical life of the city and its needs were mentioned. Perhaps the most useful work next to procuring guarantors was the formation of the Auxiliary. These women were elected and asked to become season seat holders. The reports of the sale of boxes and season seats show thousands of dollars secured in new orders during the first years and frequent comment is made upon the improved appearance of the house through the filling of the boxes. The Friday house has been sold out for a number of years, but the Saturday house was a more difficult problem and only recently has been filled by season subscribers.

The list of activities was never-ending, and included visits to music schools, circulars, appeals, the co-operation of libraries, orchestra clubs, special rates for students, parlor meetings, of which Mrs. Keffer became Chairman in 1905, letters to friends in other cities where the orchestra was to appear and many more. The results were good. Between 1904–05 and 1907–08, the total sales of new orders for seats and boxes amounted to $29,670.00, and new guarantees amounted to $37,500.

The Germantown and Chestnut Hill Women's Committee

The activity of the Women's Committee during its first year of existence and the great need of the Association brought about the formation of a second Committee in Germantown and Chestnut Hill, on March 28th, 1905, under the leadership of Mrs. Francis Howard Williams, a woman prominent in every good cause.

Mrs. Francis Howard Williams, *President**
Miss Anna Hazen Howell, *Recording Secretary*
Mrs. Henry W. Raymond, *Corresponding Secretary*
Mrs. Augustus Stoughton, *Treasurer*
Miss Frances A. Wister, *Secretary* for the
Guarantee Fund

No sooner were these women organized than they threw themselves enthusiastically into work in their section and have since co-operated with the Women's Committee in every undertaking. They raised $26,825 for the Million Dollar Endowment Fund.

Mrs. Williams declined to be a candidate for the presidency in 1916 and was succeeded by the Countess of Santa Eulalia, who still holds that office. The Committee has recently celebrated its Twentieth Anniversary.

The West Philadelphia Women's Committee

Shortly afterwards, on April 6th, 1905, the spirit moved the women of West Philadelphia to form a third Committee. Mrs. C. Lincoln Furbush, daughter of Mr. and Mrs. Wm. Burnham, staunch supporters of the orchestra, organized it at her mother's house, and became its first president and the youngest of Women's Committee presidents.

The officers were:

Mrs. C. Lincoln Furbush, *President**
Miss Margaretta Hinchman, *Vice-president*
Miss Helen Fergusson, *Corresponding Secretary*
Miss Edith Schoff, *Recording Secretary*
Miss Grace Atlee, *Treasurer*

After one year of service Mrs. Furbush, Miss Schoff and Miss Atlee resigned, and Mrs. Monroe Smith, now Mrs. L. Howard Weatherly, Mrs. Charles L. Mitchell and Mrs. Samuel S. Fels succeeded them and still hold those offices.

*For present membership see Appendix K.

[51]

This active Committee has constantly been inaugurating new plans. In 1915, to commemorate its Tenth Anniversary it presented to the Association the stage setting completed in 1918, which was used until the new plans of Mr. Stokowski made a complete change of size and shape necessary.

Entertainments of many kinds have been given and the Twentieth Anniversary was celebrated in May, 1925.

THE MEDIA, CHESTER AND WEST CHESTER WOMEN'S COMMITTEE, SINCE 1923, THE DELAWARE COUNTY WOMEN'S COMMITTEE

At the Annual Meeting of the Women's Committees and their Auxiliaries in April, 1911, Mrs. J. Claude Bedford, an active amateur musician, then living in Media, proposed that a Women's Committee should be formed in Delaware County. She had become convinced that work of value could be done there and with the help of Mrs. Arnett, she formed a Committee with members from nine towns within twenty-five miles of Philadelphia, including West Chester, Glen Mills, Media, Wallingford, Swarthmore, Primos, Lansdowne, Darby and Chester.

The task was a hard one. Many residents of the district were unable, on account of the distance and of poor train service, to attend the concerts. Yet there was enthusiasm and much hard work in Delaware County. After several years, Mrs. Bedford was obliged to relinquish her position and Mrs. Matthew H. Cryer, of Lansdowne, succeeded to the office of President, which she still retains. The work of this Committee has been extraordinary and beset with obstacles. No enterprise has ever been entered into by the other Committees, in which the Delaware County Committee has not done its share and more, including bringing in its quota of $20,000 for the Million Dollar Endowment Fund. The Tenth Anniversary was celebrated in May, 1911 by a reception given at the house of Mrs. Cryer.

These four Committees are actively engaged in working for the Philadelphia Orchestra in Philadelphia, but they have been instrumental in helping the out-of-town concerts by persuading women in other places to foster concerts given there. The first of these was formed in Wilmington, Delaware.

Mrs. Lewis C. Vandegrift, President; Mrs. Joseph Swift, Vice-president; Mrs. William Betts, Secretary; Miss Annie T. Flinn, Treasurer.

Concerts were given in Wilmington as early as the season of 1902–03, but they were not thriving as they should. The Women's Committee therefore sent a mission to Wilmington, where Mrs. Joseph Swift, a composer and an amateur musician of prominence, called a meeting at her house. Mrs. Dixon, Mrs. McCollin and Miss Wister were the emissaries and the visit resulted in the formation of the Delaware Committee, with the above officers and twenty-three Directors.

For fifteen years this Committee continued its active work under the successive leadership of Mrs. Lewis C. Vandegrift, Mrs. Swift, and Mrs. Robert B. Bird. It was active in selling seats, procuring the Guarantee Fund for the Wilmington Concerts, without which the orchestra could not appear, in arousing interest by giving receptions for our leaders and in other ways. It was of immense help to have an organized group of people furthering the interests of the orchestra in Wilmington. The Committee continued its labors until the concerts had to be given up on account of the press of engagements. This Committee was affiliated with the Philadelphia Women's Committee, and always sent a representative to the Annual Meetings.

The Baltimore Committee
Formed May, 1906

Baltimore and Washington were considered fruitful fields and Philadelphia's by right of propinquity. The Boston Symphony Orchestra had established a large clientele in these cities, but it had years of reputation, and of artistic achievement, with which to attract audiences. Not so with a new and little known orchestra. Mrs. Dixon, Miss Wister and Mrs. Thomas S. Kirkbride, Jr., paid a visit there in December, 1905, on the occasion of an afternoon concert at the Arundell Club, at which two members of the orchestra, with Mrs. Kirkbride at the piano, played trios. In the following spring, Miss Mary B. Shearer organized a Committee and became the Chairman*.

The Washington Committee

In Washington, Miss Aileen Bell, after a meeting at which Mrs. Dixon spoke, organized a group of women to assist in popularizing the orchestra, and also secured many patronesses.*

Washington, the abode of representatives of foreign countries and with a fluctuating population, was an easier field than Baltimore. Neither of these Committees has been active lately, because the necessity is past, but their help was much appreciated then.

The Atlantic County Committee

This Committee, which was affiliated with the Women's Committee, was formed in Atlantic City, after a concert by the Philadelphia Orchestra in 1912, and was active until 1915.

A Committee of five women was appointed, with Mrs. Joseph H. Ireland as President, to take charge of a permanent series of concerts in Atlantic City. During the three years of its existence, they sold the tickets, carried on educational work in the schools, arranged for special students' tickets, distributed programmes in advance as a basis for study, managed the publicity and indulged in other forms of activity.

The Women's Committees for the Philadelphia Orchestra have been an important part of the work at home and abroad. There have been twelve:

1902: Women's Committees in Harrisburg, Lancaster, Allentown, Pennsylvania, and Trenton, New Jersey.

1904: The Women's Committee for the Philadelphia Orchestra.

1905: The Germantown and Chestnut Hill Women's Committee, the West Philadelphia Women's Committee, the Delaware Committee.

1906: The Baltimore Committee, the Washington Committee.

*See Appendix K.

1911: The Media, Chester and West Chester Women's Committee (now Delaware County Committee).

1912: The Atlantic County Committee.

The Women's Committee, pioneer of the four in Philadelphia, celebrated its Twentieth Anniversary in March, 1924. The event was marked by a series of entertainments, beginning with a luncheon given by the Officers and Directors of the Philadelphia Orchestra Association on March 11th. After a number of speeches an anonymous gift of one thousand Dollars to the Pension Fund from a member of the Committee, in honor of the occasion, was presented to the President of the Association. By vote of the Board of Directors this has been placed in a separate fund bearing the donor's name and the Women's Committee has the privilege of designating a special use for the income each year.

The next event was the reception given by the Women's Committee, in the Foyer of the Academy of Music, on March 14th, in which the members of the Auxiliary joined, and at which the guests of honor were the Officers and Directors of the Association, Mr. Leopold Stokowski and the members of the Philadelphia Orchestra.

The Treasurer's Report at the Twentieth Annual Meeting in 1924, showed that since 1904, for dues and subscriptions to special entertainments and gifts by the Committee, $11,432.00 had passed through her hands. While for special funds such as the Scheel Memorial Bas-relief, the Philadelphia Orchestra Chorus and the Opera Supper Dances, an additional amount of $25,335.00 was received and expended, making a grand total in twenty years of $36,759.00. This does not include any money for the Guarantee or Endowment Funds, or money for tickets sold by the Committee. Two interesting items are those of $6,456.00 for the Fritz Scheel Memorial raised by the three committees; and of $7770 raised for the Philadelphia Orchestra Chorus in 1921–22.

"The time has come to talk of many things" when an account of the work of the women is to be given; for the things they have done have been as diverse as the "ships and shoes and sealing wax and cabbages and kings" which so puzzled "Alice in Wonderland."

They have ranged from guarantors, ticket selling and parlor meetings, to balls, dances and selling post cards. Not to mention the two Endowment Funds and the silhouettes, the contribution toward the Chorus in 1921, and the receptions for the various conductors and soloists during twenty-one years. While thousands of dollars have passed through the Women's Committees for the maintenance of the orchestra, apart from the tickets they have sold, the women had no fund to fall back on until 1921, when the Women's Committees Fund was established, to which the proceeds of the Opera Supper Dances are added each year.

In speaking of the Endowment Funds it should be recorded that the first gift ever made for such a fund came to the Women's Committee in 1906, from Mr. Theodore N. Ely.

"RESOLUTION ADOPTED DECEMBER, 1906

"RESOLVED: That this Committee send to Mr. Theodore N. Ely, their most sincere and appreciative thanks for his most generous contribution towards the cause for which this Committee exists.

"And further resolved, that the Committee appoint a Sub-committee of four, to urge upon the Executive Committee of the Philadelphia Orchestra, the desirability and great appropriateness of starting the Permanent Endowment Fund for the perpetuation of the Philadelphia Orchestra, with this generous contribution in memory of one of the first members of the Board of Managers of the Women's Committee, Mrs. Theodore N. Ely.

"And further resolved, that copies of this resolution be sent to Mr. Ely, and to the Executive Committee of the Orchestra.

"In pursuance of this, our President has appointed the following ladies a Committee to confer with the Executive Committee of the Orchestra concerning this matter, Mrs. Yarnall, Mrs. Widener, Miss Wister and Mrs. McCollin."

THE AUXILIARIES

With the exception of raising money for the various funds the most important feature of the four Women's Committees is their Auxiliaries, now numbering 1985 women, attending the three Philadelphia series. It was through these that the Friday audience was built up, for Auxiliary members must have season seats. There are no dues and no other duties; but some of the best work done for the Endowment Fund and for the Anniversary Ball, was done by Auxiliary members, who for years have had a deep regard for the orchestra. All women season ticket holders are eligible.

The Women's Committees have given many entertainments, beginning with a reception in honor of Fritz Scheel on March 6th, 1905, followed by House Music under Mr. Scheel's direction.

Others have been given in the following order:

Mr. Carl Pohlig, 1908;

Mme. Pohlig and her daughter Mme. Maillard, 1909.

Mr. and Mrs. Leopold Stokowski, 1912.

Luncheon to celebrate Tenth Anniversary of the Women's Committee, March 6th, 1914.

Reception to Mr. Stokowski and soloists and members of the Mahler Chorus, March 4th, 1916.

Supper for Mr. Stokowski and assisting artists, March 4th, 1916, at which many out-of-town guests were present.

Receptions at the houses of Mrs. Alexander J. Cassatt, the Countess of Santa Eulalia, Mrs. Weatherly and Mrs. Cryer, in the interest of the Seven-Year Endowment Fund, October, 1916.

Reception to Mlle. Guiomar Novaes, 1917.

Receptions for Mme. Olga Samaroff, M. Alphonse Catherine, M. Sergei Rachmaninoff, 1919.

Luncheon to celebrate Fifteenth Anniversary of the Women's Committee, April 24th, 1919.

Reception at house of Mrs. Matthew H. Cryer, Lansdowne, to celebrate Tenth Anniversary of the Media, Chester and West Chester Women's Committee, 1921.

Musicale and reception at the house of Mrs. L. Howard Weatherly, to celebrate Tenth Anniversary of the West Philadelphia Women's Committee, May, 1915.

Luncheon for Mr. Frederick A. Stock, guest conductor, January 19th, 1924.

Reception to celebrate Twentieth Anniversary of the Women's Committee, March 14th, 1924.

Reception to Mr. Igor Strawinsky, January 30th, 1925.

Luncheon to celebrate Twentieth Anniversary of Germantown and Chestnut Hill Women's Committee, March 31st, 1925.

Reception to celebrate Twentieth Anniversary of West Philadelphia Women's Committee, May 13th, 1925.

Among the artists whom the Women's Committees have entertained, the most popular one is Mme. Olga Samaroff. She is beloved by all the members, and admired, not only because she is a great artist, but on account of her unusual and delightful personality. The women will never forget what she did for the orchestra during her years of residence in Philadelphia.

THE ANNIVERSARY BALL
FOR THE BENEFIT OF THE CHORUS

No mention of the entertainments of the Committees would be complete without an account of this. It was held January 24th, 1921, to mark the Sixty-fourth Anniversary of the opening ball of the Academy of Music, on January 26th, 1857. It should be called a study in co-operation, for besides the four Women's Committees, almost the whole city joined to make it a beautiful affair and a success. The feature of the evening was the quadrille in the costume of the period to which a number of persons contributed sets, as well as the following organizations.

The Co-operating Societies were:

Matinee Musical Club, Mendelssohn Club, Musical Art Club, Musical Fund Society, Philadelphia Music Club, Philadelphia Orchestra Chorus, Philadelphia Choral Society, Treble Clef, Fortnightly Club, Pennsylvania Academy of the Fine Arts, Sketch Club, School of Industrial Art, School of Design for Women, Plastic Club, T Square Club.

Old trunks were overhauled and old papers assiduously read to get the local color of the time, so that when row after row of the dancers began to march down from the dais at the back of the stage and take their places on the floor there was a scene of beauty which brought forth rounds of applause. Mr. Charles S. Morgan, Jr., impersonated Mr. Hlasko, Master of Ceremonies, and took charge of the quadrille which he had trained.

A Loan Exhibition of much interest was held in the Foyer for which many treasures were unearthed, including "Miss Ethel Newcome," of London, the doll dating from the Sanitary Fair. Various business firms assisted by contributing materials and allowing the Committees to use their windows for publicity of a unique kind, such as dolls and jewelry of the period. Twenty years before such a joint undertaking would not have been possible, and it was a mark of the general good-will felt for the Philadelphia Orchestra.

The Opera Supper Dances

A word should be said about these Dances, the Sixth Series of which has just begun. They are held in the Foyer of the Academy, after performances of the Metropolitan Opera Company. The subscription and supper are moderate in price and the affairs are much patronized. The object is to raise money yearly and have a fund that can be used when necessity arises. _____

When the war came a loss of interest might have been expected, but it was the reverse. Not only the weekly respite at the concerts proved a boon, but the activities of the Committees were a relief from the anxiety and rush of war work.

The Women's Committee has had good friends in the Board of Directors. When they had no means of support, Mr. Richard Y. Cook for many years contributed towards their expenses. Without his assistance they would have been in a serious situation.

Mr. Wm. Jay Turner, the Vice-president, was an important person at the Anniversary Ball which he led with Miss Frances A. Wister, president of the Committee.

Mr. Edward W. Bok spurred the women on to victory for the Fund with a kind but firm hand. Mr. Andrew Wheeler is always friendly and interested, and so the story might go on naming every director.

First and last is Mr. Van Rensselaer, who has never lost an opportunity to assist the women's enterprises and who is regarded as the patron saint of the Women's Committees. Mrs. Van Rensselaer's interest has been a great help.

The members of the Committee deserve individual mention, but space is lacking. In the early days Mrs. McCollin and Mrs. Keffer were untiring. Mrs. Yarnall and Mrs. Allen have held office for twenty-one years. Mrs. Henry is an adapt at managing entertainments. Mrs. Cassatt was a most valuable officer, possessing courage and judgment and her loss is constantly felt.* Mrs. Arnett's direction of the

_____
*See In Memoriam

work for the Auxiliary, passed on from Mrs. McCollin, has been a quiet labor with little public notice. The Recording Secretaries, Mrs. Ashton and Mrs. Wood, have been efficient in keeping the minutes.

The woman who bore most of the burden of the pioneers was Mrs. Alexander J. Dallas Dixon, whose recent death has left a gap in their ranks. Although she gave up the presidency some years ago, her influence was always noticeable and her fulfillment of the task was appreciated. A special meeting was held on October 8th, 1925, to pass resolutions for Mrs. Dixon.* At the concert of October 16th, these were inserted in the programme and the audience stood while the Chopin Funeral March was played, in memory of the first president of the Women's Committee.

The four Committees and their Auxiliaries have an Annual Meeting each April, and the President of the Women's Committee presents a general report to the Association in May. The names of some of the reports are indicative of the work, for instance: "A Calm Sea and a Prosperous Voyage," "The Adventures of the Women's Committees, or How We Financed the Chorus," "Twenty Years at Hard Labor, a Motion Picture, with a Prologue and an Epilogue and Continuous Music by the Philadelphia Orchestra." Their work has been strenuous, but the women have had many thrills and good times in the doing of it. There are pleasures in the chase only known to those who hunt, even when the quarry is an Endowment Fund.

Women are needed in every household to attend to the personal side of life, the entertainment of guests, the timely gifts, the flowers and many other things. They have even been known to help to support the establishment when the struggle seemed too hard for the men. This has been much the position occupied by the Women's Committees during the last twenty-one years. Their entertainments have made many artists welcome to this city. Their gifts have come at just the right time: the share in the loving cup to Mr. Van Rensselaer; the silver plates to Mr. Stokowski on the completion of his tenth year as conductor; the silver vase to Dr. Rich after eighteen years of service; the porringer to little Sonia Marie Noël Stokowski, engraved with a verse from Wordsworth, all give a human touch to the Associa-

*See In Memoriam

[60]

tion. And when the men were spent in the battle, the women worked to support the establishment.

The Women's Committees rejoice in the work they have done for the Philadelphia Orchestra, and in blazing the trail for women elsewhere. When the first was formed twenty-one years ago it was a pioneer and a unique organization, unknown anywhere in connection with a permanent orchestra. Many persons looked on it with, at least, a question. Now the questions are of a different nature, and come from other cities where orchestras are being formed.

The value of women's efforts in fostering music, and in making orchestras popular, seems to be recognized. Women's work for art in America is rapidly expanding; the torch has been borne by the Women's Committees for the Philadelphia Orchestra.

Chapter V

The Guarantors and the Guarantee Fund

There are a few satisfactory ways of financing an orchestra, but there are a number of unsatisfactory ways, and maintaining or trying to maintain a Guarantee Fund is one of them. The devotion of the guarantors of the Philadelphia Orchestra through sixteen years of financial embarrassment is a part of the story of which Philadelphia may be proud. A group of one hundred and twenty men and women* constituted the first guarantors in 1900–1901.

At the close of the season this notice was issued:

"The Philadelphia Orchestra
"Fritz Scheel, *Conductor*
"Call for the First Guarantee Fund
"Philadelphia, June 15th, 1901

"Dear Sir:

"The accounts of the Treasurer of the Philadelphia Orchestra Association, for the season just closed, shows a total expenditure for all purposes of $27,729.33, and total receipts from all sources of $14,429.85, leaving a deficit of $13,299.48, to be met by the Guarantee Fund.

"A copy of the report of the Auditors is hereto appended.

"The Guarantors are to be congratulated upon the success of this experimental season—made possible only by their generous support. The musical success of the concerts has surpassed the most sanguine anticipation, but the most important and far-reaching result of the undertaking has been the formation of the recently organized Philadelphia Orchestra Association, with its well-assured plans for weekly concerts and public rehearsals during the winter seasons of the next three years.

"The total Guarantee Fund amounts to $15,720.00, upon which a call of 84.61 per cent is necessary to meet the above deficit. Will you, therefore, please mail to Mr. John H. Ingham, Assistant Treasurer, No. 505 Chestnut Street, your check drawn to his order, for $_____ being 84.61 per cent of your subscription of $_____

"Very truly yours,

"John H. Ingham
Oliver B. Judson
Edward I. Keffer
Oscar A. Knipe
Edward G. McCollin
Henry Whelen, Jr.
"*Executive Committee*"

---

*See Appendix D.

"Philadelphia, 12th June, 1901.

"The undersigned, being two of the Guarantors for the first series of Concerts of the Philadelphia Orchestra, and having been requested to act as Auditors, have examined the accounts of the Treasurer and the vouchers for disbursements.

"We find same in order and correct, and are satisfied that the business management of the Orchestra has been efficient, and that the expenditures were proper and necessary.

"The accounts show receipts from sales of tickets and incidentals amounting to $14,429.85, and payments as per receipted vouchers amounting to $27,729.33, leaving a deficit of $13,299.48.

"JOHN H. CONVERSE
"C. HARTMAN KUHN
"Auditors"

When the business of this season was settled, a new fund had to be procured; forty-three Philadelphians were found who were willing to risk a three-year pledge for an untried experiment, and a number more for shorter terms.

When this three-year guarantee expired the Association was facing a crisis and was on the point of disbanding the orchestra. Then the newly formed Women's Committee was appealed to with the information that an addition of ten thousand dollars to the Guarantee Fund, secured within two weeks, was the only hope of saving the orchestra. An account of this first effort by the women has been given in a previous chapter. They succeeded in securing a number of new guarantors for one, two and three-year terms, and completed the amount within the required time.

The story of the next sixteen years is one of constant begging on the part of everybody connected with this institution. Many methods were used to explain the financial condition. The Minutes, the programme book, and the numerous letters issued bear witness to this fact. Many were the meetings called "to consider the financial status of the Association."

"Dear Sir or Madam:

"At the end of the second season the Directors of the Philadelphia Orchestra find that the deficit will practically be the same as at the end of the first year, viz: $68,000 or $70,000. The expense of managing the organization has been reduced as much as possible, and if the organization is to be maintained on the same standard of excellence, the management feel that a large guarantee fund is necessary.

[63]

"It is proposed to increase the guarantee fund from $40,000 to $100,000, and by so doing we would not have to call on the entire guarantee fund, possibly 50 per cent of such fund would be necessary. The prices of admission for boxes and seats in the various parts of the house are as low as it is possible to make them, so that the concerts are within easy reach of students of music.

"The Orchestra during the past year has completed a season of 20 weeks, having given 71 concerts in all, 43 in Philadelphia and 28 outside of the City. In addition to these performances the orchestra or a large number of them have appeared at concerts of the Orpheus Club, the Choral Society, the Temple Chorus and the Maennerchor under their several conductors."

* * * * *

"The management have done their utmost to make the orchestra a success, being aided in their efforts by the excellent conductorship of Herr Scheel. Private individuals and those interested in music have generously contributed, but it is to the public that we now look. By an increased season sale the receipts will be greatly increased, and consequently there will be more money to defray the expenses.

"If you have not as yet become a guarantor of the Philadelphia Orchestra, will you not aid us by doing so and communicate with Mr. John Ingham, Secretary, 505 Chestnut Street, who will furnish you blanks for that purpose. The guarantee fund covers a period of three years only.

"If the orchestra is to be continued, and it would be a disgrace to Philadelphia to allow a fine organization of its kind to slip away from us, two things are necessary: a larger guarantee fund and the support of the public by an increased season sale. The outlook for the latter, we are glad to say, is most encouraging for next season."

* * * * *

Of course, it must be understood, that unless a sufficient guarantee fund be raised, they would not feel justified in continuing the Orchestra indefinitely.

* * * * *

"Hoping you will, if you have not already done so, aid us in furthering and maintaining this orchestra, we remain

Yours truly,

"GEORGE BURNHAM, JR.	A. J. CASSATT
JOHN H. CONVERSE	ECKLEY B. COXE, JR.
WM. L. ELKINS	MISS MARY K. GIBSON
JOHN H. INGHAM	OLIVER B. JUDSON
EDWARD I. KEFFER	C. HARTMAN KUHN
EDWARD G. McCOLLIN	THOMAS McKEAN
CLEMENT B. NEWBOLD	JAMES W. PAUL, JR.
MRS. F. H. ROSENGARTEN	RICHARD ROSSMAESSLER
EDGAR SCOTT	SIMON A. STERN
MISS ANNE THOMSON	A. VAN RENSSELAER
HENRY WHELEN, JR.	P. A. B. WIDENER

CLEMENT A. GRISCOM"

"The management of the Philadelphia Orchestra Association, at the end of the third season of concerts, feel that they may now claim that they have fulfilled their original promise to supply the community with an orchestra of the first class. There are but three other orchestras of this rank in the country, those of Boston, Chicago and Pittsburg.

"A great orchestra is as much a civic institution as a great library or art museum. It is the backbone of the whole musical organism. No large city can afford to be without one."

* * * * *

"The artistic success of the past season is unquestioned, the work of the orchestra under Mr. Scheel, a leader admittedly second to none in the country, received flattering comment wherever it has been heard, both at home and in other cities, New York especially envying us the possession of an orchestra of the first rank."

* * * * *

"The deficit is practically the same as that of the preceding season, viz: sixty-eight to seventy thousand dollars. While this is a large sum, it compares favorably with the deficits of the three other large orchestras of the country during their initial seasons, and is not a cause for discouragement."

* * * * *

"An orchestra of the first class, however, can never be entirely self-supporting, and must be dependent upon the guarantees or contributions of those who take pride in their city and look upon its work as necessary to the education of the community."

* * * * *

"Up to the present time the amount of the deficit over and above the guarantee fund has been paid by a few (three or four) generous and public-spirited members of the Association. It is not fair, however, that the burden of such an undertaking should be borne by a few when the whole community is benefited, and the Directors appeal to the public generally to aid in this work.

"In a city of the size, wealth and culture of Philadelphia, it does not seem unreasonable to hope that a sufficient number of people can be found to assist in retaining the orchestra and increasing its usefulness. One hundred additional subscriptions of a Thousand or Five Hundred Dollars each, per annum, for three years, would go very far toward enabling the management to establish the orchestra on a permanent paying basis, but without such support from the public, the Directors do not feel that they would be justified in continuing the orchestra indefinitely."

* * * * *

"As it is impossible to ascertain and approach personally all who are interested in the cause, those who wish to subscribe to the guarantee fund are requested to write to the Secretary, Mr. John H. Ingham, 505 Chestnut Street, for blanks. The intention is to raise a fund for three years.

"On the success of this appeal will depend the future of the orchestra."   (*Signed as before.*)

[65]

"PHILADELPHIA ORCHESTRA ASSOCIATION

"Philadelphia, April 15, 1905.

"TO THE GUARANTORS OF THE PHILADELPHIA ORCHESTRA ASSOCIATION:

"In closing the Fifth Season of the Philadelphia Orchestra, the Executive Committee think it is proper to report the result of the season to the Guarantors and to the members of the Association."

* * * * *

"The total cost this season, including salaries of
musicians and conductor, office expenses, rental
of Academy of Music, etc., amounted to......$99,746.28
"The total receipts from all sources were........ 45,877.57

Showing a DEFICIT of...................... 53,868.71
"The Guarantee Fund is...................... 48,627.50

Leaving a DEFICIT of......................$ 5,241.21*

which we have every reason to believe will be provided for in the near future.

"The loss in season 1903–04 amounted to $58,530.23, so that we can show a distinct gain this year of $4661.52. The gain, however, was really much greater, inasmuch as our fixed charges were increased nearly $5000 due to increase in salary of conductor, increased rent of Academy of Music and increased charges for advertising, etc."

* * * * *

"Owing to the unflagging energy and enthusiasm of our Women's Committee, not only has our Guarantee Fund been substantially increased, but the season's sale of boxes and seats, etc., was larger than for any previous year."

* * * * *

"All this is very gratifying, but the fact remains that an efficiently maintained orchestra will always cost in the neighborhood of $100,000, with the possibilities of only $60,000 *maximum* receipts secured from full houses at every performance."

* * * * *

"There is no question whatever that the Orchestra is gaining in prestige and popularity among the people of this city, and it is the earnest hope of the Committee that the work should spread and that the Orchestra should be put on a permanent basis.

"It has been decided to re-engage Mr. Scheel, and contracts have been authorized with the members of the Orchestra, so that as far as possible the present personnel may be retained.

"It is the hope of the Committee that you will continue to favor the organization with your support as before, and that you will renew your subscription to the Guarantee Fund.

"By Order of the *Executive Committee*

"(Signed) A. VAN RENSSELAER, *President*"

*See Page 69.

PROGRAMME BOOK

"THE PHILADELPHIA ORCHESTRA ASSOCIATION

OWES MUCH OF ITS SUCCESS TO THE DEVOTED

LABORS OF THE FOLLOWING

WOMEN'S COMMITTEES

ANY MEMBER OF WHICH WILL BE GLAD TO RECEIVE

YOUR SUBSCRIPTION OF TWENTY FIVE

DOLLARS, OR MORE, TO THE

GUARANTEE FUND

OF THE

PHILADELPHIA ORCHESTRA

"WHAT THE PHILADELPHIA ORCHESTRA IS DOING
FOR PHILADELPHIA

"The breadth of a city's culture is measured by its point of view toward the arts that interpret life. Music is one of them—with Painting and Literature. It is the function of THE PHILADELPHIA ORCHESTRA to carry forward the musical tradition that has been Philadelphia's for five generations—

"And more, to keep its musical consciousness alive and virile, by presenting the noblest works of the composers of today—composers who are expressing life in the terms of the present day."

* * * * *

"It has warm friends, enthusiastic audiences, the appreciation of musicians. Its influence is far more than local.

"But more than this—it needs financial support.

"It is not a private enterprise for private gain, but a public organization for public service.

"In the nature of things such an institution cannot be self-supporting. Its box-office receipts are fixed by the customary scale of prices—while its expenses are the creatures of time and circumstance.

"The resulting deficit is made up each season by The Philadelphia Orchestra Association, whose members guarantee sums ranging from $25 to $5000 each, annually, for this purpose.

"The Association is thus the instrument through which any one may help to perform this public service. It needs more members—of whom you are invited to be one.

"THE INFLUENCE OF YOUR NAME
AND YOUR MONEY ARE NEEDED."

[67]

"THE CALL TO CIVIC PRIDE IS IN THE AIR. 'Learn to know Philadelphia and work for her,' is heard on every hand, and our people are urged to form and join 'Patriotic Societies,' all of which is good, and well worth-while.

"BUT DO YOU KNOW that for several years a zealous Patriotic Society—one that evinces the truest Patriotism, the Patriotism of the Pocket-book and Bank Account—has been quietly at work doing all it could in its own way for the good name of Philadelphia and for the enjoyment and welfare of her citizens?

"THE MEMBERS OF THIS SOCIETY have demonstrated the soundness of their Patriotism, the reality of their Civic Pride, and their zeal for the people's good, without boasting and without complaint, by contributing from their private means, in the past nine years, approximately $468,000 to maintain and operate THE PHILADELPHIA ORCHESTRA, an institution of which every good Philadelphian has reason to be proud.

"THE MEMBERSHIP OF THIS SOCIETY of liberal and public-spirited citizens known as THE PHILADELPHIA ORCHESTRA ASSOCIATION, numbered 43 in the season of 1901–02. Last season there were 263 members."

* * * * *

"WILL YOU NOT SHOW YOUR PATRIOTISM, your Civic Pride, your desire 'to know and work for Philadelphia,' by joining the honorable roll of this Association? A subscription of Twenty-five Dollars, or more, toward the Guarantee Fund, will make you a member.

"YOUR NAME AND MONEY ARE NEEDED!
"THEY ARE NEEDED NOW!

"Write today to the Manager for a Subscription Blank."

One of the difficulties was the attitude of business men who felt that after a few years the orchestra should be making a return on the investment, or at least be self-supporting. Their opinion was that an institution which was a constant expense did not deserve the support of the community. Fortunately for music, the people of Philadelphia now understand that an orchestra never can be anything but a public charge.

Beginning with 1904 the number of guarantors ranged from two hundred and fifty to three hundred and sixty per season. The Guarantee Fund ranged from forty-five to fifty thousand dollars. During some seasons there was that most intolerable of all things, an extra deficit: during a few, a certain per cent of the fund only was called upon.

The discouraging part of the Guarantee Fund method of financing an orchestra lay in the fact that the work was never-ending. A certain number of guarantees expired each season and the guarantors had to be persuaded by all the arts of man and woman to renew their pledges. The fact that their money was to be immediately spent, militated, in the minds of many people, against the Fund. It is so much pleasanter to think of one's gift safely ensconced in a permanent fund yielding an income year after year for a favorite cause.

The Women's Committees worked hard for the Fund. Besides procuring new guarantees each year for twelve years, amounting to thousands of dollars, they obtained renewals of old guarantees or made good the loss by new ones. In 1905, they defrayed the extra deficit of $5300.00; no doubt taxing everybody's generosity and patience to the utmost.

Much of the financial burden in the first years was borne by a few men and women, who time after time put their hands deep into their pockets. Among these may be named Mr. Alexander Van Rensselaer, the president; Mr. Thomas McKean, Jr., for some years vice-president; Miss Anne Thomson and Miss Mary K. Gibson, directors. The treasurer, Mr. Henry Whelen, Jr., was always optimistic and advanced money constantly. What the result would have been if Mr. Whelen had not done this is problematical. His untimely death in 1907 robbed the orchestra of a devoted friend.

Mr. Whelen was succeeded as treasurer by Mr. Arthur E. Newbold, of Drexel and Company, who arranged loans and advanced money and took endless trouble for the Association. The same can be said of Mr. Robert K. Cassatt, the present treasurer, who attends to many details of business.

From 1905–06 until 1910–11, Mr. Horace Churchman was the Controller of the finances, which he administered with ability and much to the satisfaction of the Board.

A glance at the figures is all that is needed to learn the story of those years so discouraging from a business point of view.

Season	Concerts	Total	Number of Guarantors	Amount Collected	Extra Deficit
1900–01	6	$15,720	120	$13,299 (84%)	$40,000
1901–02	14 pairs	32,000	43	32,000	30,000
1902–03	14 "	38,000	113	38,000	16,000
1903–04	14 "	42,000	137	42,000	5,300
1904–05	15 "	48,000	259	48,000	
1905–06	18 "	50,000	315	47,000 (95%)	
1906–07	20 "	46,840	281	41,900 (90%)	
1907–08	22 "	42,285	273	40,100 (95%)	
1908–09	22 "	45,125	352	42,800 (95%)	
1909–10	22	44,800	359	44,800	
1910–11	25	42,400	311	42,400	
1911–12	25	42,100	309	42,100	
1912–13	25	43,200	314	43,200	
1913–14	25	46,000	335	46,000	
1914–15	25	45,300	323	45,300	
1915–16	25	49,100	310	49,100	
		Total		$618,699	

During these distressing days Scheel was asked to dine at the Rittenhouse Club to meet some prominent men of affairs, at a time when desperate efforts were being made to procure guarantors. The hour arrived, but no Scheel and it was learned that he had not gone home to dress. His friends started out to find him, and he was discovered teaching the second bassoon player to play a syncopated passage in a Tschaikowsky symphony. The dinner was entirely forgotten in the absorption of the lesson, but he rushed home to dress and arrived only thirty minutes late. The result of the dinner, however, was an addition of several thousand dollars to the Guarantee Fund.

The total number of guarantors who defrayed the annual deficit during sixteen years was about seven hundred and fifty, and to them Philadelphia music lovers are deeply in debt. Many sighs of relief were heard when this unstable way of financing an orchestra was ended by the offer of the "Unknown Donor," which made possible a more permanent method.

CHAPTER VI
THE DEATH OF FRITZ SCHEEL

But while the Board of Directors was in a continuous state of anxiety about the expenses; and the guarantors were being kept up to the mark; and the three Women's Committees then in existence were straining every nerve to help; and the orchestra was constantly improving through the untiring efforts of the conductor, all was not well with Fritz Scheel. In looking back over his term of leadership of the Philadelphia Orchestra, his friends realize now that his illness began at least one year, and perhaps more, before the final breakdown came. He became irascible with his players, erratic in conduct, and his good judgment in matters musical seemed to forsake him. During the first months of 1907 his programmes had to be constantly supervised to guard against excessive severity; and on one occasion he had to be restrained from playing five symphonies at one concert.

The first knowledge the public had that he was in a peculiar mental condition was at a concert of the Eurydice Chorus, held in Horticultural Hall on February 6, 1907. He had been much upset by the death of a violinist in the orchestra, who disappeared and was found drowned. During the concert he asked the audience to rise and then played a funeral march in memory of this man. He constantly talked to the audience and to the singers. It was immediately seen that he was not responsible for his actions, and a specialist was consulted. He was taken to Atlantic City for a week, but did not improve.

The news of Scheel's illness brought forth universal expressions of regret, as witness the following:

March 3, 1907.

"FRITZ SCHEEL"

"Fritz Scheel's illness is not only a personal tragedy; it is a public calamity. The fine orchestra which he has created for Philadelphia, and into which he has poured to exhaustion his own nervous energy, remains the pliant instrument he made it, ready to the hand of whatever master may be found to carry on his work, if he should not return to it. But the orchestra has been so peculiarly the expression of

Scheel's artistic personality, that his withdrawal at the end of what had been a most prosperous and buoyant season leaves the great constituency built up for it in these seven years with a sense of bereavement and depression.

"Mr. Scheel is a remarkable instance of a concentrated musical temperament, that views all life and thought through its own medium alone. In the years that he has spent in Philadelphia, he has been scarcely known beyond the immediate circle of the orchestra and the musical societies that he has directed."

* * * * *

"It is not enough to refer to the wide field of modern music that he has made familiar to us, through his lucid presentation of the works of the French, the Russian and other Continental composers, including the most recent Germans, such as Strauss, whose recondite music he read with a clearness and significance that the composer himself failed to convey. Scheel's peculiar insight is still more characteristically expressed in that fact that he has made Brahms a popular composer in Philadelphia, and he has triumphantly shown that the great 'classics' are not antiquated, but that real musical thought may speak to modern ears as well through ancient as through modern forms, if felt and interpreted with modern understanding.

* * * * *

"The orchestra, of course, goes on, and the best present hope is that Scheel may be restored to health before another season. No doubt another conductor will be found if this hope should fail, but he will necessarily be different and there is no one now known in this country whom with an equally broad musical outlook, could be counted upon to make all the work of the orchestra so unfailingly and often surprisingly interesting as Scheel has done. Such artists as he are rare in any time or place, and it is to the honor of Philadelphia that he has received not only from the few, but from the many, some measure of the appreciation that is his due."

Public Ledger, February 10, 1907

".............Scheel's collapse, however, came as a shock to everyone connected with the orchestra, and yet they all realized that he could not endure for a much longer time. For three weeks he had been unable to sleep.

"Never a moment of freedom did he allow himself. In Odd Fellows' Temple each morning he rehearsed one group of players, in the afternoon another group and in the evening the entire orchestra. At his meals he arranged the sugar bowl so that it would keep the score of some symphony or other in an upright position where he could study while eating.

"In Harrisburg, only three weeks ago, Scheel had the grip, and when the business manager, Charles Augustus Davis, went to see him, he found the leader lying in bed with water bags over his heart and a

[72]

score in front of his eyes. All this time Scheel was also attending to his work as leader of the Eurydice and the Orpheus Clubs, rehearsing and leading at concerts.''

* * * * *

"LOOKS HAGGARD"

"Mr. Scheel was seen by the *Public Ledger* correspondent as he returned to his hotel after a swift stroll down the boardwalk with his physician. He looked haggard and spoke in an excited, almost hysterical tone.

'' 'Please tell my friends in Philadelphia that I am not a sick man,' and greeted the newspaperman effusively. 'All this talk about my mental condition is absurd. I needed a rest, that was all, and the directors very kindly allowed me to come to the seashore. I will be all right in a few days, won't I, doctor?'

"The concluding sentence was directed to Doctor Goodman in a tone of pitiful appeal. Dr. Goodman nodded good-naturedly, as he does to all the proposals and plans that the sick musician unfolds in his illusions, when he talks about purchasing several beach playhouses for great music festivals.''

After conducting a last concert in Reading, Scheel was taken to a sanitarium where he died of paresis on March 13th, 1907.

One of his last hallucinations was to write letters to prominent musicians in Europe, offering them large sums to come to Philadelphia and teach in a conservatory that he was about to found. During his stay at the sanitarium he organized the nurses and orderlies into a chorus and made them sing part songs, grouped about his bed. This was a unique occurrence in the conduct of sanitariums, and he was soon much beloved by the attendants, whose tears at his funeral bore witness to their feeling for him.

"Fritz Scheel, Fighter," would have been a good name for the first leader of the Philadelphia Orchestra. His death was generally attributed to overwork, but modern psychologists insist that no man ever came to his death by work. It was the strain of conquering, handicapped by the financial condition of the Association, that killed Scheel— conquering first his musicians, then the musical public, then the opposition to a Philadelphia Orchestra, and last the general apathy, most difficult foe of all to subdue. If he had not been a fighter, the Twenty-fifth Anniversary of the Philadelphia Orchestra would still be several years ahead.

[73]

Philadelphia Inquirer, March 14, 1907,

"SCHEEL, MARTYR TO ORCHESTRA HE CREATED, IS DEAD. CONDUCTOR
KNOWN THROUGHOUT THIS COUNTRY AND
EUROPE SUCCUMBS TO PNEUMONIA

"Fritz Scheel, conductor and creator of the Philadelphia Orchestra, who during the seven years which he headed that organization won the affection of local music lovers as no other musician ever gained it, died shortly before one o'clock yesterday afternoon in Dr. Francis X. Dercum's sanatorium, at 1929 Wallace Street. Double pneumonia was the direct cause of his death.

"There is little doubt that the real cause of the sudden end of the brilliant career of Mr. Scheel was his devotion to the orchestra, of which he was the conductor, for had it not been for the nervous and physical breakdown of a month ago, brought on by overwork, his ordinarily sturdy constitution in all probability would have shaken off the pneumonia which conquered him in his weakened condition.

"During the month before his nervous breakdown, Scheel, encouraged by the artistic and financial success which was attending the season's performances, redoubled his efforts to make the remaining concerts even outshine in brilliancy and attendance the preceding ones.

"There is no doubt that he would have succeeded, for he had not only imbued both the musicians in the orchestra with his zeal, but had also wrought the music lovers of Philadelphia up to a high pitch of enthusiasm."

Philadelphia Press, Thursday, March 14, 1907:

"MAGIC OF SCHEEL'S BATON STILLED BY LEADER'S DEATH"
"Double pneumonia ends life of gifted musician who brought the Philadelphia Orchestra to a high plane of excellence.

"Philadelphia music lovers suffered perhaps the severest loss in the city's musical history yesterday, when Fritz Scheel, director of the Philadelphia Orchestra, succumbed to double pneumonia."

* * * * *

"The news was received with sorrow among rich and poor alike, among those who were regular subscribers to the season of symphony concerts, as well as among those, who loving music, waited patiently in line for the doors to the family circle and amphitheatre of the Academy of Music to open, to hear the diverse program which it was Scheel's wont to perform.

"The maestro had made a brave fight for his life, his vitality, according to his physicians, having been remarkable."

* * * * *

"Mr. Scheel added to the technical equipment, which is the natural product of German life and training, a poetic temperament and a broad outlook on matters musical, which not only gave great vivacity and variety to his programmes, but which made for such insight in the matter of the meaning of any given composition, as to produce the most illuminating and inspiring results.

"A course of seven seasons under his baton was, therefore, not only pleasurable in the highest sense of the meaning of the word, but instructive and educational to a marked degree, the entertainment however, marked, being as it were, incidental to a greater purpose of not only creating, but of satisfying the desire for the higher things in the most glorious of arts. In this sphere of endeavor Mr. Scheel's singleness of purpose was well known. His devotion to musical ideals was manifest in everything he did, and his concentration on what he considered his lifework was of so energetic and absorbing a character as to make serious inroads on his health and strength. His death places the musical world peculiarly in his debt, since he arrived in Philadelphia at a critical period in our musical history and met the situation admirably.

"It is natural that those interested in music should feel a personal loss, but there is also a larger loss, in that every city must conserve those influences which keep the fire burning for the finer things of life. Hence, although those who are not of the musical world may not so realize it, they are also the losers through the passing of so striking a personality, for nothing is more certain than that any community does not live for or by bread alone, and it is a hopeful sign when any city is the scene of activities which include men and movements that look beyond mere material comforts.

"It is fortunate that at this juncture Philadelphia has a large group of self-sacrificing citizens who realize this. Mr. Scheel had his reward in life in their support and appreciation, and the best tribute to him, now that he is dead, will be that the good work will go on on the lines laid down by him, so that what he stood for shall not be lost, and the vantage ground attained to be held in all certainty."

Funeral services for Fritz Scheel were held on March 16th in the Lutheran Church of the Holy Communion, on Chestnut Street above Twenty-first. The immense gathering was a tribute to the conductor and a proof of his personal, as well as musical, popularity in Philadelphia.

The list of honorary pall-bearers was a long one and included representatives from almost every branch of musical activity in Philadelphia:

Executive Committee of the Orchestra: Mr. Thomas McKean, Mr. Henry Whelen, Jr., Mr. Richard Y. Cook, Mr. John H. Ingham, Mr. Andrew Wheeler, Jr., Dr. Edward I. Keffer, Mr. Edward G. McCollin, Mr. A. J. D. Dixon.

Orchestra Guarantors: Mr. F. T. S. Darley, Mr. S. Decatur Smith, Mr. Richard S. Brock, Mr. John H. Converse.

Business Office: Mr. Chas. A. Davis, Mr. Horace Churchman.

Orchestra Members: Mr. Thaddeus Rich, Mr. Anton Horner, Mr. Jan Koert, Mr. C. Stanley Mackey.

Philadelphia Symphony Society: Mr. Charles A. Braun, Mr. J. H. Michener, Jr., Mr. Joseph M. Mitcheson.

Orpheus Club: Mr. Charles W. Baily, Mr. Arthur L. Church.

Eurydice Club: Mr. Louis F. Benson, Mr. F. H. Rosengarten.

Mendelssohn Club: Dr. W. W. Gilchrist.

Choral Society: Mr. Henry Gordon Thunder.

University of Pennsylvania: Dr. Hugh A. Clarke.

Philadelphia Press: Dr. A. C. Lambdin, Mr. Max Heinrici, Mr. George Rogers, Dr. Martin Darkow.

Philadelphia Musicians: Mr. Philip H. Geopp, Mr. Maurice Leefson, Mr. Richard Zeckwer, Mr. Wassili Leps.

Personal Friends: Dr. Victor Loser, Dr. John H. Musser.

Besides these, the Board of Directors of the Association and the Women's Committees for the Philadelphia Orchestra attended in two large groups.

Although the orchestra had disbanded for the summer enough of the musicians were still in Philadelphia to play the slow movement of the Eroica symphony as the cortège entered the church. The Orpheus Club sang "The Long Day Closes," by Arthur Sullivan, and "Holy Peace," by Abt. At the grave the horn quartette of the orchestra played Mozart's Ave Verum." His baton and the score of the Ninth Symphony were buried with him.

Telegrams and messages of sympathy poured into the offices of the Association from musicians in all parts of the country and from foreign artists, sojourning here.

A special meeting of the Board of Directors was held on March 14th, 1907, and this resolution adopted:

"The untimely death of Fritz Scheel has deprived this Association of the services of a Conductor, who, by his genius and devotion to his art, has successfully forwarded our efforts to establish an orchestra that is a credit to Philadelphia and to the contributors whom we represent.

"Artistic both by temperament and inheritance, the devotion to his profession by which this community has profited so much has been indirectly responsible for the untimely ending of his career. Had he been less insistent upon the full performance of every detail involved in a complete and conscientious fulfillment of his duties, the great drain upon his powers that left him without sufficient vitality to withstand the attack of his last illness, might have been avoided.

"If it be for us to write his epitaph, we would place devotion to his art as his most prominent trait of character, and loyalty to his orchestra and to our Association as its closest companion.

"In many respects the Philadelphia Orchestra stands as a monument to his work and memory, for he must long be remembered as its first, and for seven years its only Conductor."

Scheel's devotion to Beethoven was well known, and if he had been told to arrange his last concert no doubt he would have chosen a Beethoven programme. Was it more than coincidence that the following programme was his last?

BEETHOVEN PROGRAMME
February 7 and 8, 1907
DR. OTTO NEITZEL, *Pianist*

QUARTET

MARIE KUNKEL-ZIMMERMAN, *Soprano*   NICHOLAS DOUTY, *Tenor*
EMILY STUART KELLOGG, *Contralto*   FREDERIC MARTIN, *Bass*

THE MENDELSSOHN CLUB

(Through the courtesy of Dr. W. W. Gilchrist, Director)

LUDWIG VON BEETHOVEN (1770–1827)

1. Phantasie for Piano, Orchestra and Chorus, Op. 80
    Adagio   *Piano*
    Finale
        Allegro
        Allegro molto
        Adagio ma non troppo
        Marcia assai vivace   *Piano and Orchestra*
    Allegretto ma non troppo
    Presto   *Piano, Orchestra and Chorus*

Prefatory Remarks by Dr. Otto Neitzel

2. Quartet from "Fidelio" ("Mir ist's so wunderbar")
                        For Two Sopranos, Tenor and Bass
3. Symphony No. 9, in D Minor (Choral), Op. 125
                Finale on Schiller's "Ode to Joy"
            For Soli, Chorus and Orchestra
    Alletro ma non troppo, un poco maestoso
    Molto vivace
    Adagio molto e cantabile
    Allegro assai   *Quartet and Chorus*

Prefatory Remarks by Dr. Otto Neitzel

The predicament of the Board of Directors during Scheel's illness and after his death can hardly be described. Apart from the feeling of personal loss, the Association was pledged to give a series of concerts in Philadelphia and elsewhere. All the best conductors in America were engaged in mid-season and the best European ones, if available, were to be had only at impossible prices.

[77]

The concerts of February 7th and 8th during the first week of his illness were conducted by August Rodemann, the assistant conductor and first flutist; and Dr. Otto Neitzel, who was included in the programme as lecturer, directed the Ninth Symphony. The remaining ones were led in an atmosphere of sadness and apprehension by Leandro Campanari.

THE SCHEEL MEMORIAL TABLET

Immediately after the death of Fritz Scheel the Women's Committee proposed to raise a fund for a memorial to him to be placed in the lobby of the Academy of Music. A committee was appointed with Mrs. Wm. W. Arnett as Chairman. The circular printed below was sent out, to which there was an immediate and generous response.

FRITZ SCHEEL MEMORIAL FUND
UNDER THE AUSPICES OF
THE WOMEN'S COMMITTEE FOR THE PHILADELPHIA ORCHESTRA

"The Women's Committee for the Philadelphia Orchestra has decided to erect in the Academy of Music a life-sized bronze bas-relief portrait of the late Fritz Scheel, three-quarters length figure, at a cost of $5000; $2000 of which has already been contributed. This memorial will have great value as a work of art, as it will be executed by Mr. Charles Grafly, of Philadelphia, the eminent American sculptor. It will also be a lasting and visible monument to the first conductor of the Philadelphia Orchestra, who was beloved by the musical public not only of Philadelphia, but of other neighboring cities. It is right and fitting that so great a man, representing so great an organization, should have an adequate monument in our historic Academy of Music.

"The music-loving public is asked to help erect this monument to Mr. Scheel, and all lovers of Art who have the interest of the great enterprise of their city at heart, will wish to have their part in this Memorial.

"Messrs. Drexel & Co., Fifth and Chestnut Streets, have kindly consented to receive contributions to the 'Fritz Scheel Memorial Fund,' as also have Heppe & Son, 1115 Chestnut Street, and Theodore Presser, 1712 Chestnut Street. Contributions may also be sent to the office of the Philadelphia Orchestra Association, Room 1313, Pennsylvania Building, Fifteenth and Chestnut Streets, or to Mrs. Alfred Reginald Allen, Treasurer, 111 South Twenty-first Street, Philadelphia. Contributions of any amount, large and small, are solicited.

"It is important that all contributions be made by June 1st in order that the bronze may be completed before the termination of the next Orchestra season."

* * * * *

Mr. Charles Grafly had taken a death mask of Scheel and produced a fine work of art and a most excellent likeness of the man. The setting was designed by Mr. Edgar V. Seeler. The Tablet cost six thousand dollars, and enough money was raised in addition to purchase a lot in West Laurel Hill Cemetery, and to place on Scheel's grave a suitable tombstone and some shrubbery. Perpetual care was arranged for, a great satisfaction to Miss Scheel and to all his friends and admirers. For many years the Women's Committee has placed a wreath on the memorial tablet on the anniversary of Scheel's death, thus keeping alive the memory of the man and what he did for music here.

One year after Scheel's death a memorial meeting was held at the Academy of Music at which time the tablet was unveiled.

PROGRAMME OF CEREMONIES

"FRITZ SCHEEL MEMORIAL

"ACADEMY OF MUSIC
WEDNESDAY, MARCH ELEVENTH
NINETEEN HUNDRED
AND EIGHT
AT THREE O'CLOCK"

———

"FRITZ SCHEEL

"A TRIBUTE
"By Florence Earle Coates

"He gave his life to Music—gave—
  For love, not hire—himself denying;
His body rests, o'er wearied, in the grave,
  But Music lives and gives him life undying.

"In the deep silence, may he hear
  Such harmonies as he could wake,
And O, may some faint accents reach his ear
  From the great City's heart that sorrows for his sake!"

———

"IN MEMORIAM
"By Harrison S. Morris

"Broken in twain the ordered sum of years,
  The baton fallen, the chords forever stilled;
Vanished the master, mourned of human tears,
  Enduring what to Art his spirit willed.

"The hand that swept the strings
  Like unto dust shall be;
The stricken chords vibrate
  Eternally."

[79]

"Program

"In Memoriam
"Fritz Scheel
"Born Lübeck, 1852; Died Philadelphia, 1907"

"Richard Wagner—Vorspiel, "Parsifal"
"Address
"Mr. Owen Wister
"Richard Strauss, Tone Poem, Opus 28,
"Tod und Verklärung,
"(Death and Transfiguration)."

* * * * *

"Unveil Memorial to Fritz Scheel"

Great Throng at Academy of Music to Participate in Honor of First Conductor of Philadelphia Orchestra

"One of the greatest tributes ever paid to a musician in this city was the Fritz Scheel memorial celebration at the Academy of Music yesterday afternoon. It was a tribute to a man who was much beloved for the years of hard work he had done in bringing the Philadelphia Orchestra to its present perfection, as well as a tribute to his own personality, which won for him hosts of very warm admirers here."

"Great Crowd Gathered"

"The memorial services at the Academy yesterday, modest and impressive as they were, were remarkable for the vast crowd that assembled to honor the master. Long before the doors were opened, hundreds of people had gathered at each of the entrances, which were rapidly increased to thousands and when admission was finally gained, it was only a short time before every bit of available space was taken, with sufficient people on the outside to fill the place twice over.

"That the Academy was filled to capacity was announced at the different entrances by attaches of the Academy, and although hundreds turned away disappointed, an equal number of them remained during the entire hour of the memorial services, and to repay them for their patience, they were finally allowed admission, not to get a chance to hear any of the ceremonies, but to view the handsome tablet.

"The tablet was unveiled while the audience listened to the brief but impressive address of Mr. Owen Wister.

* * * *

"Mrs. Roosevelt Sent a Wreath"

"Encircling the tablet was a festooning of laurel sent by the Women's Committee, and underneath a large wreath of beautiful white roses sent by Mrs. Roosevelt.

"Mr. Wister's address was a brief but eloquent effort. After a few introductory remarks, he said among other things:

[80]

" 'Great poems survive the poets who wrote them; great pictures and statues survive their creators, as symphonies survive the masters who composed them. In all these arts the work of genius lives on, while the brain where it was born goes to dust. Not so is it with another sort of artist, the enterpreter. He who interprets—the actor, the singer, the player—be he never so great, be he Garrick, or Mario or Paganini, still must he perish with the generation that heard him, and sometimes he does not even leave a name.

" 'The lot of the orchestral conductor is the same, for he belongs to the class of interpreters, with the Garricks, the Marios, the Paganinis. No matter what magic comes from the baton that he waves, once that baton is laid down, the magic is dead.'

"Reviewed Mr. Scheel's Work"

"Mr. Wister then went on to sketch briefly the work of Mr. Scheel from the time he came to this country and of his residence in Philadelphia for nine years, beginning with the conducting of the Amateur Symphony Orchestra and including the years he was at the head of Philadelphia Orchestra. He said:

" 'Arduous were the pioneer steps, but between each one lie many struggles, many examples of generosity, of munificent giving on the part of private citizens; some gave their time and some their purse and some both. Without their persmission (for they would refuse it), let the names of the pioneers be mentioned:

" 'Mrs. A. J. Cassatt and that hardworking committee of four: Messrs. Edward Keffer, Edward McCollin, John Ingham, Oliver Judson. Let us remember next the boundless generosity of Alexander Van Rensselaer and Thomas McKean, who poured their thousands out like a royal gift; nor let us ever forget Miss Anne Thomson and Miss Mary Gibson; to let any of these names go in silence today, would be to fail in due appreciation. And for Henry Whelen, his untiring devotion of time and purse, let a special word of remembrance be said.'

" 'But for the loyal help of all these we might not be here—nor should we, if, in a dark hour, when masculine endurance gave out, feminine energy had not stepped in.'

"Mr. Wister then followed with a eulogy of Mr. Scheel, the 'artist' as well as Mr. Scheel the 'man.' In conclusion he said:

" 'So did his work end. Many must be sitting here today who well remember those years when Theodore Thomas played to a mere handful of listeners in this house; when tickets were given away by the dozen and the fifty, in order that there might not be a desert of empty seats.

" 'But it was not a barren field that Theodore Thomas sowed the seed in. He made it ready for the Boston Orchestra, and thus at length arrived the man and the hour for a Philadelphia Orchestra. We have grown to understand the great value of such music, not only the pleasure it gives, but its educational and civilizing importance; and, although now and again some benighted voice is raised against systematic musical instruction in our schools, the day of the municipal savage draws to its close!

[81]

" 'Older governments assist symphonic art, liberally subsidizing it; but in our Republic it is proper for the citizens to take this upon themselves, and all over the country they are beginning to do so. But Philadelphia's progress since the days of Theodore Thomas is the most extraordinary of all, and her citizens will see that it goes on.

" 'And so Fritz Scheel passes from this desk into bronze, where the artist has caught his look with admirable and living skill; the very look he had so often when he turned half round the moment before he raised his baton. At this desk now stands his eminent successor, worthy to perfect the work so worthily, so loyally begun. At future concerts when we come in we shall see Fritz Scheel looking down from his bronze, and imagine upon his face a look of serenity and approval.'

"Mr. Wister was heartily congratulated for his address, and the ladies of the committee in charge of the memorial celebration received many favorable comments as to the admirable way in which they had carried out their work, not only in the collecting of the money, but in providing such a fitting tribute to the late conductor."

* * * * *

Evening Bulletin, March 11, 1908:

"THE MEMORIAL TABLET"

* * * * *

"The seats in the parquet circle, with the exception of the boxes, had been reserved for the subscribers to the Fritz Scheel Memorial Fund, and the Guarantors for the Philadelphia Orchestra.

"The balcony and family circle were for the regular ticket holders of both series of concerts, while tickets for the amphitheatre had been distributed to the music students of the various musical conservatories.

"Proscenium Box No. 2 had been reserved for Mr. and Mrs. A. J. Dallas Dixon, Miss Margaret Scheel, Mr. and Mrs. Alexander Van Rensselaer, Mr. and Mrs. Andrew Wheeler, Jr., Mr. and Mrs. Arthur Newbold, Dr. and Mrs. Edward I. Keffer and Miss F. A. Wister.

"Proscenium Box No. 3 for Mr. and Mrs. Thomas McKean, Mr. John H. Ingham, Mr. Clement B. Newbold, Mr. and Mrs. Edgar Scott, Mr. E. T. Stotesbury, and Miss Anne Thomson, representing the Board of Directors of the Philadelphia Orchestra Association.

"Proscenium Box No. 4 had been allotted to the following ladies representing the Honorary Vice-Presidents of the Women's Committee for the Philadelphia Orchestra: Mrs. George F. Baer, Mrs. Alexander W. Biddle, Mrs. John Cadwalader, Mrs. Charles B. Coxe, Miss Mary K. Gibson, Mrs. Clement A. Griscom, Mrs. Austin S. Heckscher, Mrs. C. E. Ingersoll, Mrs. Frank H. Rosengarten, Mrs. Cornelius Stevenson, Mrs. Theodore Voorhees and Mrs. L. C. Vandergrift and Mrs. Oscar R. Jackson of Wilmington, Del.

"The parquet circle and balcony boxes were reserved for the officers of the Women's Committee for the Philadelphia Orchestra and their guests. The list of Philadelphia guests included the following: Mr. and Mrs. John E. Reyburn, Mr. and Mrs. Edward H. Coates, Mr. and

Mrs. Charles Grafly, Mr. and Mrs. C. C. Zantzinger, Mr. and Mrs. Charles L. Borie, Mr. and Mrs. Edgar V. Seeler, Mr. and Mrs. Harrison S. Morris, Mr. John Luther Long, Mrs. Owen Wister, Jr., Mr. and Mrs. H. B. Fine, of Princeton, N. J., Miss Alice Nevin, Lancaster, Pa., Mr. and Mrs. Frederick Martin, of Harrisburg, Pa.

"The following ladies had charge of the memorial services: Mrs. W. W. Arnett, chairman; Mrs. A. J. Dixon, Mrs. H. E. Yarnall, Mrs. Thomas S. Harrison, Miss Anne Thomson, Miss Nina Lea, Mrs. F. H. Rosengarten, Mrs. George Widener, Mrs. John B. Miles and Mrs. W. L. McLean.

THE FUTURE

The Board of Directors immediately began to look for a successor to Fritz Scheel. Various proposals were made, among them one to Franz Kneisel, who was forced to decline by a storm of protest from his New York admirers. At the Annual Meeting held May 14, 1907, this announcement was made:

"Though the association has sustained a great loss in the death of Mr. Scheel, who labored with untiring zeal, achieving successful results in bringing our orchestra to a high plane of musicianship, the public may be assured that his place will be worthily filled. At the present moment, however, the Executive Committee is compelled to face a question of some embarrassment in selecting the successor to the late Mr. Scheel. Fortunately, your committee is in receipt of applications that include many of the representative conductors in the world of music, and, in consequence of this wealth of material from which to select a conductor, the question of arriving at a decision is rendered somewhat puzzling. The public may rest assured, however, that a conclusion may be speedily reached, and a conductor named who will meet with the approval of all."

THE MUSICAL RECORD
1900—1907

Fritz Scheel's musical achievements were outstanding, considering that he was organizing a new orchestra under difficulties, both artistic and financial. The list of important works presented by him is of interest, for besides the compositions of European composers, he also brought forward those of American and Philadelphia musicians.

1900–01: Edward A. MacDowell: Concerto for Piano.

1901–02: Dvorak: "Heldenlied."**

1902–03: Beethoven Cycle, including Ninth Symphony with Chorus
Mozart, Aria for Contralto piano and orchestra. Martinu
Van Gelder* Symphony, A major (dedicated to Mr. Scheel)

1903–04: Beethoven: Ninth Symphony; Jan Sibelius, Swan of Tuo
nela;** Frank G. Cauffman,* "Salammbo;" Camille W
Zeckwer,* Concerto for piano and orchestra (composer a
the piano).

1904–05: Vincent d'Indy, Second Symphony, B flat.**

1905-06: Mozart Programme:

One Hundred and Fiftieth Anniversary of the
Birth of Mozart.

January 26–27, 1906.

Soloist: Mme. Charlotte Maconda, Soprano

1.   Symphony, G minor

2.   Recitative and Aria from "The Marriage of Figaro"

3.   A Short Serenade (Eine kleine Nachtmusik)
for two violins, viola, violoncello and bass

4.   Aria from "The Magic Flute"

5.   Overture to "The Magic Flute"

_____

Wassili Leps;* "Andon" (poem by John Luther Long*).

1906–07: Beethoven; Ninth Symphony.

Scheel possessed a fine music library, which was an asse
to an orchestra just starting out in an almost penniless con
dition. It contained standard orchestral scores of symphon
ies, overtures, violin and piano solos with orchestra, a
well as music suitable for popular concerts, operatic selec
tions, and smaller orchestral works. He was never handi
capped on account of the lack of music for besides this the
Association was constantly purchasing what was needed
In addition to first performances in America, there were
constant novelties at the concerts and the artistic standard
was high from the outset. A glance over the programmes
shows that while on occasion minor works were presented
which are now not generally played, the works of the great
masters predominated. In this way the taste of the audience
was trained and for this education Philadelphia owes to
Fritz Scheel much of its ability to appreciate and enjoy
music today.

_____

*Philadelphian

**First performance in America.

SCHEEL MEMORIAL TABLET

"The man who really made The Philadelphia Orchestra from a musical standpoint is Fritz Scheel. I never knew him personally, but he must have had very high musical ideals. They are evident in everything he did. Also, he must have had a wonderful faculty for choosing the highest type of artists for the orchestra; he set a standard then which has been difficult to live up to musically. Such artists as Rich, Horner, and Schwar (to mention only a few of the many who are still remaining in The Philadelphia Orchestra from Fritz Scheel's time) are absolutely in the first rank for their instrument, not only in America but in the whole world. It was Scheel's vision that laid such a wonderful foundation for this orchestra; that was very difficult, but in most cases I feel that we have at last succeeded; but we never can sufficiently recognize the debt we owe to Fritz Scheel; the good work he did and the influence of his ideals seem to live on forever.

LEOPOLD STOKOWSKI."

PART II

CHAPTER I
THE NEXT STEP

The Board of Directors was now obliged to find a new conductor for the Philadelphia Orchestra. A survey of America did not bring fruitful results. Orchestral conductors were few in this country in those days, and the Board was determined to engage no man but one competent to carry on the work so well begun. Therefore it was decided to send the business representative of the Association, Charles A. Davis, abroad on this quest. After visiting Steinbach in Cologne and Mottl in Munich, who both recommended Carl Pohlig, Mr. Davis went to Stuttgart, where Pohlig was the director of the Court Orchestra of the King of Würtemberg. After consultation with the officers, an offer was made to him to become the leader of the Philadelphia Orchestra for a term of three years, which was accepted.

Carl Pohlig was born at Teplitz, Bohemia, in 1864. Like Robert Schumann, he was the son of a bookseller. His first musical studies were at the piano. Early in life, while attending the gymnasium at Weimar, the talented boy was cordially received by Franz Liszt, and was permitted to accompany the master on his journeys to Rome, Budapest and other cities, this privilege being shared only by Tausig, von Bülow and Rubinstein. He thus learned many Liszt traditions.

After having toured Germany, Austria, Russia, Scandinavia and Italy, he became Kapellmeister at Graz. Later he was associated with Mahler at the Opera in Hamburg: then at Covent Garden, and Bayreuth, where he trained artists for the Wagner Festival. Pohlig conducted symphony concerts following this operatic experience and appeared in Coburg, Stuttgart, Berlin, Frankfort, Munich and other cities. Finally he was offered the position of First Court Kapellmeister to the King of Würtemberg, whence he came, by permission, to Philadelphia.

The "Neue Musik Zeitung," one of the best musical journals in Germany, speaks thus of Carl Pohlig as conductor:

"In the symphony concerts he directs with equal fervor the works of Beethoven, Mozart and Haydn, as well as the creations of the later great masters. It goes without saying that Liszt is especially dear to him."

* * * * *

"Pohlig directs with fire and deep feeling, and with a certain clearness that can only spring from a quiet insight into the innermost content of the music; into the finest fibre of its design."

The new conductor entered upon his duties in Philadelphia in the autumn of 1907, presenting for his first concert the following programme:

THE PHILADELPHIA ORCHESTRA

Carl Pohlig, *Conductor*

First Afternoon Symphony Concert
Friday Afternoon, October 18th, 1907, at 3.00

First Evening Symphony Concert
Saturday Evening, October 19th, 1907, at 8.15

Programme

1. Ludwig Van Beethoven (1770–1827)
    1. Overture "Fidelio"
    2. Overture "Leonore No. 3"
    3. Symphony No. 5, in C minor, Op. 67
        I. Allegro con brio
        II. Andante con moto
        III. Allegro-Allegro, Presto

2. Richard Wagner (1813–1883)
    4. Vorspiel, "Meistersinger"
    5. "Siegfried Idyll"
    6. Overture, "Tannhaeuser"

Pohlig was warmly received by the audience and acclaimed by the critics as the following will show:

North American, October 19, 1907:

"Society, Fashionable and Cultured, Cheers Pohlig.
Music Lovers Turn Out in Force to Hear This
Season's Philadelphia Orchestra's First Concert

"Conductor Carl Pohlig came, waved his baton and conquered at the Academy of Music, yesterday afternoon—the first concert of the Philadelphia Orchestra's regular season. The new musical director's local début was a brilliant success and an artistic triumph."

CARL POHLIG

"The house was crowded. It was apparent almost from the outset that Conductor Pohlig was a master artist and craftsman. He knew his business—'the first among German conductors,' as Felix Mottl styled him. The great audience, representing fairly Philadelphia's highest artistic culture, quickly recognized the new orchestral director's high and rare quality. By the time the 'Leonore' Overture was ended, mystic cords of sympathy between conductor and audience were flung out and firmly fastened. The immortal Fifth Symphony, mightiest of musical creations—was awaited with pleased expectation."

* * * * *

INTERPRETATION OF WAGNER

"Mr. Pohlig's initial programme was too long—two hours of solid music. He does not think so—he broke his watch crystal in an energetic explanation.

"There was some weariness over the Wagner music—Mr. Pohlig has not yet got his band keyed up to the marvelous complexion of the master of Bayreuth. But again it was quite clear that conditions of Wagnerian interpretation were as familiar to him as were the canons of classical music."

* * * * *

"There was no uncertainty of tempo, and when the tremendous finale of the 'Tannhaeuser' prelude was stilled, the people rose in their seats and acclaimed the new conductor in vociferous accents."

* * * * *

Name and date of newspaper unknown:

"CITY TAKES COMMANDING PLACE IN COUNTRY'S MUSICAL GROWTH. CARL POHLIG, NEW SYMPHONY CONDUCTOR, THINKS AMERICA'S FUTURE PLACE WILL BE FIRST

"A dozen years ago, a symphony concert in Philadelphia meant the arrival of an out-of-town organization, and the gathering of a sparse audience, dismally scattered through the Academy of Music. The writer remembers when on one occasion, in 1899, the Boston Symphony Orchestra played to a handful of people in our city because of inclement weather. The reports of the inception of orchestras like the Pittsburgh, the Chicago, the New York Philharmonic and others reveal what an uphill struggle was forced upon these musical bodies because of the lack of interest in music in the various large communities.

"So different is the story today, that one is almost puzzled to account for a change, which has led Herr Pohlig, the new Conductor of the Philadelphia Orchestra, to remark: 'Musically speaking, Germany is the land of the setting sun; America the land of the rising sun.' His enthusiasm is not the result of the newcomer's optimism, for Europe has kept track of our musical progress, and is acquainted with the fact that in a few years Philadelphia has been able to inaugurate season upon season of successful concerts given by its own orhcestra, that Chicago's magnificent organization created by Theodore Thomas, is now on a self-supporting basis, and that Pittsburgh, Boston, New York and Minneapolis are musical communities of great importance."

* * * * *

"Asked about his plans for the concerts to be given this winter, Mr. Pohlig talked unhesitatingly and with enthusiasm. The first question put to him involved the type of music he would arrange for Philadelphia music lovers, and was a query whether this would be of the same nature he would have furnished a German audience. He said promptly: 'Of course, Philadelphia should get the best and previous programmes show it has been getting it. And, of course, it must get everything. All schools of music should be represented. If anything, a modern conductor must be cosmopolitan.'

"His mode of arranging his programmes will be new to Philadelphia concert-goers, who have been accustomed to a programme with the symphony either at the opening of the concert or at the end. Mr. Pohlig will have the symphony divide the programme into two, where it serves the purpose of balancing the music of the recital. He intends, if the opportunity offers, to combine with local singing organizations for the production of music for chorus and orchestra hitherto unheard in America. His belief in the great spirit of modern music will give Philadelphians the chance of hearing the compositions of European contemporaries . . . . ."

* * * * *

Pohlig's first New York concert on November 5th, 1907, did not meet with approval, which considering the programme presented is not strange, but the comments were of such a nature as to call down the wrath of at least one Philadelphia newspaper which retorted in kind. As New York has since capitulated this can be inserted.

A Philadelphia Newspaper, November 7th, 1907:

"POHLIG IN NEW YORK. FLINGS BY MUSICAL CRITICS AT THE PHILADELPHIA ORCHESTRA AND ITS NEW CONDUCTOR

"The views of the musical critics of New York concerning Carl Pohlig upon his first appearance with the Philadelphia Orchestra in that city on Tuesday evening are not altogether flattering. The *Sun*, as might be expected, leads in its light-hearted attack. Pohlig 'is employed in the pleasant city of Philadelphia, where he conducts the local orchestra. Its work was so rough as to cause wonder that the organization should have been brought all the way across the State of New Jersey.'

"The *Times* says that 'the orchestra is a good assemblage of musicians that clearly brought all of Mr. Pohlig's intentions to realization. He is a strenuous conductor of advanced view as to the treatment not only of Liszt but also of Beethoven.'

"The *Tribune* says: 'It was a rather unfortunate conjunction that of the Philadelphia Orchestra with its new conductor, Carl Pohlig;

[92]

Richard Buhlig, pianist, and Carl Klein, violinist, at Carnegie Hall yesterday afternoon. Coming alone, and at a more opportune time, each might have won a more dignified hearing and more serious consideration than were possible under the conditions which prevailed yesterday.'

"The New York public is 'already booked for three-score and ten of the kind of concerts which it gives.' However, Mr. Pohlig 'presented himself as a conductor of quite admirable capacities so far at least as a command of the technics of his art is concerned (leaving all questions of interpretation open).'

"The *World* speaks of the incapacity of the orchestra, who seriously hampered the soloist, by as wicked an accompaniment as was ever heard at a first-class concert.

" 'Provincial was writ large over the whole proceeding, and one felt tempted to inquire: "Why Herr Pohlig; why the Philadelphia Orchestra; why Richard Buhlig?"—at any rate in New York.'

"In Beethoven's Fifth Symphony, however, Herr Pohlig 'effectually removed previous impressions and stamped himself at once as a thorough musician, a graphic conductor of real distinction, possessing authority, temperament, magnetism, poetic feeling and imagination. One could quarrel with his rather slow tempi and liberties of phrasing, if inclined to be captious, but the interpretation of this great work was so well planned and coherent, that it aroused decided enthusiasm.' "

EDITORIAL

The Same, November 7th, 1907:

"NEW YORK SNOBBERY"

"It is not pleasant to utter harsh judgments against a neighboring city, but New York does much constantly to deserve them at the hands of Philadelphians. The smug self-sufficiency of the three or four millions of people who reside on or in contiguity to Manhattan Island, is comical to witness, and we are again reminded of this attitude by the unjust criticism which the newspapers have launched against the Philadelphia Orchestra upon its first visit to New York under its new conductor. This accomplished musician has had the leadership of excellent organizations in Europe, where this form of art was more or less known and enjoyed while New York was inhabited by the Indians. He came here not without some right to a respectful hearing, and since his arrival has received it in this city from a public, which, we venture to say, is as discriminating as any that can be assembled upon the tongue of land which is bounded by the Hudson River and Long Island Sound. Remarks such as we reprint elsewhere today do not fall under the head of criticism. They are a form of cheap wit, which is supposed to be demanded by the inhabitants of this arrogant and insular community at the expense of the people, the products and the institutions of Philadelphia.

"The slurs of the press at our music, books, art and much besides, do this city no particular harm. We are above any need of the endorsement of the self-centered elements which congregate in New York. The support which it gave to the union during the war was notably reluctant. Its patriotism was always in doubt. It was the centre of disloyal conspiracy. A spirit of selfish commercialism rules its affairs, and it was only by force made to observe its national duty. Since that time it has been under foreign government, and it is without a doubt the least American of our cities. It has less love for our history as a nation; it is more willing to sell its birthright for a joke or a dollar than any community which has yet been established within American borders, and its swaggering air causes it to be loved by the citizens of other portions of the Union about as much as they love a produce market or a Midway Plaisance.

"It is nothing at all to Philadelphians whether New Yorkers like our orchestra, our books, our poets, our historical personages, our pictures, our homes, or anything else that is ours. They may go on their sneering way amusing themselves from day to day, as they see fit. They will find, if they make the effort to inquire, that most of the mind and the soul, as well as the body of this nation have lain and still lie in lands that they do not dominate. They may say what they will, but their manners might be mended to their own conspicuous advantage. That is all."

At the expiration of Pohlig's contract the Association renewed it for three years more.

Pohlig was a fine-looking man of German military style, more popular in America previous to 1914 than it has been since. His platform manner was excellent and his appearance was elegant, and he made a good impression on his audience. He was, however, of a difficult disposition, which made dealings between him and the musicians, and the Board of Directors, trying and difficult. This was the final cause of his resignation, presented on June 10th, 1912.

THE MUSICAL RECORD, 1907–1912

Under the direction of Carl Pohlig, the orchestra continued to develop and improve. He was a competent and well-trained musician, and was on his mettle to do his best in an artistic way to keep up the precedents established by the first conductor. He continued to give unusual performances and to keep abreast of the day by producing modern works, among them his own symphony, "Per Aspera ad Astra" ("A Hero's Death and Apotheosis"), in which members of the Eurydice Chorus took part.

1907–08: Carl Pohlig, Symphony, "Per Aspera ad Astra."
1908–09: Frank G. Cauffman*, "Legende"; Philip H. Goepp*: Academic March.

*Philadelphian.

Feb. 26th – 27th, 1909: Mendelssohn Centenary: Midsummer Night's
Dream with Ben Greet Players.
Chaminade: Concertstück, piano and orchestra (composer
at the piano).

1909–10: November 26th – 27th, 1909: Rachmaninoff, Symphony
No. 2, E minor, conducted by the composer; Moussorgsky,
"La Nuit sur le Mont Chauve," Rachmaninoff, guest conductor; Wm. W. Gilchrist*, Symphony No. 1, C major,
conducted by the composer.

1910–11: November 11th – 12th: Schumann: to commemorate the
One Hundredth Anniversary of his birth 1810, Symphony
No. 1, B flat major: Henry Hadley, guest conductor, Cantata
"The Culprit Fay," Op. 62, after Joseph Rodman Drake,
conducted by the composer: November 11th and 12th, 1910,
St. Saëns, Symphony No. 3, in honor seventy-fifth birthday
of composer: Louis von Gaertner*, Tone Poem "Macbeth."
Celeste D. Heckscher,* "Dances of the Pyrenees."

1911–12: October 27th – 28th: Liszt Centenary. Henry Hadley, Symphony No. 3, B minor.

March 8th – 9th: Brahms Symphony No. 3, F major, to celebrate
seventy-ninth anniversary of his birth, March 7th, 1833.
Herman Sandby, Prelude to "The Woman and the Fiddler"
(play by Mrs. Sandby).

---
*Philadelphian.

PART III

CHAPTER I

THE COMING OF LEOPOLD STOKOWSKI

The summer of 1912 brought the Board of Directors, for the second time in five years, face to face with the problem of securing a conductor. Again the place was waiting for the man, but under far different conditions from those in the summer of 1899, when Fritz Scheel was found at Woodside Park. Philadelphia had a good orchestra, a growing audience tended carefully by the four Women's Committees, and a Guarantee Fund in a more or less satisfactory condition. It was an opportunity. The Board of Directors looked around the field again. They had heard of a young man, Leopold Stokowski, recently conductor of the Cincinnati Orchestra, and heard well of him. Mr. Andrew Wheeler knew him and suggested approaching him. He was then in Europe, so he was cabled to, and accepted the position.

The first concerts under Mr. Stokowski took place on October 11th and 12th, 1912, with the following programme, which inaugurated the third period of the Philadelphia Orchestra, and one which has been a story of constant artistic development, until now this orchestra ranks with the great orchestras of the world.

THE PHILADELPHIA ORCHESTRA ASSOCIATION
(INCORPORATED)

MAINTAINING

THE PHILADELPHIA ORCHESTRA
(Founded 1900)

LEOPOLD STOKOWSKI, *Conductor*

FIRST PAIR OF SYMPHONY CONCERTS

Friday afternoon at 3.00   Saturday Evening at 8.15
October 11th and 12th, 1912

PROGRAMME

1. LUDWIG VAN BEETHOVEN............Overture, "Leonore No. 3"
   (1770–1827)
2. JOHANNES BRAHMS.........Symphony No. 1, in C minor, Op. 68
   (1833–1897)

[99]

I. Un poco sostenuto; Allegro (6/8)
II. Andante sostenuto (3/4)
III. Un poco allegretto e grazioso (2/4)
IV. Adagio-piu andante; Allegro non
troppo, ma con brio (4/4)

3. MICHAEL IPPOLITOW-IWANOW......"Sketches from the Caucasus'
(1859–   )
I. In the Mountain Pass
II. The Mountain Village
III. March of the Sirdar
(First Time at These Concerts)

4. RICHARD WAGNER....................Overture "Tannhauser'
(1813–1883)

Public Ledger, October 12th, 1912.

"NEW CONDUCTOR OF PHILADELPHIA ORCHESTRA
TENDERED OVATION IN ACADEMY

"Leopold Stokowski made his début yesterday afternoon at the
Academy as conductor of the Philadelphia Orchestra, in the opening
concert of its thirteenth season. Every seat was taken and the extra
chairs had been placed within the orchestra rail. There was much
enthusiasm, manifesting itself at the beginning in prolonged applause
as Stokowski came forward with bowed head, evidently pondering
the content of his musical message. Those who went forth to see a
hirsute eccentricity were disappointed. They beheld a surprisingly
boyish and thoroughly business-like figure, who was sure of him
self, yet free from conceit, who dispensed with the score by virtue
of an infallible memory, and held his men and his audience from first
note to last firmly in his grasp.

"Mr. Stokowski has known the players, and they have known
him, for only four days of actual rehearsal, and it was not to be
expected that the organization at the outset would manifest the
homogeneity to be expected later. Yet in this brief time the new
leader has been surprisingly successful in welding the several choirs
into a single coherent entity. They played yesterday with a unity of
purpose—particularly among the first violins—not usually attained
until mid-winter. They brought out the full value of the lights and
shadows. The climaxes were duly accentuated, the pianissimos with
the utmost delicacy and refinement were contrasted with the full
throated polyphony.

"METHODS OF CONDUCTOR

"Mr. Stokowski's conducting is after the order of Nikisch, whom
he frankly admires. He does not tear a passion to tatters. He holds his
thunders and the winds of Aeolus in a leash. His gestures are graphic,

the arcs and parabolas he describes tell of a kind of geometrical translation going on in his mind, whereby he visualizes the confluent rhythms in outward action. At impassioned moments his movements have the freedom of a violinist's bow arm; at other instants he brings his fists against his shoulders with vehement concentration, or his uplifted eloquent left hand pleads with some suppressed choir to come forward and assert itself in power. There is, from first to last, no languor or slackened moment; he directs with a fine vigor and intensity that mounts to ecstasy yet does not lose its balance or forget its sane and ordered method.

* * * * *

"Tribute Presented

"At the close of the symphony a laurel wreath was laid on the dais ere Mr. Stokowski found his way to the footlights in response to the tumultuous applause. The wreath was so large that he stood in it while he called upon his musicians to rise, himself applauding their efforts and modestly disavowing his leonine share of the credit."

It soon became apparent that Philadelphia had something very unusual in Leopold Stokowski. He was young, but rarely gifted, and he dedicated himself to reaching a high artistic goal for the Philadelphia Orchestra. His plans were of a daring character and at times almost took away the breath of the Board of Directors; for instance, when the idea of giving Mahler's Eighth Symphony was presented and Mr. Stokowski announced that it would cost $14,000. There was much discussion, as the Board was convinced that this performance would be unpopular and not a success from a financial point of view. However, the desire to have the name of the orchestra connected with productions of an unusual nature and to keep ahead of the times musically, won the day, and it was decided in 1915 to produce this gigantic choral work in March 1916.

The story of this production is dramatic from the moment that Leopold Stokowski, after having secured the rights for the first American performance, escaped from Munich in August, 1914, with the score in a handbag, all he had time to pack. Mr. Stokowski was at that time still a British subject, having only taken out his first papers for American citizenship.

Having secured the consent of the Board of Directors to produce this symphony, this announcement was issued.

[101]

THE PHILADELPHIA ORCHESTRA

LEOPOLD STOKOWSKI, *Conductor*

First Performances of the Mahler Eighth Symphony
Academy of Music, Philadelphia
Thursday Evening—Friday Afternoon—Saturday Evening
March 2, 3, 4, 1916
Metropolitan Opera House, New York
Sunday Evening, April 9, 1916

With Orchestral and Choral Forces of Over One Thousand
and the Following Soloists:

FLORENCE HINKLE, Soprano	ADELAIDE FISCHER, Soprano
INEZ BARBOUR, Soprano	MARGARET KEYES, Contralto
SUSANNA DERCUM, Contralto	LAMBERT MURPHY, Tenor
REINALD WERRENRATH, Baritone	CLARENCE WHITEHILL, Basso

First Chorus—The Philadelphia Orchestra Chorus, 400
Children's Chorus, 150

Second Chorus—Philadelphia Choral Society, Mendelssohn Club
and the Fortnightly Club, 400

"The Philadelphia Orchestra Association takes pleasure in announcing three performances in Philadelphia of Gustav Mahler's Eighth Symphony and, under the auspices of the Society of Friends of Music, one performance in New York. The first Philadelphia performance is the first presentation of this work in America, and is given under an exclusive contract with the publishers. Although other famous organizations had approached the Universal-Edition in Vienna, to the Philadelphia Orchestra fell the honor and artistic responsibility of presenting this work for the first time to the American public. The production of the work, requiring three choruses aggregating 950 voices, an orchestra of 110, and 8 soloists, entails a cost for the Philadelphia performances alone of approximately $15,000."

* * * * *

"The New York performance owes its possibility to the public spirit and generosity of the Society of Friends of Music, and will be given with the complete forces employed in Philadelphia. This single production will cost approximately $12,000.

"Owing to the great magnitude of the work and the great demand which it makes on the musical forces employed, it is extremely doubtful whether it can receive many performances in America. Two years have been spent in preparation in order that the rendition of the work might realize the ideals of the composer. That the value of the work is appreciated is shown by the fact that orders for seats have been received from all over the eastern and middle western sections of this country. The Friday and Saturday performances in Philadelphia are sold out and many mail orders have been received for Thursday night. An early application for seats should be made.

Work with the two choruses which sang in German and
in Latin began in October, 1915. Hitherto the orchestra had
had no chorus of its own, but was obliged to depend on the
good will of Philadelphia choral organizations to co-operate in producing choral works. Now for the first time the
name "Philadelphia Orchestra Chorus" appeared, and, as
the first chorus of 400 members, was trained by Mr.
Stokowski. The second chorus of 400 voices was rehearsed
by Mr. Henry Gordon Thunder.

The requirements were severe as to personnel and rehearsals. The spring was occupied in the selection of
voices. When rehearsals began in October, men and women
were rehearsed separately until January. After that they
had weekly rehearsals together. Singers who were inatten-
tive or who skipped rehearsals were not retained, and towards the end everybody was over-worked and wrought up
to a pitch of excitement.

NINETEENTH PROGRAMME

Friday, March 3rd, at 3.00   Saturday, March 4th, at 8.15

THE PHILADELPHIA ORCHESTRA
LEOPOLD STOKOWSKI, *Conductor*

PROGRAMME

Symphony No. 8................................GUSTAV MAHLER
(1860–1911)

Part I. Hymn, "Veni, Creator Spiritus"
Part II. Final Scene from Part II of Goethe's "Faust"

(First performance in America)

[103]

Una Poenitentium, FLORENCE HINKLE, Soprano
Magna Peccatrix, INEZ BARBOUR, Soprano
Mater Gloriosa, ADELAIDE FISCHER, Soprano
Mulier Samaritans, MARGARET KEYES, Contralto
Maria Aegyptiaca, SUSANNA DERCUM, Contralto
Doctor Marianus, LAMBERT MURPHY, Tenor
Pater Ecstaticus, REINALD WERRENRATH
Pater Profundus, CLARENCE WHITEHILL, Basso

Augmented Orchestra of 110

First Chorus:
THE PHILADELPHIA ORCHESTRA CHORUS, 400

Second Chorus:
PHILADELPHIA CHORAL SOCIETY, MENDELSSOHN CLUB
and THE FORTNIGHTLY CLUB, 400

CHILDREN'S CHORUS OF 150
The English version (by Mr. Philip H. Goepp) of Specht's Analysis
may be obtained in the lobbies of the Academy

MR. CONSTANTIN VON STERNBERG at the Piano
MR. HENRY GORDON THUNDER at the Organ
MR. WILLIAM SILVANO THUNDER at the Harmonium
MR. HEDDA VAN DEN BEEMT at the Celesta

While there were varying opinions about the musical value of this symphony, the manner of producing it evoked but one. In order to make the event national in character, prominent musicians from all parts of America were invited to be present at the first performance. Among the many notable persons from other cities were: Mr. and Mrs. Ossip Gabrilowitsch, Mr. and Mrs. Harold Bauer, Mr. and Mrs. Josef Hofmann, Mr. and Mrs. Ernest Hutcheson, Dr. and Mrs. Ernest Kunwald, Mr. and Mrs. Harold Randolph, Mr. and Mrs. Ernest Schelling, Mr. and Mrs. David Mannes, Mr. and Mrs. Samuel Untermeyer, Mr. and Mrs. Gustav Strube, Judge and Mrs. J. Butler Woodward, Mr. and Mrs. J. Fred Wolle, Mrs. Werrenrath, Mrs. William M. Bannard, Miss Kitty Cheatham, Dr. A. G. Rolfe, Oscar G. Sonneck, Albert Spalding, Kurt Schindler and Theodore Spiering.

THE PHILADELPHIA ORCHESTRA AND MAHLER CHORUS

Public Ledger, March 3rd, 1916:

"MAHLER'S WORK AND STOKOWSKI SCORE TRIUMPH

THOUSANDS AT ACADEMY OF MUSIC AROUSED TO HIGH PITCH OF
ENTHUSIASM. NOTED MUSICIANS GIVE PRAISE TO PRODUCTION
PROMINENT PERSONS FROM ALL OVER COUNTRY ATTEND
RENDITION HERE

'Every one of the thousands in the great building was standing, whistling, cheering and applauding, when Leopold Stokowski, his collar wilted, and his right arm weary, but smiling his boyish smile, finally turned to the audience in the Academy of Music last night.

"He had scored, so famous musicians agreed, the greatest triumph of his career, the greatest triumph the Philadelphia Orchestra has known in its sixteen years of life and he had done it on a stupendous scale with the American première of Gustav Mahler's Eighth Symphony. He carried along with him to triumph an orchestra numbering 110 pieces and a chorus of 958 singers, to say nothing of the city's music lovers and scores of musical pilgrims from other cities.

"For every one who is any one in musical America was here for the Mahler American première last night or will be here when the tremendous work is repeated this afternoon and tomorrow night. The boxes were filled with famous musicians and musical authorities. One and all stood, applauding Mr. Stokowski and the symphony, while the orchestra members blared a 'touche' in honor of their leader.

"The scenes at the Academy set nerves tingling. Two weeks before the performance every seat had been sold. Fifteen minutes before Mr. Stokowski swung his baton upon his augmented orchestra and upon the great chorus, banked 24 tiers high, horns blew a fanfare in the foyer of the Academy of Music, following an ancient custom at Bayreuth. The curtain rose and the audience gasped.

"The 958 singers filled the great stage from footlights to roof and the orchestra was upon an apron that has been built out into the house.

"The first twelve rows of singers were women, dressed in white. Above them were twelve rows of men, with a gardenia-like spot of girls, members of the children's chorus, pinned, it seemed in their midst."

* * * * *

"Alexander Van Rensselaer presented a wreath for the orchestra. It was inscribed 'To Leopold Stokowski in commemoration of the first performance of Mahler's Eighth Symphony in America, March 2nd, 1916.'

MR. VAN RENSSELAER'S REMARKS

"In presenting the wreath, Mr. Van Rensselaer said:
"'The directors of the Philadelphia Orchestra Association feel that the presentation of this Eighth Symphony of Mahler this evening for the first time in America, marks an epoch in the musical history of Philadelphia to which no other event is comparable.

"'This occasion is memorable not only because the Mahler Symphony is such an extremely difficult work, but because we have here in Philadelphia been able to follow out the precise instructions of the composer in welding into one vast instrument these great choral and orchestral forces which are here assembled. These two choruses of 400 trained voices each, together with the large chorus of boys and girls selected from the best choirs of this city, the eight soloists of metropolitan reputation, and the augmented orchestra of 120 instruments, all have been trained into one vast harmonious instrument by you.

"'We of Philadelphia are indebted for the production of this great work to you, our brilliant and talented conductor. It was you who first conceived the idea more than two years ago of producing this work; it was you who made the arrangements with the publishers and guaranteed to them that we would produce it in the manner indicated by the composer and obtained from them the rights for the first performance in this country; it was you who chose and trained Chorus No. 1 and intrusted chorus No. 2 to the able direction of Henry Gordon Thunder, to whom our thanks are also due; it was you who arranged with the best choirmasters of Philadelphia to train this large body of boys and girls in their respective parts and it was you who brought together these large agencies and trained them in the final ensemble of this great work.

"'We feel that not only the musical public of Philadelphia, but the entire city, owe you a debt of gratitude that never can be repaid. And as a testimonial from the Board of Directors of the Philadelphia Orchestra Association, and as an expression from them of their thanks to you for the successful completion of this grand work, I have pleasure in presenting the victor's crown of laurel, made in perpetual bronze.'

Reply of Mr. Stokowski

"Mr. Stokowski lifted the wreath, and when the applause died down, turning to Mr. Van Rensselaer, said:

"'It is impossible for me to put into words my emotions tonight. This stupendous and noble work was written six years ago. For six years I have been meditating the possibility of its performance and hoping, some day, to have the opportunity of giving it, although I knew the requisite forces would be extremely difficult to obtain.

"'Through a generosity for which I can never sufficiently express my gratitude, Mr. Van Rensselaer and the directors of the Philadelphia Orchestra Association made the great undertaking possible at last. The dream still would have remained unfulfilled, however, had it not been for the hard work and willingness of the orchestra; of all these dear people in the chorus, who have worked for more than a year, training for this night; of all the soloists, and of Henry Gordon Thunder, who has supported and helped me with most wonderful generosity. To the committee that tried thousands of voices, choosing this magnificent chorus, we are particularly indebted.

"'My final and greatest debt, a debt so great that I feel I never can express it, is to you, the public, for your warmth and understanding at the first hearing of this great work. It is a great inspiration.'

[106]

Offers of $100 to Obtain Seats

"Popular interest in the Mahler Symphony's American première was evidenced by offers of $100 a seat, reported from several of the large hotels, just before the Academy doors were thrown open, and by more than 1000 persons, lucky holders of general admission tickets who stood in Locust Street, or sat on newspapers spread on the Academy steps, for hours before the performance was scheduled to start. At least 100 persons were waiting at 3.30 o'clock in the afternoon, braving the drizzle, for a chance at a good seat.

"From 7 until 8 o'clock there was a steady stream of automobiles stopping at the Academy doors. All society and all musical Philadelphia streamed into the building. The stage door was besieged by the nearly 1000 chorus members, who were marshaled without a hitch or the raising of a voice into their places. Necessary readjustments on and off the stage, seating arrangements, provisions for the wardrobing of the great chorus and the engaging of understudies for each of the eight soloists cost, it was said, close to $4000. This sum, of course, did not include the great expense entailed in training the voices during the last twelve months.

"Mr. Stokowski was given two great demonstrations; the first during the intermission, the second at the conclusion of the performance. Both lasted for more than five minutes. The noise was so great that the Academy doormen said it could be heard across Broad Street in the foyer of the Walton.

Miss Florence Hinkle Applauded

"Mr. Stokowski bowed until it seemed his back would break. Then he led forward Henry Gordon Thunder, William Silvano Thunder, Constantin von Sternberg and Hedda van den Beemt. The audience wanted more. They wanted the soloists, so forward came the eight of them, and as they went back Florence Hinkle, who was being wildly applauded by the great chorus, kissed her fingertips to them. Above the crescendo of applause could be heard members of the chorus, crying, 'Hinkle!'

"One of the most interested persons present was Mrs. J. F. D. Lanier, president of the Society of Friends of Music, the New York woman chiefly responsible for the invasion of New York with the Mahler Symphony on April 9. She sat in the same box with the pianist, Harold Bauer.

"In a nearby box was the pianist, Ernest Schelling. Aline van Barentzen, the pianist, also was on hand. Ernest Hutcheson, Harold Randolph, Joseph Hofmann, Ossip Gabrilowitsch, Director Bodansky, of the Metropolitan Opera and of the Cincinnati Symphony, are expected to be present at today's performance. Other prominent guests were entertained last night and will be entertained today by the Women's Committee of the orchestra.

"It was announced last night that all seats for the extra performance of the Mahler Symphony on April 4th have been sold.''

After the third performance the Women's Committees fo
the Philadelphia Orchestra gave a reception to Leopolc
Stokowski, and the soloists, in the foyer of the Academy
This was followed by a supper at the Bellevue-Stratford it
their honor and for a few distinguished guests.

The news of this production spread over America anc
Europe, and in Philadelphia created more excitement that
had arisen in a generation. The demand for seats was sc
great, that it became necessary to announce extra perform
ances in this city, and four more were given, making a tota
here of nine, including two public rehearsals. After the last
orders for seats, amounting to over $10,000 in Philadelphi;
alone, had to be refused. The dress rehearsal on Wednesday
was open to the families of the performers and some other
at a special price. A dress rehearsal was later given for pub
lic school children. The first performance was on a Thursday
night, and then followed two in the regular season series
By the time four audiences had heard the symphony, all who
had not heard it were seized with an overpowering desire to
witness this extraordinary event.

The New York Performance

Such a journey was never before undertaken in musica
circles here or abroad. Twelve hundred people left Philadel
phia by private trains, totalling seventeen cars, about noor
on Sunday, April 9th, reached New York in time to have ;
rehearsal and dine and dress at a hotel and at 8.15 appeared
before a packed audience which included all the musician;
then in America.

It was an inspiring occasion and one long to be remem
bered. That evening New York unreservedly acclaimed the
Philadelphia Orchestra. Scenes of enthusiasm followed the
first half, after a tremendous burst of applause when the
curtain rose. But at the end the audience let itself go in ;
way never seen in Philadelphia.

There were many musicians in the house, including Ignace
Paderewski, the members of the Flonzaley Quartet, Mme
Alma Glück and Efrem Zimbalist, Pablo Fasals, Henry Had
ley, Mr. and Mrs. Ossip Gabrilowitsch, Rubin Goldmark
Dr. Frank Damrosch, Victor Harris, Harold Bauer, George
W. Chadwick, Mischa Elman, Emma Eames, Leopolc
Godowsky, Rudolph Ganz, Arthur Foote, David Bispham

Percy Grainger, Arthur Hinton, Alfred Hertz, Franz Kneisel, Daniel Gregory Mason, Ernest Schelling, Walter K. Spalding (Department of Music, Harvard University), Josef Stransky, Arthur Whiting, Marcella Sembrich, Antonio Scotti, Cornelius Rübner (Columbia University), Fritz Kreisler, Mme. Schumann-Heink, and others.

New York Sun, April 10th, 1916:

"EIGHTH SYMPHONY BY MAHLER HEARD

"Society of Friends of Music Gives Concert at "the Metropolitan. Sent by Philadelphia

"The Society of the Friends of Music, which has performed a valuable function in the artistic musical life of this metropolis by bringing to the notice of a circle of trained listeners compositions not to be heard at public entertainments, emerged from its privacy to give an ambitious concert last evening in the Metropolitan Opera House. The novelty chosen was Gustav Mahler's Eighth Symphony, which recently had its first hearing in this country in Philadelphia.

"When the huge symphonic and choral creation of Mr. Mahler was produced in Philadelphia, it was praised with emotion and thanksgiving, the interpretation was considered with reverence and rapture, and the concert had to be—or at any rate was—repeated several times. Upon the heels of this excitement, the whole show came to New York.

"The entire cast, chorus, orchestra and conductor were brought across New Jersey. The Philadelphia Orchestra, numbering for this occasion 110 players; the Philadelphia Orchestra Chorus, a Children's Chorus, the Philadelphia Choral Society, the Mendelssohn Club and the Fortnightly Club, constituted the choral forces. The presiding genius of all was Leopold Stokowski, the gifted and accomplished young conductor of the Philadelphia Orchestra.

"Not a Box Office Symphony

"Mahler's Eighth Symphony quite properly belongs to the class of compositions sought by the Society of the Friends of Music. It does not court the attention of musical directors, who must consider the wishes of the general public or the demands of the box office. New Yorkers may regret that a local orchestra and local choruses were not chosen for the presentation of the work; but only by preparing for more than one performance could the projectors of this production have hoped to complete their undertaking without losses too heavy to confront. Mahler was not troubling himself with practical considerations when he wrote the composition. He had a purpose, which he carried out in the seclusion of his study. And if Hector Berlioz might write a requiem mass fit only for festival occasions, why not Mahler an Eighth Symphony?"

"After the New York performance, W. J. Henderson said: "If Phila
delphia believes that Mr. Stokowski is essential to her musica
development, let her decline to permit him to conduct great concert
in New York. This is a piece of perfectly disinterested advice.

"The *Sun's* musical chronicler would be delighted to see Mr
Stokowski a New York conductor. He has personality, force, author
ity, temperament, scholarship and imagination. His conducting c
the Mahler Symphony was masterly. He would be a valuable facto
in the musical life of New York."

Although the Philadelphia Orchestra is a serious work
ing organization, it has its moments of relaxation and plea
sure. Such a one was the reception and dinner given by Mr
Van Rensselaer to the members of the Mahler Chorus or
March 16th, 1916, at which the following programme wa
presented:

HORTICULTURAL HALL
BROAD STREET, PHILADELPHIA

PROGRAMME OF

MR. ALEXANDER VAN RENSSELAER'S
BUFFET DINNER

Thursday Evening, March 16th, at Seven o'Clock

Given to the Members of the Mahler Choruses and
the Philadelphia Orchestra
(dismembered)

Philadelphia Orchestra

Soloists

Horsecar Schwer!!! that's all
Ham Byndler!! Solo-Killest

PROGRAMME

Symphony "Ein Musikalischer Spass"......................MOZART
1787, German

Allegro
Minuetto Maestoso
Adagio cantabile
Presto

(Ten Minutes Intermission at this Concert Only)

Concerto Brosso (1916)......................Composer unknown
Probably an American, Philadelphian Preferred

(First time at these concerts)

Adagio
Andante Soustenuto
Large-o

Tone Poem "Tausend Künstler".......................Schreiner
(Augmented Orchestra)   1850–1916, Bavarian

Conductor............Sig ad Lib. RIDDEUS THATCH, *Actor-conductor*

"Note—Owing to the exceptional acoustic properties of the Hall, the Audience is requested to refrain from hilarity as the slightest murmur might be disconcerting to the performers. It is earnestly requested by the 'Damagement' and the 'Board of Erectors' that all vegetable offerings and tokens be of a firm nature.

"The personality of the orchestra will be found on the next page among the Programme notes composed by Professor YEPP.

Yes, my dear! The Piano is a Steamway

"The next 'Mahler-ia' concert will take place next week at 2 o'clock. Owing to the Philadelphia Blue-laws a very limited number of tickets will be available. The Knaben-chor will be heard to great advantage at this concert.

"ANDREW WHEEL-HER, *Secretary*"

SPECIAL MAHLERATE PROFUNNYGRAM
HORTICULTURAL HALL
March 16, 1916

PROGRAMME NOTES

"Ein Musikalischer Spass"............................ MOZART
Born 1756, died 1791.

"This symphony pictures Mozart in his most happy mood. Where he got his inspiration from I do not know. What a pity he cannot be with us tonight; he would surely have an inspiration. But who knows what kind!

The symphony, or, rather, first movement, opens with '*Some Chords*.' However, they are in the key of 'C', so we are pretty safe. These opening chords are for the 'FULL orchestra and are very effective, provided they are 'FULL ENOUGH.'

* * * * *

"The second movement is a minuet. You will notice that there is three in a bar, but six in the orchestra, so you see we are at least mathematically even, which ought to insure a fine rhythm—SOME-TIMES (?). There is much fervor in this movement and some wrong notes in the horns, but why worry; they are printed in the score, and are consequently correct.

* * * * *

"Tausend Künstler"................................Schreiner
Bavarian

(First time in America)

"This work really requires 'more men,' but Herr Schwer thinks he can handle it alone. The principal theme is of a martial and military nature. Mr. Schwer only had one rival, and that man died long ago. You will not have much difficulty in following Mr. Schwer, for in this work the performer is very much in evidence at all times. He is very familiar with all of the instruments required for this composition. He has 'hit them' very often and possesses an unusual amount of

originality. 'To See it is to Appreciate It.' Mr. Schwer will depic
thunder claps, echoes, bombardments, combats, cavalry charges
charge accounts, railroad wrecks, and many other scenic effects whil
performing this work."

* * * * *

PERSONNEL OF ORCHESTRA

"Mozart Symphony

> J. K. Witzemann, Schroon Lake, N. Y.
> F. W. Cook, Hampton Beach, N. H.
> Emil Hahl, Willow Grove, Pa.
> Louis Boehse, Profile House, N. H.
> Anton Horner, Stone Harbor, N. J.
> Joseph Horner, Tent City, Cal.

"Conductors—(negotiations pending)."

This occasion was much enjoyed by about 1200 guests, to whom an evening of musical fun was somewhat of a novelty

After the production of the Mahler Symphony the Philadelphia Orchestra became the most talked of orchestra in America. Its reputation was made. This success, however did not bring about any abatement in the conductor's zeal or make him relinquish his aims for the perfection of the orchestra.

On the part of the Board of Directors the result was a determination to put the orchestra on a firm financial basis This desire was so great on the part of one of them, who wished to remain unknown, that he planned a course of action which involved a large expenditure on his part, bu which with the co-operation of 1200 Philadelphians made it possible to roll up in seven years a fund of approximately $800,000.

Chapter II

The Seven Year Endowment Fund, 1916

The question of placing the Philadelphia Orchestra on a firm financial foundation had been under consideration for a long time by the Board of Directors. Each year the Guarantee Fund was becoming more difficult to secure and more of a burden; besides which hand-to-mouth financing is not a very creditable path to travel indefinitely. When these discussions arose, the first question always was "How can we solicit money for a permanent fund and beg for a Guarantee Fund at the same time?" That question always ended against a blank wall. No answer suggested itself until in May, 1916, Mr. Van Rensselaer received a communication from a person who wished to remain unknown, so he later received the title "Unknown Donor."

The proposition was accepted by the Board and later by the Association, and was issued in a circular of which a copy is printed below.

"Endowment Fund

"To the Friends of the Philadelphia Orchestra:

"A friend of the Philadelphia Orchestra Association, who desires to remain unknown, has offered to meet any deficit of the Orchestra for each of five years, beginning with the season of 1916–1917.

"The conditions under which this gift will become available are as follows:

"1. That an Endowment Fund of $100,000 yearly for five years shall be created by the Orchestra Association, so that the total Fund may be $500,000 at the end of this period.

"2. That the contract of the present conductor, Leopold Stokowski, shall be extended to cover this period of five years.

"3. It is earnestly desired that each friend of the Philadelphia Orchestra will pledge a generous amount in order to create this Endowment Fund. Heretofore, all subscriptions to the Philadelphia Orchestra have been spent year by year, to meet the annual deficit. Under this offer the money now contributed will not be so spent, but will be invested to insure the permanency of the Orchestra as an institution of Philadelphia.

"The Orchestra is a civic asset. If it is to fulfill its destiny and place Philadelphia in the front rank among the musical cities of the world, it must be endowed. In order to do this, the Orchestra Association must depend upon the generosity of its friends. We ask that the enclosed blank be signed and returned to us at your earliest opportunity. While it is hoped that all gifts may be for a period of five years, yearly contributions will be gratefully accepted. Payment of subscriptions will be on November 1st and March 1st of each year, beginning with November, 1916.

"ALEXANDER VAN RENSSELAER
FRANCES A. WISTER
EDWARD W. BOK
Endowment Committee"

The way out was found—at least the beginning of the solution was in sight.

The proposal was widely circulated and everybody connected with the Association began to work to raise the amount, which was to reach $500,000 in five years. This was later extended to seven years and now bears the name of "Seven Year Endowment Fund." All persons connected with the Association threw themselves enthusiastically into the work of fulfilling the agreement with the Unknown Donor.

A meeting was called of the four Women's Committees and their Auxiliaries, at the auditorium of the Curtis Building through the courtesy of Mr. Bok; the plans were explained and met with a vigorous response. The women were to raise money in two ways. One was to procure five-year subscriptions of large sums. The other was to secure small subscriptions by the Group Plan. This idea was suggested because the business management could not arrange to take care of sums of less than $25.00. The accumulation of such, therefore, was undertaken by the women, with Mrs. Arnett as Chairman. This piece of work was as trying as any ever entered upon, on account of the detail of keeping small accounts yearly for so long a period.

A group might include any number of persons but the minimum amount for each group could not be less than $25.00 yearly, for five years. The sum of $14,632.00 was raised by seventy-nine Groups, including two Junior Groups but the most important feature of the plan was that it secured the interest of a number of hundred people who would otherwise have been deprived of the pleasure of assisting this cause. This was of infinite value to the Association. To Group Captains, who kept up their quotas of $25.00 yearly for five years, the orchestra owes much, for members often had to be replaced. The Women's Committees have long acted on the principal that the active interest of many people was a necessity in building up an orchestra, and never was their belief more justified than at that time.

The work of the women was prosecuted with enthusiasm and the response was remarkable, not only from Philadelphia, but from Pennsylvania towns as far west as Harrisburg and in New Jersey as far south as Atlantic City.

Other ways of raising money were resorted to, such as chains of card parties, inaugurated by Mrs. John B. Thayer, Jr., whose own chain amounted to $2870, and various entertainments and concerts given by young people. These were necessarily gifts for one year and could not be included in the required $100,000.

The amount including large subscriptions and groups collected by the four Women's Committees was a total for five years of $186,000, this being twenty-five per cent of the Fund.

In November, 1916, it was announced that the amount guaranteed for five years was over $500,000, more than stipulated under the contract with the Unknown Donor. It was then decided to ask the contributors to extend their yearly subscriptions two years longer, and many responded heartily. The name was changed to Seven Year Endowment Fund, and in 1923, the total had reached $788,400. About twelve hundred individuals contributed at this time, and through the groups over five hundred more.

The "Unknown Donor" disclosed himself in 1920, and proved to be Mr. Edward W. Bok. The satisfaction was great of knowing at last the name of this generous friend of music, who had enabled the Philadelphia Orchestra to place itself on a firm foundation.

Chapter III

The Orchestra During the World War

One year after the offer of the Unknown Donor had been accepted by the Board of Directors, the United States was in a state of war. The condition of Europe during the past three years had in a way been disturbing in orchestral circles, because no men could leave Europe and players were scarce. Also, foreign men were called home, leaving vacancies that were difficult to fill. Still, the orchestra had flourished and continued to advance artistically under Mr. Stokowski's guiding hand.

In April, 1917, however, musical organizations in America were facing a different and a serious situation. In everybody's mind the questions lingered and would not be put away: "How is the Philadelphia Orchestra going to survive a war?" "Will there be any players, and will there be any money for music?" Philadelphians spoke not these words aloud, but they feared for the existence of the city's most beloved art organization.

In December, 1917, the four Women's Committees were desirous of making a patriotic demonstration with the orchestra, and at the suggestion of Mrs. J. Sellers Bancroft, an American flag was presented at each of a pair of concerts.

"PRESENTATION OF FLAG
To the Philadelphia Orchestra Association by the Women's Committees for the Philadelphia Orchestra
Presentation of Flag
Miss Frances A. Wister, *President*
The Women's Committees for The Philadelphia Orchestra
The audience is requested to join in singing the National Anthem:
The Star Spangled Banner
(1 verse)
Acceptance of flag for The Philadelphia Orchestra Association:
Mr. Alexander Van Rensselaer, *President*
The Philadelphia Orchestra Association
Acceptance of Flag on behalf of the Orchestra:
Mr. Leopold Stokowski, *Conductor*
The audience is requested to join in singing 'America' "
(2 verses)

Ledger, December 23rd, 1917:

"Viewed in the light of all that has been written, said and done regarding the relation of the musical art and its interpreters to the war and the conception of the majority as to what constitutes patriotism, the public action of the Women's Committee of the Philadelphia Orchestra last week, on December 14th and 15th, when their president, Miss Frances Wister, introduced by Alexander Van Rensselaer, president of the Philadelphia Orchestra Association, presented the orchestra with a flag which was accepted by Leopold Stokowski, seemed full of deepest significance. In presenting the flag, Miss Wister made a graceful little speech about the relation of patriotism and art and said, among other things:

" 'In order to express our loyalty to our country's cause and to the Association which we have fostered so long, and to testify to our belief in the necessity for music as a mighty inspiration, a profound solace during times of stress, we take pleasure in presenting to the Philadelphia Orchestra Association and to the Orchestra a flag.

" 'This is the visible demonstration of the patriotism of this organization and of the Women's Committees during our period of national peril.'

"Both Mr. Van Rensselaer and Mr. Stokowski spoke words of appreciation of the Women's Committees' offering. The former read the resolutions adopted by the Association, and the most popular of musical leaders, Mr. Stokowski, on behalf of the orchestra announced that he and the men meant to give their services in a concert for the benefit of the American Red Cross, which statement naturally was greeted with responsive applause by the huge audience.

"The remarks by which Mr. Stokowski declared the Orchestra's loyalty to the United States were gracefully made, and his action necessarily was profoundly appreciated by his many friends and admirers whose numbers have already increased accordingly.

"The ceremonies closed with two verses of 'America' in which everyone joined heartily. The effect was thrilling. Many eyes were moist and many hearts were moved.

"These are trying times that test men's souls and it does not take much to force to the surface deep, pent-up emotions that long training had suppressed."

* * * * *

At a special meeting of Board of Directors, December 13th, 1917, the following Resolution was unanimously adopted:

"WHEREAS the Women's Committees for the Philadelphia Orchestra are presenting to the Philadelphia Orchestra Association and the Philadelphia Orchestra two American flags as an expression of the patriotic spirit animating their organization of two thousand women,

"BE IT RESOLVED by the Board of Directors of the Philadelphia Orchestra Association in behalf of the fifteen hundred contributing members of the Association, that these flags be accepted in the spirit with which they are given, with the thanks of the Association, and that the management be instructed to display them on the stage of the Academy at each concert given by the Orchestra.

"BE IT FURTHER RESOLVED by the Board of Directors, that it pledges the loyalty of the Association to the Government and people of the United States in this crisis in the affairs of the nation, and offers its services to be made use of in any way in which the Government of the United States may deem wise."

The next patriotic demonstration was the concert at Camp Dix, N. J.

Public Ledger, January 3rd, 1918:

"ORCHESTRA PLAYS FOR CAMP DIX MEN
100 MUSICIANS UNDER LEOPOLD STOKOWSKI
ENTERTAIN 3000 SOLDIERS

"The Philadelphia Orchestra, led by Leopold Stokowski, aroused more than 3000 khaki-clad men here in the big Y. M. C. A. auditorium to outbursts of enthusiastic applause, when they concluded an entire Tschaikowsky programme, including the Symphony Pathétique, the famous 'Nutcracker' Suite, and the stirring overture Solennelle. The concert was made possible through the courtesy of the Philadelphia Orchestra Association.

"The large auditorium was crowded to the doors with the privates in training for the National Army, while the officers occupied a square patch of seats in the center. Alexander Van Rensselaer, President of the Orchestra Association, and Edward Bok and Charles D. Hart, directors, were among the officials who accompanied the orchestra. With the party also was Noah Swayne of the Orpheus Club. The party arrived in Camp on a special train, and the musicians were escorted to the Y. M. C. A. hostess house and served a luncheon by society girls.

"Mr. Van Rensselaer, Mr. Bok, Mr. Stokowski and Mr. Swayne were entertained at the division headquarters mess.

"When Mr. Stokowski took his place at the stage, he was given an ovation, and throughout the four movements of the symphony, the men watched the discipline of the players with an interested eye.

"The contrast of the dark evening suits of the orchestra with the mud-stained puttees and brown uniforms of the thousands of enlisted men formed a novel sight. One officer was overheard saying to another:

" 'How would you like to be captain of those collective artistic temperaments?'

"After the first movement of the symphony was ended in a crash of tympani, the same officer said:

" 'Well, if we can train a million men of the National Army to such precision and such discipline as that, we will have no trouble in beating the Huns.'

"During the intermission, the entire audience did a sort of 'eyes right' when a group picture of the concert was taken."

Besides this concert, men in the service stationed at Philadelphia were given many opportunities to enjoy the orchestra. Beginning in November, 1917, subscribers were requested through a notice in the programme to send tickets that they could not use to the manager, to be placed at the disposal of soldiers and sailors and it was a common sight to see men in uniform at the Saturday evening concerts.

On January 23rd the promised Red Cross Concert was given at the Metropolitan Opera House before a large audience. The affair was most successful financially, the amount turned over being $7045.00.

LIBERTY LOANS

The subject of Liberty Loans was more and more occupying the public mind and soon claimed the attention of musicians.

The first booth during the Third Liberty Loan of May, 1918, was in front of 1427 Chestnut Street, and was presided over by Mr. and Mrs. Stokowski on two Saturday mornings. A quartet of trombones from the orchestra offered their services at the booth and attracted large crowds. The result of these two mornings was $114,000.

During the next loan, the Fourth, the booth, which was a shell dug-out in front of the Union League, was in charge of the four Women's Committees. For the first time in their existence the Committees diverted their minds from the orchestra for a brief space to participate in a patriotic act. This loan occurred at the time of the influenza epidemic and the women who served did so at some risk. No member, however, contracted the disease, or was the worse for the experience.

The booth was open for two weeks only, but with the assistance of members of the orchestra, the amount collected was $896,000.

When the Victory Loan was announced for May, 1919, the Women's Committees were asked to again take charge of a booth for three weeks at the same place. Miss Frances A. Wister acted as Chairman for the second time, and they were assisted by a Committee of Musicians from the orchestra, when their engagements permitted; and a Committee from the Business Management. Seventy-six members of the Women's Committees served during the Loan, as follows: Women's Committee 27; Germantown and Chestnut Hill, 13; West Philadelphia, 22; Media, Chester and West Chester, 14. The total number of subscriptions received was 825, amounting to $691,300.

This, added to the total of $896,000 for the Fourth Loan and that of $114,000 at the Third Loan, made a grand total of $1,701,300.

Music at the booth was furnished without expense by members of the Philadelphia Orchestra, and ten other well-known artists, including Mr. David Bispham. Mr. Albert N. Hoxie gave a patriotic demonstration one day, with a parade and a chorus of one thousand, and the First Regiment Marine Corps Band.

THE TRIBUTE TREES

Another patriotic enterprise in which the Board of Directors and the Women's Committees took part was the planting of tribute trees in honor of men in the service, on Fairmount Parkway, at the invitation of the Civic Club of Philadelphia. Fifty-five trees were planted on the Parkway at Twenty-second Street, and the Board and the Committees were represented at the ceremonies on April 25th, 1919.

The Association did all in its power to assist in war time. Nearly $300,000 of the Endowment Fund was invested in Liberty Loans. On account of railroad congestion traveling was largely eliminated, but this was the only American orchestra permitted to cross the Canadian border, which journey was made for the Toronto Festival.

The audience was not allowed to forget the nation's situation, as Mr. Stokowski had at the first concert of the season inaugurated the ceremony of playing the Star Spangled Banner, orchestrated by himself, at the beginning of every concert, while the house stood. Later he organized and led a band of nearly two hundred pieces at Franklin Field, when funds were being raised for a special War Chest, and he did the same for the Service Star parade.

Eight of the musicians went into the service.

To mark the signing of the Armistice, special ceremonies were held at the concert of November 15th, 1918. Representatives of the Allied Nations appeared on the stage with their flags while their national anthems were played. The audience stood during the playing of MacDowell's "Dirge," from the Indian Suite, which was played in memory of those Americans who had died in the war.

When Philadelphia realized that the orchestra had survived in its full strength and with little curtailment of its schedule, except for out-of-town concerts, and the postponement of two pairs of Philadelphia concerts on account of the epidemic, there was a sigh of gratitude. After such labors to procure an orchestra for Philadelphia, its abandonment would have been a tragedy and a calamity.

CHAPTER IV

THE TWENTIETH ANNIVERSARY
MILLION DOLLAR ENDOWMENT FUND, 1919

During the war the Seven-Year Endowment Fund continued to be paid in showing that Philadelphians were learning to prize what they had. But the Board of Directors was now faced with another problem, the fact that the increased cost of everything in life made it evident that even the Seven Year Fund was going to be insufficient to meet the yearly deficit. Mr. Edward W. Bok then suggested that the Association should conduct a campaign to raise $1,000,000 during the month of October, 1919, in honor of the twentieth season of the Philadelphia Orchestra. This was in January, 1919, and after the Board of Directors had decided to take this bold step, a Campaign Committee was appointed by Mr. Van Rensselaer, of which Mr. Bok was made chairman, in such fashion do one's sins return to one.

This Committee met at intervals during the winter, and Mr. Bok, fertile in ideas, formulated his plan of action. This was to have a Committee of Fifty Campaign Chairmen, men and women, each of whom should raise $20,000. Luncheons were to be held twice each week during the month at which reports were to be made. Chairmen having less than $2000 were obliged to announce "No report."

A circular was widely distributed in order to inform the public of the plans of the Association.

"THE PHILADELPHIA ORCHESTRA
ENDOWMENT CAMPAIGN

"The next season of the Philadelphia Orchestra marks the Twentieth Anniversary. To mark this event, the people of Philadelphia will be asked to complete the Endowment Fund begun in 1915, which was interrupted by the war. For nineteen years, a group of Philadelphia men and women have sustained the annual deficit of the Orchestra. This group has maintained the Orchestra until it reached its present unquestioned position as the leading symphony orchestra in the United States. The Association now feels that the Philadelphia public should place the Orchestra, once for all, on a permanent financial basis. This can be done by completing the Endowment Fund."

"The Endowment Fund as it Stands

"The present Endowment Fund consists of $500,000. In addition to this, there are pledges not yet matured which will bring the amount, within two years, to $800,000. Carefully invested, this total fund will insure the Orchestra a net income of approximately $36,000 a year. This is not sufficient to carry the annual deficit.

"The Orchestra's Annual Deficit

The cost of the Orchestra per season is....... $304,000
The income per season is.................... 238,000
Last year's defict was, therefore............ 66,000

"With increasing costs, the estimated deficit for future years will be $80,000.

"What the Complete Endowment Fund Will Mean

"To the present Endowment Fund, therefore, must be added ONE MILLION DOLLARS. This would mean an estimated income of $81,000, on a total fund of $1,800,000.

"It is this additional
One Million Dollars
that it is now proposed to ask the Philadelphia public to subscribe.

"It should be borne in mind that not a penny of this amount is spent; all is permanently invested, and only the interest therefrom is used to maintain the Orchestra.

"Where the Money Goes

"93 cents out of every dollar of income is spent on the Orchestra; put back into the Orchestra, in other words, in order to increase its efficiency:

Salaries of Orchestra members................55.61%
Expense of rentals, etc., of concerts at Philadel-
    phia and out-of-town......................34.61%
Miscellaneous expenses (Orchestra music, insur-
    ance, etc.)................................. 2.78%
Administration expenses.................... 7.00%

"The Smallness of the Orchestra Deficit

"The annual deficit of the Philadelphia Orchestra of $66,000 is one of the smallest of any of the large symphony orchestras of the United States. These deficits average from $85,000 to $125,000 per year. And yet, with one exception, the Philadelphia Orchestra is the largest symphony orchestra in number of musicians, in the United States, and plays a longer season.

"The Details of the Campaign to Raise
One Million Dollars

"It will begin October 1st, 1919, and continue throughout the month.

"The amount to be raised is One Million Dollars.

"There will be 50 Committees, each Committee to raise a minimum of $20,000.

"These 50 Committees will be under the general chairmanship of Dr. Charles D. Hart.

"The headquarters will be, during October, at the Hotel Ritz-Carlton, Broad and Walnut Streets.

"The territory for the campaign will include the counties of Philadelphia, Montgomery, Delaware, Chester and Bucks.

"Pledges will be payable in cash (much preferred) or 50% payable January 1, 1920, and 50% payable May 1st, 1920.

"The Depository for the Fund will be Messrs. Drexel & Company, to whom all checks should be drawn.

"All pledges should be delivered to Dr. Charles D. Hart, or Miss Frances A. Wister, at the Ritz-Carlton Headquarters.

"THE ENDOWMENT CAMPAIGN COMMITTEE

EDWARD W. BOK, *Chairman*

JOHN F. BRAUN	DR. CHARLES D. HART	MISS FRANCES A. WISTER
SAMUEL S. FELS	EFFINGHAM B. MORRIS	CHARLTON YARNALL
	ALEXANDER VAN RENSSELAER	

General Chairman of Committees
DR. CHARLES D. HART"

Mr. Joseph E. Widener provided the Campaign Headquarters in the Ritz-Carlton Hotel where an office force was installed and the bi-weekly luncheons held.

Dr. Hart worked hard to procure the fifty Chairmen and fifty-three people consented to serve, but some dropped by the wayside. At the opening campaign luncheon, on September 29th, 1919, there were in actual service only forty-two. As was to be expected, some collected more than their quotas and some less. Women chairmen predominated, there being twenty-eight of these to fourteen men. Their names should be recorded.

CHAIRMEN

Messrs. Edward W. Bok, John F. Braun, Charles D. Hart, Henry McKean Ingersoll, Alexander Van Rensselaer and Andrew Wheeler of the Board of Directors; and from outside, Messrs. Henry G. Brengle, W. W. Fry, J. B. Henkels, Jr., George I. Bodine, G. H. Lang, Maurice Speiser, Herbert J. Tily and Wm. Jay Turner.

WOMEN CHAIRMEN

Mrs. Alfred Reginald Allen, Mrs. Wm. W. Arnett, Mrs. Thomas G. Ashton, Mrs. Charles Carver, Mrs. Herbert L.

[124]

Clark, Mrs. Matthew H. Cryer, Mrs. Joseph M. Gazzam, Mrs. Charles W. Henry, Mrs. Henry S. Jeanes, Miss Lea, Mrs. Joseph Leidy, Mrs. Wm. S. Newcomet, Mrs. Thomas Robins, Countess of Santa Eulalia, Mrs. Wm. A. Slaughter, Mrs. John B. Thayer, 3rd., Mrs. L. Howard Weatherly, Miss F. A. Wister, Mrs. Harold E. Yarnall and Mrs. Camille Zeckwer, all members of the Women's Committees.

In addition to these women, able assistance was given by Mrs A. J. Dallas Dixon, Mrs. L. Chandler Williams, and six women who had not up to this time been connected with the Philadelphia Orchestra, except as enthusiastic patrons. These were Mrs. Frederic W. Abbott, in charge of the Matinee Musicale Club Committee, Mrs. Frank T. Griswold, Mrs. Joseph N. Snellenburg, Mrs. John B. Thayer, Mrs. J. William White, and the Motor Messenger Service under Mrs. Thomas L. Elwyn.

The Germantown and Chestnut Hill and the Media, Chester and West Chester Committees acted under their own presidents. The work of this committee under Mrs. Cryer and that of Mrs. Wm. A. Slaughter in West Jersey deserve special mention on account of the distances covered.

Synopsis of the Results:

Twenty members of the four Women's Committees, as individual chairmen............$396,292.36
Women Chairmen outside of Women's Committees...................................191,832.55

Total for 28 Women Chairmen. $588,124.91
This was 53% of the Fund, but the women Chairmen were two to one against the men.

Besides the collections made by the Committee of Fifty, amounts came in from other sources, such as, members of the Philadelphia Orchestra Chorus, the Van Rensselaer Tribute, the two Wister Tributes, the Van Rensselaer-Bok Telegram to business firms, the Telephone Circular, the Main Line Bonds, other Liberty Bonds, contributions received at the office, etc.

A unique feature of the campaign was the memorials and tributes which gave people an opportunity to place the names of family or friends on special tablets to be placed in the Academy of Music. No less than $1000 was accepted for each memorial.

MEMORIALS AND TRIBUTES

in

The Philadelphia Orchestra Endowment Fund

1919

MEMORIALS TO THE FALLEN IN THE WORLD WAR
MAJOR ALFRED REGINALD ALLEN, U. S. A.
THE AMERICAN HEROES IN THE GREAT WAR,
    UNKNOWN AND UNSUNG
LIEUTENANT MORTIMER P. CRANE, B. A.
LIEUTENANT WILLIAM BOULTON DIXON, U. S. A.
ENSIGN GEORGE B. EVANS, JR., U. S. N. Air Service
LIEUTENANT ROBERT H. GAMBLE, U. S. A.
LIEUTENANT WILLIAM B. KUEHN, U. S. A.
LIEUTENANT PAUL BORDA KURTZ, U. S. A.
RALPH LESLIE MELVILLE, B. A.
MAJOR TALBOT MERCER PAPINEAU, M. C.
CORPORAL ABRAM K. STREET, U. S. A.
LIEUTENANT ARTHUR RICHMOND TABER, U. S. A.
MEMBERS OF STRAWBRIDGE & CLOTHIER CHORUS
ARTHUR HOWELL WILSON, U. S. A.
TWELVE PHILADELPHIA BOY SCOUT HEROES

TRIBUTES OF THANKSGIVING

for the safe return of

LIEUTENANT WILLIAM CURTIS BOK, U. S. N.
HAMILTON DISSTON CARPENTER, U. S. A.
LIEUTENANT LEONARD E. POWELL
LIEUTENANT SYDNEY THAYER, JR., U. S. M. C.
LIEUTENANT GEORGE BOWER, U. S. M. C.
JOHN FREDERICK SIEBERLING, U. S. A.
HAROLD FRANCIS WESTON, B. A.

PERSONAL MEMORIALS AND APPRECIATIONS

In Memory of

JOSEPHINE L. S. ADAMS
BLANCHE BALDWIN
BEULAH HECKER BANCROFT
GEORGE BARRIE
MAUDE ECKERT BENSON
RUDOLPH BLANKENBURG
JOSEPH B. BLOODGOOD
MARY FRANCES BLOODGOOD
SIEKE GERTRUDE BOK
ELIZABETH S. BRAUN
LOUIS BRÉGY
ARTHUR BROCK
CHARLES HALL BROCK

G. MARTIN BRILL
RICHARD VAUX BUCKLEY
WILLIAM BURNHAM
LOIS BUCHANAN CASSATT
WILLIAM T. CARTER
FREDERICK TAYLOR CHANDLER
MRS. ANNA L. COMEGYS
RICHARD Y. COOK
HUGH CRAIG, JR.
MICHAEL H. CROSS
CHARLES HOWE CUMMINGS
HARRY K. CUMMINGS
LOUISE KNAPP CURTIS

ENDOWMENT FUND MEMORIAL TABLET

EDWARD TONKIN DOBBINS
FRANKLIN DUANE
GEORGE W. ELKINS
ADAM H. FETTEROLF, LL. D.
SIMON B. FLEISHER
ROBERT H. FOERDERER
REV. FREDERIC GARDINER
DR. W. W. GILCHRIST
ANNE STARR GRISCOM
HARRY B. HALL
JOHN WILLIAM HALLAHAN, 3RD
GEORGE W. HARRAH
THOMAZINHA E. HARRAH
MARIA AMES HARTE
SARAH KENT HOW
MAX LIVINGSTON
HARRIET ANNE LUCAS
MABEL ELEANOR McCAHAN
JOHN R. McDOWELL
HENRY J. MARIS
DR. CHARLES MOHR
JOHN PAUL MORRIS
JOHN THOMPSON MORRIS
HARLAN PAGE
RIEHLÉ MEMORIAL FUND
HELEN HAMILTON ROBINS
THEODORE ROOSEVELT

RICHARD ROSSMASSLER
EDWARD COLLIN ROSSMASSLER
JOHN C. SCHAEFER
FRITZ SCHEEL
MRS. FRANCIS SCHROEDER
MRS. WILLIAM SIMPSON, JR.
HENRY M. STEEL
JOHN M. STEFFAN
JOHN B. STETSON
DR. REUEL STEWART
WILLIAM STOLL, JR.
ROLAND LESLIE TAYLOR, JR.
ARCHIBALD GRAHAM THOMSON
FRANK THOMSON
JAMES TILY
S. LETITIA TILY
EDWARD K. TRYON, JR.
ALICE DOUGLAS TURNER
ISABEL G. WALKER
FREDERICK WEBER
J. WILLIAM WHITE, M. D.
ELEANOR MERCER VANDERBILT
WILLIAM F. VACHE
MARY CHANNING WISTER
WILLIAM BREWSTER WOOD
HAROLD ELLIS YARNALL

IN APPRECIATION OF

EDWARD W. BOK
LEOPOLD STOKOWSKI
OLGA STOKOWSKI

ALEXANDER VAN RENSSELAER
FRANCES ANNE WISTER

Miss Wister's name was placed on the tablet by the contribution of two large amounts, one from the Women's Committee and one from the Auxiliary.

The tablets beautifully designed by Mr. Paul Cret, the noted architect, are placed on each side of the entrance to the inner lobby.

The delightful luncheons held bi-weekly instilled in the workers much enthusiasm and were attended by from 300 to 400 people each time. At these the following well-known public and private individuals and artists appeared, all giving freely of their time and often of their money to help the great cause:

Miss Margaret Anglin, Mr. David Bispham, Mrs. A. J. Cassatt, Mrs. Edward H. Coates, Mr. Cyrus H. K. Curtis, Mr. Walter Damrosch, Mrs. Minnie Maddern Fiske, Sir

Johnston Forbes-Robertson, Mr. Walter Hampden, Dr. John Grier Hibben, Mr. Josef Hofmann, Miss Estelle Hughes (Winner of Stokowski Medal), Mr. Sascha Jacobinoff, Mr. Otto H. Kahn, Mr. Hans Kindler, Rabbi Krauskopf, Mme. Matzenauer, Miss Violet Oakley, Judge Patterson, Bishop Rhinelander, Dr. Thaddeus Rich, Mme. Samaroff, Mr. Oscar Schwar and a group of men from the orchestra.

The thrill of these occasions will never be forgotten by the campaigners. Only those who participated can have any idea of the enthusiasm and excitement prevailing among the workers who eagerly awaited the reports. After speeches and music of a very delightful nature, the chairmen were called by name and saw their totals written on a large blackboard. Many of them went to bed the night before with nothing in their pockets and arrived at headquarters in the morning to find their able assistants had brought in the required two thousand and more. It is marvellous that Mr. Bok could, besides running a campaign, manage such brilliant affairs as these were, twice each week. It was no unusual sight to see four hundred men and women come in exhausted and discouraged, and go forth with renewed vigor to beg money. The spirit of excitement ran through it all, for raising money is as uncertain as gambling in that the pursuer never knows when he accosts a victim what the outcome will be, large, small, or nothing, and many surprises were experienced. The competition was great, for Mr. Bok had offered $1,000 each to the first ten committees to raise their quotas.

The Officers and Directors and the members of the Women's Committees and their Auxiliaries swarmed at the Ritz. Over it all was the influence of Mr. Van Rensselaer, with a courteous and cheerful word for all the harassed.

Philadelphia Press, September 28th, 1919:

"400 Enlisted for Campaign to Save Philadelphia Orchestra.
Volunteer Workers will Receive Final Instructions at
Ritz-Carlton Luncheon Tomorrow
$1,000,000 Fund the Goal
Failure may Mean Loss to City of Asset of Incalculable Value

"Musical Philadelphia is watching with a great deal of interest and anxiety, the movement on foot to 'make the Philadelphia Orchestra safe for Philadelphia' by raising the endowment of $1,000,000, for

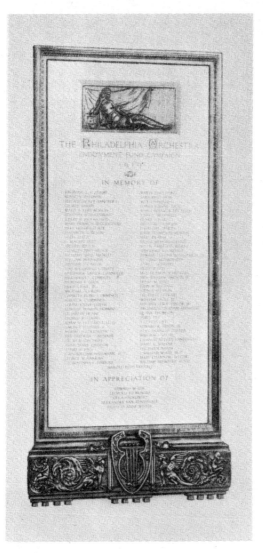

ENDOWMENT FUND MEMORIAL TABLET

otherwise, it has been announced that this organization must be seriously curtailed in its activities."

* * * * *

"Many cities sustaining an orchestra are greatly aided by the work and philanthropy of one or two men, but in the case of the Philadelphia Orchestra, the burden of making up the yearly deficit is distributed among a number of people.

"The Committee of fifty Chairmen who will meet tomorrow at the get-together luncheon' are each pledged to turn in for his Committee a sum of $20,000. Each Chairman has a group of co-workers, including prominent social and philanthropic leaders of this city.

ORCHESTRA'S VALUE TO CITY

"The campaign to save the Orchestra for Philadelphia has set loose a flood tide of arguments as to the value of this organization to the city's life. To business-men the argument that the Philadelphia Orchestra is a great advertisement to the city will make the strongest appeal, while to the great number of people interested in the artistic life of the city the argument that its pre-eminent place in the world of music merits their greatest support will naturally serve to stir them to action."

* * * * *

"The realization that the possession of an orchestra of high standing is a great commercial as well as a great civic asset to a city, has caused a number of cities to build up an organization similar to the one Philadelphia already possesses."

* * * * *

RANKS WITH WORLD'S BEST

"By a most consistent plan of development under the direction of Alexander Van Rensselaer, the Philadelphia Orchestra, now in its twentieth year, has earned the reputation of being 'the first orchestra in America.' No less a critic than H. T. Parker, of Boston, writing in the Boston *Transcript* says, 'there can no longer be any doubt that the Philadelphia Orchestra is today the first of all American orchestras. In fact, it may be said now to rank among the five great orchestral organizations in the world.' Mr. Ossip Gabrilowitsch, famous no less as a conductor than a pianist, says that 'it is now a most important factor in the musical life of this country, and has set a standard of excellence which all other symphony orchestras in America, no matter how famous, must bear in mind, if they wish to maintain their places in the front rank.'"

* * * *

"Under Stokowski the Orchestra has made a rapid step forward. The first performance in America of the Mahler Symphony, using a chorus of over one thousand singers, made the whole country 'sit up.'"

* * * * *

"One element that the committee in charge of this endowment fund campaign must combat, is the confidence that the $1,000,000 can be easily raised. This is unpsychological. This same notion has frequently spoiled some of the best organized campaigns for endowing other worthy institutions in this city."

The publicity for the campaign was brilliantly conceived and executed by Mr. Bok.

In the spring "The Orchestra News" began to appear monthly, with the idea of making the story of the organization much more widely known than it had heretofore been. Its pages were "instructive and entertaining" as the expression was in old times. So were the various folders and leaflets sent out during the campaign itself. Persons of importance in the business world helped with the publicity as well as with large contributions.

"THE ORCHESTRA NEWS

"Published Every Once in a While in the Interests of the Philadelphia Orchestra at the Pennsylvania Building, Philadelphia

Why I Came to Philadelphia

"Because—America was fast becoming (and has since completely become) the great music-making country of the world.

"Because—Fritz Scheel (with his instinct for choosing exactly the right artist for each position in the orchestra) had laid the foundation of a wonderful orchestra. Since then many fine artists have been added but the main structure of the personnel remains as Scheel created it.

"Because—I felt in Philadelphia the existence of a warm hearted and genuinely music-loving public which I believed would grow. This it has done amazingly in the last few years.

"It is my ardent hope that this development will continue, and that we may soon welcome among us the great number of music-lovers in Philadelphia, who have not yet come to us.

"Leopold Stokowski"

"To The Business Men of Philadelphia

"We are convinced that the Philadelphia Orchestra is entitled to the support of the business men of Philadelphia. The Orchestra is now the leading symphony orchestra in the United States, and has become a distinct civic asset of signal value to Philadelphia. The impression made by the Orchestra in the largest cities in America which it visits and where it plays before 100,000 persons during each season has been proven to be of the most pronounced advertising value to our city. To place this Orchestra on a permanent financial basis such as the Endowment Fund of One Million Dollars now asked will accomplish, is a distinct investment for the business interests of the city. To compel so valuable a municipal asset to be discontinued for lack of this fund cannot be considered.

"We ask, therefore, that the business men of Philadelphia will join us in the support of the Orchestra in this campaign.

"SAMUEL REA	"W. W. ATTERBURY
EFFINGHAM B. MORRIS	E. PUSEY PASSMORE
JOHN GRIBBEL	JOHN H. MASON
SAMUEL T. BODINE	JAMES CROSBY BROWN
SAMUEL M. VAUCLAIN	SAMUEL S. FELS
CYRUS H. K. CURTIS	ELLIS A. GIMBEL
WILLIAM A. LAW	WILLIAM P. GEST"

"WE DO IT IN NEW YORK
By OTTO H. KAHN

"A business man should realize that he makes a definite investment, yielding interest to him and to his city in civic and business advantage, when he supports a worthy art organization in his community.

"In New York we have come more and more to realize the value, the merit and the obligation of such investments.

"The Metropolitan Opera, for instance, and our several symphony concert organizations were started and have always been and are now being supported financially by business men.

"These and similar art enterprises have become not only genuine assets in the lives of the people who support and patronize them, but distinct and profitable business assets to the city.

"Of late, another organization, the Philadelphia Orchestra, has entered into friendly and successful rivalry with the old-established symphonic organizations of New York.

"The public and press of New York are one in acknowledging gladly and cordially that Philadelphia has now in its Orchestra, under its eminent leader, one of the greatest organizations of the kind in the United States, or, indeed, anywhere.

"Its visits to New York are welcomed and looked forward to.

"It has taken an honored place in the musical life of New York.

"In what it has achieved, it has served and proclaimed Philadelphia.

"It carries the message of Philadelphia wherever it appears: a high and fine message of credit and renown to the city which gave it being and supports it.

"The civic value and the business value of the investment which is represented by the Philadelphia Orchestra are definite and great.

"The eminent position and conspicuous reputation which it has attained are assets of great price to its home city.

"The business men of Philadelphia should take pride in coming forward unhesitatingly and generously to the full support of the splendid musical organization which bears the name and enhances the fame of Philadelphia.　　　　　"OTTO H. KAHN."

The newspaper publicity was very fine and the programme books were also pressed into service, to further the campaign. Mr. Bok's and Mr. Stokowski's clever appeals kept the subject well in the minds of the audiences during that month by the following appeals:

"A Personal Invitation

"Much as we would like to do so, we cannot naturally reach personally every resident of Philadelphia for their contribution to the Million Dollar Endowment Fund to save the Philadelphia Orchestra.

"In case we have not reached you, will you regard this as a personal invitation to help in our efforts to save our beautiful Orchestra by filling in the blank below and mailing it to the address given?

"Please remember that not a penny of your money will be spent: every dollar is carefully invested, and will work year in and year out, for all time, only the interest being used to pay the expenses of the Orchestra. Your subscription, therefore, is a legacy to yourself, your children, the Orchestra and the city.

"The Philadelphia Orchestra Endowment Campaign Committee."

Programme, October 17th, 1919:

"A Personal Message From Mr. Stokowski

"We are facing two possibilities today:

"One: Shall we continue the Orchestra as it is?

"The other: Shall we reduce it?

"Let me tell you exactly what these two things mean, so that we will know exactly what we are leading to.

"Suppose we reduce the orchestra: which we must do if we do not raise this Endowment Fund. That means that your first men in the orchestra, the chiefs of each section, would not remain, because there are orchestras being formed all over the country now, and these orchestras will naturally take away the splendid first men that we have in our Orchestra.

"You would naturally have to replace those men with second-class men. You would have to do this because the relation of supply and demand of orchestral players is tremendously intense. There is far more demand than there is supply of really great players. Having second-class men in those positions—I must speak frankly to you now—you would have a second-class orchestra.

"Now, whoever you have for conductor cannot possibly give you really first-quality results if he has a second-quality orchestra. That is impossible.

"Then you could not allow such an orchestra to go outside of Philadelphia. You could not permit a second-class orchestra bearing the name of the city to travel to the West, to New York, Washington, Baltimore, Pittsburgh, Toronto, and the various places where we play. It would be too much to our shame. We could not do it. So all the tours would have to be cut out.

"In Philadelphia itself we should not be able to give concerts of the first quality, and you would naturally become dissatisfied. And after these second-rate concerts had gone on for one or two seasons, you would say to yourself, this must stop; we must have again an orchestra like what we used to have; we must have a first-class orchestra. You would begin all over again to rebuild your Orchestra once more, and do you realize how long it takes to build or rebuild an orchestra?

"Do you realize that it took me personally all the seven years that I have been in Philadelphia to get three first-class artists for just one section of the Orchestra? And you have ninety-seven men in your Orchestra! That gives you just an idea of the work involved."

* * * * *

"Will Philadelphia give its Orchestra its needed fund, avoid the calamity I have tried to outline and let the Orchestra go on as it is, and as the generations go on, and we go from this life, we will have the feeling that its influence will go on; that it will accumulate tradition; that it will go on maturing; and that it will become more and more beautiful.   "LEOPOLD STOKOWSKI."

"P. S. In the above I have tried to tell you what must happen if the Orchestra fails to secure the Endowment Fund for which it asks.

"In the programme for next week's concerts, I want to tell you what will happen if we do get the Fund; the plan that we have so long had in mind for the Orchestra and Philadelphia."

———————

"To the Friends of
  The Philadelphia Orchestra
"We have reason to believe that it is in the hearts of a number of the friends of the Philadelphia Orchestra to leave a legacy in their wills to the Orchestra. Appreciative as we are of this beautiful thought on the part of these friends, we hope we may not be misunderstood if we suggest the thought that were such legacies now given to the Endowment Fund when the Orchestra stands at the cross-roads of its career, and when the next fortnight must determine its continuance or its dissolution, the service rendered would be greater than may be possible at any other period in its history. If ever the Orchestra has need of the kindliest thoughts of its friends it is at this time when the prestige of this superb organization may be maintained, its present excellence continued, and its strength conserved: when it is here to support and when the generosity of those who believe in it can save it and make it the permanent institution of Philadelphia that it deserves and should be."   ———————

Programme, October 24th-25th, 1919:
"It is not a campaign-slogan: it is the truth when we say:

SAVE THE ORCHESTRA
"If the Endowment Fund fails, this will be the last season that the Orchestra can remain at its present strength of excellence.
"Is that to be your gift to it on its twentieth birthday?"

"WHAT WILL HAPPEN IF WE SUCCEED
By LEOPOLD STOKOWSKI
"In last week's programme I tried to tell you how we would have to curtail the Philadelphia Orchestra, if we failed to get the Endow-

ment Fund for which we are all striving; how we would have to let our best artists go; how we would, for very shame, stop traveling to other cities because we had a second-class orchestra. All this is absolute.

"Just as absolute, however, is the other side of the picture if Philadelphia will give its Orchestra this fund.

"We would naturally not only continue the Orchestra as it is, but we would go on developing it every season to a higher quality, for in art there is no end, since, as soon as you reach the horizon which you saw a year ago, new horizons appear and new fields of beauty. The end never comes, because you are never satisfied; that is the wonderful thing about art.

"Let us in Philadelphia go forward; not backward! Let us carry this fund through.

* * * * *

"We are not asking for a fund that is raised and spent. Not a penny of the Million Dollars is to be spent; every dollar is to be invested and put away. Twenty, thirty, forty years from now it will still be there, always working, bearing interest. And only this interest is to be spent.

"Is this not a good investment for yourself, your children and your city?

"Upon this twentieth anniversary I plead for this birthday gift to the Orchestra.
"Leopold Stokowski."

The appeal sent to telephone subscribers ran as follows:

"The Present You Can Make With Two Dollars For Yourself and Children

"A handful of people, for nineteen years, have paid all the bills of the Philadelphia Orchestra until now the foremost artists and the leading music critics have proclaimed it to be the greatest orchestra in the United States, and one of the five great orchestras of the world.

"The expense of the orchestra is now too great for a few to continue to pay. This year the orchestra will be twenty years old, and, as a birthday present, it is now asked that the people of Philadelphia, as a whole, will make the orchestra permanent by completing its Endowment Fund, each contributing only two dollars, making it in a true sense the orchestra of the people.

Your Two Dollars Will Never be Spent

"It will be carefully invested, and only the interest used for the Orchestra. Your gift is, therefore, one for all the years to come: a permanent gift to a permanent institution."

In December two concerts were given for these contributors who numbered several thousand.

When October 31st arrived and the million dollars was neither in hand nor in sight, the campaign was extended for one week. The appeals became more and more urgent.

[134]

Programme October 31st, November 1st.

"For Lack of Help the Campaign may Fail!

"Owing to a lack of sufficient workers, the Million Dollars necessary for the proper Endowment of the Philadelphia Orchestra has not been raised.

"Tired, but full of courage, those who are working have decided to extend the campaign for another week.

"Campaigns usually fail because the money cannot be had. Here the money is in sight, but the friends of the Orchestra have not come forth in sufficient numbers to collect the funds.

"Is the campaign to fail for this unusual reason?

"Will you not, man or woman, give a day, two days of this extra week to help us collect the last $250,000 necessary to complete the fund?

"You cannot, at this time, render a greater service to the Orchestra. You can, at this most critical time, do your part to

Save the Orchestra."
* * * * *
"Will You Not?

"May we ask you, as a final appeal for the Orchestra, to give to it
Just One Liberty Bond
of any denomination, as your contribution to save the Orchestra for yourself and the city at this critical time in its history?

"Whether you have given previously or not, will you not do this one more act?

"The Bond you give will not be sold: it will not be spent. Not a penny of it. It will be put away under a Deed of Trust, and only the interest on it will be used to maintain the Orchestra.

"Could you put a Bond in a better, more permanent place?"

"Face to Face

"We now stand face to face with the question whether our Orchestra is to be preserved as it is or reduced to a second-class orchestra.

"The Million Dollars necessary for its preservation have not been raised.

"The campaign will, accordingly, be extended for one week.

"But the question, after all, is—Will you give? Will you help?

"We need some $250,000 more.

"The workers have done their best. Hundreds of the friends of the Orchestra have not done their part as yet. Less than 5000 have contributed!

"Is the truth clearly realized without the mincing of words: If this remaining sum is not raised, the Orchestra must be reduced; it cannot remain the glorious thing it is today."

"The Truth Is Simple and Direct

"We must tear down the beautiful Orchestra that has been so patiently and skilfully built up unless the Million Dollar Endowment Fund is raised. Only one week remains in which to do it. Whatever that tells is the answer."

Finally the goal was won and the event was celebrated by a great dinner at which there was much enthusiasm and rejoicing, when it was announced that $1,100,000 had been contributed.

The twenty-eight women Chairmen expressed their appreciation of Mr. Bok's leadership in the following letter, which was read:

"PHILADELPHIA ORCHESTRA ASSOCIATION
COMMITTEE OF FIFTY

"EDWARD BOK, ESQ., *Chairman*,
   Twentieth Anniversary Endowment Fund Campaign Committee
"Dear Mr. Bok:
   "The Women Chairmen of the Committee of Fifty desire to express their appreciation of your leadership as Chairman of the Twentieth Anniversary Endowment Fund Campaign for the Philadelphia Orchestra.
   "The luncheons alone, as arranged and presided over by you, have been the most unique and inspiring series of affairs ever conducted in Philadelphia. But these have been only a part of your labors and detail in the large plans which you have undertaken and carried out.
   "We thank you for your unfailing courtesy toward us and for your words of encouragement at moments when the result of the battle seemed to be in doubt. Your imagination and enthusiasm have led us to victory and it has been a pleasure to co-operate with you in the important work of placing the Philadelphia Orchestra on a permanent foundation.
                         Yours sincerely,
                         (Signed)

HELEN WARREN ALLEN	KATHARINE E. NEWCOMET
ELIZABETH H. ARNETT	MARIE R. ROBINS
MARY L. H. ASHTON	COUNTESS OF SANTA EULALIA
	per E. V. W
MARETTA VERNON CARVER	IRENE H. SNELLENBURG
ELIZABETH CONWAY CLARK	FLORENCE LEWIS SLAUGHTER
MARTHA G. CRYER	MARIAN M. THAYER
MARGARETTA S. DIXON	LOIS C. THAYER
NELLIE ANDREWS GAZZAM	CAROLINE CLARK WEATHERLY
ALICE GRISWOLD	LETITIA WHITE
SALLIE HOUSTON HENRY	LOUISE CHANDLER WILLIAMS
CORA BAIRD JEANES	FRANCES ANNE WISTER
NINA LEA	ADÈLE G. YARNALL
HELEN C. LEIDY	HORTENSE L. ZECKWER

                     Matinee Musical Club,
                     CLARA BARNES ABBOTT, *Chairman*
                     Motor Messenger Service,
                     NATALIE J. ELWYN, *Chairman*
Victory Dinner, Philadelphia
November 10th, 1919."

The campaign under the able leadership of Mr. Bok was inspiring and exciting to a degree. He gave time and money, but best of all, he gave ideas, and he proved himself an accomplished beggar and a clever general.

The Association was not unmindful of his masterly achievement. At a meeting of the Board of Directors held November 26th, 1919, this resolution was passed:

"WHEREAS the Directors of the Philadelphia Orchestra Association recognize that the splendid services of Mr. Edward Bok, Chairman of the Campaign Committee of the Philadelphia Orchestra Endowment Fund, were largely responsible for the triumphant success of the Campaign,

"BE IT RESOLVED that the Directors of the Philadelphia Orchestra Association place on record such belief, and, further, their appreciation of the energy, resourcefulness and self-sacrificing devotion with which he led the Campaign to success, together with a real expression of their regard for him.

Also this one passed at the Annual Meeting of the Association, May 25th, 1920:

"Mr. Edward W. Bok as Chairman of the Twentieth Anniversary Endowment Fund Campaign Committee was successful, in October, 1919, in procuring from the people of Philadelphia and vicinity, a fund of One Million Dollars for the Philadelphia Orchestra. This fund, when added to the Endowment Fund of 1916, will place the Orchestra on a permanent foundation.

"In no piece of work hitherto undertaken by Mr. Bok has he shown more decided talents of leadership, executive ability and resourcefulness, than in this brilliantly executed campaign. Future generations, only, can measure the value of the establishment of a great orchestra in this city, but certain it is that the raising of this magnificent sum for music is an achievement the like of which Philadelphia has not previously witnessed.

"Therefore be it RESOLVED:

"That the thanks of the Philadelphia Orchestra Association be hereby expressed to the Chairman of the Endowment Campaign Committee, Edward W. Bok, together with our appreciation of his great service to the Philadelphia Orchestra, to the cause of music, and to the people of Philadelphia."

Gifts ranged from one penny, given by a blind child, to $100,000. Many men and women of moderate means deprived themselves of necessities in order that the orchestra might live. Others gave time and others again gave both time and money, but never one word of regret has been heard.

The Chairman's parting shot appeared in the programm
book a week later:

November 14th-15th, 1919:

"THANK YOU!

"The Million Dollar Endowment for the Philadelphia Orchestr
has been secured with the goal passed by a generous margin. Th
result ensures not only the permanency of the present Orchestra bu
the expansion of its influence.

"To each and all who worked and gave and encouraged, we extend
individually and collectively, our heartfelt thanks.

"We asked you to save the Orchestra!

"The Orchestra IS saved!

"Thank you!

THE PHILADELPHIA ORCHESTR
ENDOWMENT CAMPAIGN COMMITTE

November 14th, 1919."

Thus the creation of an Endowment Fund was achieve
by the most extraordinary campaign ever conducted i
Philadelphia, and through the contributions of more tha
13,000 people who wished to place a Philadelphia musica
institution on a permanent foundation.

CHAPTER V

TWENTY YEARS OF PROGRESS

The Twentieth Anniversary of the Philadelphia Orchestra was celebrated on November 19th and 20th, 1920; and great was the rejoicing that this city possessed an orchestra of such attainment, brought to its present high state by a distinguished conductor, and endowed by a large number of citizens of Philadelphia and vicinity. The long labors of the officers and directors, and of the Women's Committees, were bringing their recompense. The occasion was celebrated by the playing of the first programme given by Fritz Scheel in 1900; and the presentation of a silver loving cup, bearing the following inscription, to Mr. Van Rensselaer:

"ALEXANDER VAN RENSSELAER
First President of
The Philadelphia Orchestra Association
on the Occasion of the Twentieth Anniversary Concerts
November 19th and 20th, 1920
With gratitude and deep appreciation of his invaluable services
from
The Board of Directors, the Women's Committees
The Philadelphia Orchestra, the Business Management"

THE PHILADELPHIA ORCHESTRA*

"With the concerts of November 19th and 20th, 1920, the Philadelphia Orchestra celebrates its twentieth year; a year auspiciously opened in November, 1919, by completing the Endowment Fund.

"To have sustained an honorable career during twenty years is no mean attainment for a business enterprise, a school or an institution. But for a group of people to support an orchestra for twenty years—years artistically certain, but financially uncertain—is a memorable achievement and a cause for congratulation and rejoicing.

"The first concert of The Philadelphia Orchestra was played on November 16th, 1900, and was one of the series of six evening concerts given during the season of 1900–1901. The names of the founders, Dr. Edward I. Keffer, Mr. Edward G. McCollin, Mr. John H. Ingham, Mr. Oliver Boyce Judson, and Mr. Oscar A. Knipe, who formed the Executive Committee, did not appear on the programme. Neither

---

*Programme book, November 19th and 20th, 1920.

was it publicly known that this was the Committee which ha
asked Mrs. Alexander J. Cassatt to arrange the so-called Philippin
Concerts about six months earlier, which gave Fritz Scheel his firs
opportunity to conduct in Philadelphia an orchestra composed c
professional musicians.

"On the programme for the second series of concerts, consisting c
fourteen pairs, during the season of 1901-02, the names of the abov
gentlemen appear with the additional names of Mr. Alexander Va
Rensselaer, President, and Mr. Henry Whelen, Jr., Treasurer.

"The talents of Mr. Scheel, who died after seven years of devotio
to the cause, soon placed the new organization among the first i
America; and the work thus begun has resulted in an orchestra whic
has steadily and surely advanced to its present pre-eminent positio
under the leadership of Leopold Stokowski."

* * * * *

"The history of the Philadelphia Orchestra cannot be written i
this brief space. It is a story of the pioneers who were inspired t
found an orchestra; of devotion, faithfulness and financial aid on th
part of the Officers and Board of Directors; of continuous work by th
four Women's Committees; of an 'Unknown Donor,' who is no longe
'unknown'; of loyal support from interested citizens, and of a grou
of artists, whose music speaks for them and for their leader. In shor
the orchestra, which now speaks for Philadelphia the world over, i
the result of co-operation on the part of all these groups; a co-opera
tion which has made Philadelphia one of the great musical centres c
the world."

Public Ledger, November 20th, 1920:

"ORCHESTRA GIVES BIRTHDAY CONCERT
"Programme same as that presented at First Performance
Twenty Years Ago
"Players Warmly Greeted
"Silver Urn for Mr. Van Rensselaer After His Review
of Two Decades

"The Philadelphia Orchestra gave a concert yesterday that was re
music, all of it. There was nothing 'modern' in the programme, not
ing that teased the ear with puzzle-problems or geometric exercis
wrought ingeniously. The performance celebrated the Twentiet
Anniversary of the first concert and the programme was the same a
on that fundamental occasion."

* * * * *

"After the symphony came the celebratory features. Alexander Va
Rensselaer made a graceful address in brief review of the twenty year
The finished product of the present, he held, was the outcome c
united effort. The chief credit must go to the indefatigable women'
committees. The munificence of the until recently 'unknown donor

Mr. Bok, assured us five years more of the inspiring leadership of Stokowski, and has established the endowment fund.

"Dr. Stokowski declared that the music spoke for itself and that the orchestra was heartily glad when it gave pleasure to its hearers. Dr. Hart, in behalf of a committee, made an eloquent and feeling speech in deserved tribute to Mr. Van Rensselaer, and presented a silver urn of enormous dimensions, together with a set of resolutions.

"The members of the committee standing with Dr. Hart were Miss Frances Wister, Miss Anne Thomson, Mr. Judson and Dr. Rich, and the actual presentation was made by Miss Thomson. The orchestra blew a fanfare and the audience stood and applauded."

* * * * *

Public Ledger, November 20th, 1920, Editorial:

"TWENTY YEARS IN MUSIC

"In signalizing its twentieth anniversary with a revival of the original programme directed by Fritz Scheel on November 16th, 1900, the Philadelphia Orchestra has enabled its friends to indulge in pleasurable reflections.

"It is difficult, of course, to recall accurately, the artistry of any performance, musical or dramatic, after a lapse of two decades. But a highly sensitized memory is not needed in this instance. Between the most pioneering effort of the orchestra, which ventured upon only six concerts in its first season, and the authority and artistic opulence of the present organization, there is a disparity in which the whole community can take the profoundest pride.

"Not only has the orchestra headed by Mr. Stokowski attained to a position of splendid leadership in the realm of music, but the esthetic standards of Philadelphia have admirably kept pace. Without affectation it may be said that the growth of musical culture in this city during the last score of years has been gratifyingly vigorous, unsurpassed here in any previous period of similar length."

* * * * *

"Cultural appreciation, it is said, usually follows an era of fervent inspiration. Evidently it is an age of the former in which we are now dwelling, hence the abiding charm and appeal of a twenty-year-old programme. The new honors, well worth an anniversary observance, are for the interpreters."

To those who had devoted years of effort to the orchestra, this occasion was full of interest. Their thoughts flew back to memories of Fritz Scheel and the early struggles; to the advent of Leopold Stokowski and the advance of the orchestra to its present position; to the changed attitude of the public. A procession of events seemed to march down the years; the inauguration of a Pension Fund; the Mahler Symphony and the Chorus; the Peoples' Concerts; the University of Pennsylvania Concerts; the effort for Popular and Sunday Concerts. Such recollections made the life of the Philadelphia Orchestra seem full and vigorous.

The twentieth season was especially fine musically. I marked the inauguration of the Special Monday Evening Concerts, three in number, which have gradually been increased to ten.

Other musical features of the year were Beethoven's Ninth Symphony; the playing in November, 1920, of "The Pilgrim Vision" by John Alden Carpenter, commemorating the 300th anniversary of the landing of the Mayflower: the three performances in March, 1921, of the Brahms Requiem and the presentation of Mahler's Second Symphony, both with the Chorus, trained by Mr. Stephen Townsend, of Boston.

It also marked the first appearance, as guest conductor, of the celebrated leader, Willem Mengelberg, of Amsterdam.

The year was one of great satisfaction to all lovers of the Philadelphia Orchestra. An organization founded on faith that it would succeed artistically; and on faith that Philadelphia would eventually cherish it to the extent of placing it on a permanent financial basis, had justified the hopes of the founders in both these particulars. The number of musicians had been augmented from eighty-five in 1900 to ninety-six in 1920, and the audience had so increased that hundreds of people were often turned away.

All persons therefore interested in the progress of music in the city and especially the ones whose efforts had helped to bring about this result rejoiced in the position now occupied by the orchestra.

In addition to delighting music lovers here and elsewhere, the Philadelphia Orchestra was carrying the name of Philadelphia gloriously around the world.

Chapter VI
Musical Neighbors

Occasionally philanthropic citizens express the wish that
the Philadelphia Orchestra was not conducted exclusively
for a few idle rich. Therefore, it is well to record some of
the things that the orchestra has done for the general public in this city.

The policy of the Association from the beginning has
been to make the orchestra the centre of Philadelphia's
musical life in an inclusive, not an exclusive sense. Hence it
has always been ready to reciprocate any assistance rendered to it by giving its services free of charge on numerous
occasions. Often, of course, financial conditions had to be
considered first. Among the societies that have co-operated
in choral performances, without recompense, and, no doubt,
at considerable expense to themselves, are: the Eurydice
Chorus, Fortnightly Club, Jungermaennerchor Singing
Society, Mendelssohn Club, Philadelphia Choral Society.
Outside of Philadelphia the Bach Choir of Baltimore,*
Schola Cantorum of New York, and Pittsburgh Chorus.

On its part the orchestra has given a number of special
performances without remuneration, such as the concert for
the Manuscript Music Society in 1913, the concert in
collaboration with the Mendelssohn Club in honor of Dr.
Wm. Wallace Gilchrist two years later; a performance at
Camp Dix and a concert for the benefit of the American Red
Cross, 1918; a French War Relief Benefit the next year; the
music at the presentation of the Philadelphia Award for
four years beginning in 1922, and the concert with the
Mendelssohn Club to celebrate its Fiftieth Anniversary in
January, 1925. Special concerts were given for the National
Federation of Music Clubs in 1911, and for the National
Convention of Music Supervisors in 1920.

It must be remembered that such concerts undertaken in
addition to the regular engagements for the season have
entailed special preparation and have been an added burden
to the busy conductor.

See Appendix G.

From the earliest days an effort was made to give music to the numbers of people who enjoy lighter programmes. Popular concerts at low prices were inaugurated by Mr. Scheel in 1903, at which time the name "Popular" was such a misnomer that they had to be given in the form of benefits on a fifty per cent basis of profit. Such concerts were given at intervals after this for some years, and consecutively from 1909–10 to 1914–15 inclusive. In May, 1916, an effort was made to institute "Pop" Concerts after the manner of the Boston Orchestra, at the close of the regular season. The Academy parquet was floored over and light refreshments were served at tables. The first season of eleven evenings went off brilliantly, under the alternate leadership of Mr. Stokowski, Dr. Rich and Mr. C. Stanley Mackey, and left a small surplus on hand. Prices ranged from fifteen to fifty cents. The second season the number was increased to eighteen, and for reasons not understood the Association was left with a deficit, which caused the venture to be abandoned.

An early enterprise of a philanthropic nature was the "People's Concerts" planned by the Executive Committee but placed in charge of the Civic Club, with a committee composed of Mrs. Edward I. Keffer, Chairman; Mrs. Spencer Ervin, Mrs. C. Howard Clark, Mrs. Frank Rosengarten and Mrs. Walter Horstmann.

The first programme would have pleased the most fastidious of tastes:

Labor Lyceum Hall
Second and Cambria Streets
Tuesday Evening, December 15th, at 8.15 o'clock
First of the Series of
THE PEOPLE'S CONCERTS
by the
PHILADELPHIA ORCHESTRA
FRITZ SCHEEL, Conductor
Under the Auspices of the Civic Club

PROGRAMME
1. FELIX MENDELSSOHN-BARTHOLDY.....Wedding March from
                              "Midsummer Night's Dream"
2. HECTOR BERLIOZ......................Le Carnaval Romain
3. JOSEPH GODEFROID......................Dance of the Sylphs
Solo for Harp, Alfred Kastner

[144]

4. JOHANN STRAUSS . . . . Blue Danube Waltz

5. JULES MASSENET . . . . Scenes Neapolitaines

6. GIOACHINO ANTONIO ROSSINI . . . . Overture "William Tell"

7. HENRI VIEUXTEMPS . . . . Fantaisie Appassionata
Solo for Violin and Orchestra, Hugo Olk

8. WEBER-BERLIOZ . . . . Invitation to the Dance

9. ALBERT FRANZ DOPPLER . . . . "Das Waldvoeglein"
Solo for Flute and Horn Quartette, August H. Rodemann

10. RICHARD WAGNER . . . . Overture "Tannhaeuser"
Admission 10 Cents

In the Annual Report of the Civic Club for 1904 this account is given:

"The first 'People's Concert' was held in Kensington at the Labor Lyceum Hall, Second and Cambria Streets, admission being 10 cents. It was largely through the co-operation of Mr. R. R. P. Bradford, of the Lighthouse Lyceum, his Committee and Miss Esther Kelly, that the concert proved to be such a great success. The hall was crowded and the people most enthusiastic; Mr. Scheel and his orchestra were greatly interested and gave a number of encores.

"The receipts were $236.62 up to January 1st; expenses, $103.02. We hope to have a balance of almost $100 when all returns are made. This balance to be considered a fund for the People's Concerts. The second concert will be given at Bethany Hall on January 11th, the third at Tuxedo Hall in March."

There was no doubt about the success of these concerts from the point of view of the enjoyment of the audiences. The hall was crowded almost to the danger point, and the enthusiasm was unrestrained. The Women's Committees were much interested and kept in touch with Mrs. R. R. Porter Bradford of the Lighthouse, Kensington, who knew the value of such music in a section where the shutting down of textile mills for a winter often made the price of a ticket unavailable. The Committees used their persuasive powers with the Board of Directors to continue these concerts at considerable expense, until a fight between two labor unions made it impossible to rent the hall, the only one in the neighborhood, and the concerts were no longer given. They were the means, however, of procuring a number of guarantors, who were interested in the orchestra from a philanthropic, instead of from a musical point of view.

From the first, special rates were offered to music students through the music schools of Philadelphia, for the attendance of the young was especially desired. Tickets were also distributed free, but the response was not encouraging.

Special prices were offered to boarding schools in and near Philadelphia, but they too were not eager to patronize symphony concerts.

In 1909, through the Women's Committee, about 43,000 circulars about the orchestra were sent out by the music schools and other schools with their prospectuses, a favor much appreciated.

Special Concerts were given for the students at Weightman Hall, University of Pennsylvania, from 1909-1922. These were conducted under the auspices of a committee composed of representatives of the student body, of the Faculty Tea Club (of which professors' wives were the members) and of the West Philadelphia Women's Committee for the Philadelphia Orchestra. Although the hall was unsuited to orchestral performances, and the stage inadequate in size, these concerts were very popular, and the orchestra was always treated in college style. Press of engagements combined with the unsatisfactory physical conditions there caused the abandonment of these.

Through the generosity of Mr. Cyrus H. K. Curtis two series of eight "Public Ledger Educational Concerts" were given for public school children in 1915-16 and 1916-17.

Public School Concerts have been given at the Academy of Music, with all tickets at fifty cents, during the last two seasons.

Also for many years the orchestra played for the benefit of the Stetson Hospital under a special business arrangement.

Free Sunday Concerts were inaugurated at the Metropolitan Opera House in 1915-16, with a series of three, and continued during the next season.

The Public School Concerts given in 1915-16 and led by Dr. Rich must not be forgotten. They took place at the Normal School, Wm. Penn High School, Philadelphia High School for Girls, Boys' Central High School, Germantown, West Philadelphia, Frankford and Southern High Schools.

The Young People's Educational Concerts should be mentioned. Such a series of five concerts was first given by Fritz Scheel in 1902-03, at the Broad Street Theatre, with lectures by Wm. J. Henderson, Wm. F. Apthorp, Louis C. Elson, Hugh A. Clarke and Henry E. Krehbiel. During 1903–04 and 1905–06 they were continued, and after a long intermission came to life again in the Children's Concerts, instituted in 1921. *A special committee was organized in which many associations were represented and the concerts were so successful that a second series is now given in order to meet the demand. There is no more inspiring sight than to watch the Academy filling up with eager-faced children or than to hear their quick response to Mr. Stokowski's remarks. The first series was devoted to an explanation of the instruments and the programmes are progressing educationally year by year. The principal difficulty so far encountered is to prevent grown-up children from attending.

Compositions on the Children's Concerts

"I want to tell you the lovely time I had at the concert. I want to thank you for sending the tickets. I adored the beautiful light in the Academy of Music. The conductor's name was Mr. Stokowski and he was a very nice man. I liked the part when the little boy only seven years old played the violin. He looked like Jackie Coogan. He watched the leader all the time he played. I wonder how long it took him to learn to play the violin so well.

"Mr. Stokowski is a very pleasant man. He conducted very well. He told a story of a little goat boy who played on Sand Pipes. He asked the people to sing Auld Lang Syne."

"I thought the concert was fine. I think the little boy played a good piece of music when he played his violin. I would like to play a drum, because my brother plays a drum, and I could easily learn. He used to play in a band called the "Ardmore Band." He was the best drummer they had. People could hear him far away."

"I enjoyed the concert so much. The orchestra was the largest I have ever seen. It seemed as if there were at least a hundred men on the stage. Mr. Stokowski looked very gay in his medium blue suit. I liked to watch his hands.

"He said anyone could learn to play in an orchestra if he wanted to, because it was up to the person himself."

This short account demonstrates that the Philadelphia Orchestra is a neighbor of much value to the community in which it dwells.

---

*See Appendix L.

CHAPTER VII

THE SUPPORT OF THE PUBLIC PRESS

Long before the project of a permanent orchestra for Philadelphia received any degree of public support, the newspapers of this city in a body used their influence in favor of such an institution. Some one has spoken of newspaper life as a "career for patriots," and surely the editors of the daily papers deserve this title, if any newspaper men do. No stone was left unturned to further the effort for a first-class modern orchestra in this city. Paid-for space announcing performances is one thing. Editorials by the column and general information, besides the work of the music critic for each paper are another. In the orchestra archives are scrapbooks filled with editorials of immense value to the cause. For the newspaper is a marvelous teacher of public taste and a molder of public opinion. What would the task have been for such a small number of people, first five, then eight, then twenty-four, to which were presently added twenty-one women, if such support had not been prompt and constant? The gallant list of newspapers, some of which no longer exist is, the *Evening Bulletin*, the *Evening Ledger*, the *Evening Telegraph*, the *Item*, *The Inquirer*, the *North American*, the *Press*, the *Public Ledger*, the *Record*, the *Times*. Not only was support given to the orchestra itself, but to the Women's Committees in every undertaking. For this publicity the Philadelphia Orchestra is in deep debt to the Philadelphia papers.

Of the music critics it can be said that they are human in their likes and dislikes, but have always been really interested and friendly.

One newspaper writer must be mentioned. Mrs. Cornelius Stevenson, as "Peggy Shippen" used her clever pen to further the cause and especially the work of the Women's Committees; and was an honorary vice-president from the beginning until her death. She was also one of the original guarantors. She was not a music critic, but in her youth she had possessed a fine contralto voice and she was a devoted music-lover.

So many articles and extracts have already been given that only one more will be added in order to prove that

Philadelphia newspapers and many others have been warm friends of the Philadelphia Orchestra.

Evening Telegraph, March 18th, 1901, Editorial:

"FOR A PERMANENT ORCHESTRA"

"A constituency of nearly 3,000,000 people within sight of William Penn's statue on the Public Buildings ought to be able to support all the institutions pertaining to a great modern metropolis. The newspapers, the hotels, the theatres, the great stores, the transportation facilities, and the institutions of learning and of science in Philadelphia will compare favorably with those of any other community of 2,000,000 in the world; while the Park attractions, and the galleries and exhibitions of works of art are, in some important respects, far above the standard referred to. One factor of the metropolitan order of civilization has, however, been lacking. Up to a very recent period, Philadelphia has not kept pace with the modern procession in the public recognition of the value of music as a factor of civic life. While several American cities of half the size and quarter of the wealth have each maintained a permanent orchestra of the first class, Philadelphia has not had such an organization of any class. True, the Germania Orchestra made a brave struggle for existence, aided by the Pennsylvania Academy of the Fine Arts, and, for a time, gave promise of building up a permanent orchestral structure on a solid basis, but this endeavor was made largely at the cost of the musicians. While the Germanians and others who have devoted time and money to the service of the community deserve and should be given credit and honor for their labors, it yet remains true that to establish a permanent orchestra worthy of the city, the first requirement is a solid financial foundation to build on.

"Such a foundation is the one thing we need to provide at this hour. We can today secure a permanent orchestra of the best type for our city by providing a permanent basis for its support. We are fortunate in having here at this time a musician who is at once a thorough artist and an efficient drill master—a rare combination of qualities that gave to the late Anton Seidl the highest place among orchestral leaders. It is not necessary to institute comparisons between Mr. Fritz Scheel and other conductors, but it is proper to say he has demonstrated the possession of these higher qualities that go to the making of a great leader. He has done wonders with the material at his command in this city, and that, too, under conditions unfavorable enough to discourage any less enthusiastic musician or less energetic worker. In view of what he has already accomplished in the comparatively short time he has been at work here, it is a safe and reasonable presumption that if given a guarantee of control for five years, with means enough available to warrant satisfactory contracts with competent musicians, Mr. Scheel would create for us a permanent orchestra second to none in this country. There is no question as to his ability to undertake this task; the only thing to be determined being whether we are wise enough and farseeing enough to strengthen his hands for its accomplishment."

Chapter VIII
The Listeners

The largest portion of this story has been devoted to the orchestra itself, and the people who founded it, supported it and endowed it. Now comes the turn of the party of the third part, the audience. An orchestra may be wonderfully trained, superbly led, comfortably supported, and yet miss the main point of existing. For without listeners, even in the days of radio, an orchestra is incomplete.

In 1900 it was difficult to lure listeners into a concert hall, where symphonic or severely classical music was to be played. Philadelphians began by listening to symphonies in bits and in the late nineties it was the custom for the Germania Orchestra to play one movement of a symphony each week for four weeks, and play the entire work in the fifth week. Theodore Thomas did not do this, but he could not get an audience in 1876 or even in 1881.

It is an inspiring sight of a Friday afternoon or Saturday evening to see the crowds bound for the Academy of Music. Equally inspiring, is it to see the audience standing on the steps of the Academy and on the street for two and three hours before admission can be had to the Amphitheatre for fifty cents. True lovers of music these.

One of the methods employed to persuade people to take season seats was the membership in the Auxiliary of the Women's Committees. Another was the lure of big soloists. Year by year, this musical organization was obliged to attract by advertising the appearances of great artists. But once the audience was procured, it stayed; and today soloists are on the verge of becoming unpopular. Such is the influence of symphonic music.

The right to interrupt the progress of a concert by demands for repeated encores was one which the audience gave up with little grace. In 1913 a paragraph appeared on the programme, stating that:

"The management has decided in no case to permit more than one encore."

And again:

"As encores tend to disturb the unity of an orchestral programme the patrons of the Philadelphia Orchestra Concerts are respectfully informed that encore demands cannot be granted."

The conductor had one or two bad experiences, which occupied some minutes, but finally patience won the day and the audiences realized that this pleasure, if it was a pleasure, was over forever at a symphony concert.

Next came the hat question. It is not a new one, for in 1841 the Musical Fund Society placed this notice in one of its programmes:

"Ladies are particularly requested not to wear their bonnets in the concert room."

This makes one realize that Philadelphia women were always devoted to their hats. The war on hats was a merry one and began as early as 1906, at a time when hats were large. It is rumored that the fashion at the moment required pinned on hair, so hats could not be removed. This matter was taken up in the Women's Committee, thought by some to be like the complaint desk of a department store; a situation of which they are proud, as it shows how the public turns to the women. Much discussion arose and notices began to appear in the programmes:

"For the greater convenience of all concerned, it is earnestly hoped that the women patrons of the Orchestra WILL REMOVE THEIR HATS during the performance. In many cities local ordinances compel, by legal means, the removal of head coverings that obstruct the view in places of amusement."

"Madame Homer as a Heroine

"Louise Homer, the popular contralto of the Metropolitan Opera Company, who was the soloist at the Symphony Society's concert in the New Theatre," writes a New York critic, "proved herself a heroine. SHE TOOK OFF HER HAT! To herself and to every woman in the house, probably, the big creation, or confection, or whatever it is called, which she wore as she came upon the stage was a triumph in the art of millinery. Mere men knew only that it hid her lovely face. If the audience hadn't been as well bred as it was musical, there would have been a demonstration when she pulled out the pins, removed the hat and placed it at the foot of the conductor's stand. Instead there was only an audible sigh of delight. Is it too much to hope that Mme. Homer's sister artists will hasten to follow her example, and that the hosts of her sex who attend concerts and recitals may be moved to accede to the request of the managers: 'Ladies will please remove their hats'?"

The "hat question" would not down, but in Philadelphia the situation was nothing to what it was in Boston, for the management was obliged to put the following alarming announcement in the Programme Book:

"His Honor, the Mayor, has notified the Management of Symphony Hall that, unless the law relating to the wearing of hats by ladies at public entertainments is obeyed at the Symphony rehearsals and concerts, he may be forced to revoke the license of Symphony Hall!"

"THE HAT AT THE CONCERTS
"An Earnest Request of Our Women Patrons

"A number of complaints have reached the Orchestra Association regarding the practice of women wearing their hats at the Orchestra Concerts, particularly at the Friday afternoon concerts, despite the notice printed each week in this program asking that for the comfort of others the hats shall be removed. This complaint has become so general that it now bids fair to result in a city ordinance, the same as in Boston and in Chicago, enforcing the removal of hats at all occasions of public amusements. This legal enforcement of what should be a matter of polite request ought not to be made necessary and the Orchestra Association earnestly asks of all its woman patrons that they will not permit this very simple matter to reach this acute stage. The Association would exceedingly regret to be compelled to carry out such an ordinance and it is within the power of each of our woman patrons to keep what after all is a matter of simple thoughtfulness within the bounds of politeness and consideration for others."

Hats today are small, but all the listeners are not yet converted.

The next most disturbing element was, and is, the restlessness of the audience.

There is a mistaken idea that coming late and leaving early is peculiar to the modern era, and this day of haste. Far back in 1882 we know that people left concerts early from this notice in a programme of that year:

"NOTICE

"The patrons of the Germania Orchestra Concerts are respectfully requested to be in their seats, on the evenings of the concerts, by eight o'clock punctually.

"Those persons who are unable to comply with this request, will kindly wait in the lobby until the close of the First Movement of the Symphony, when a pause will be made to enable them to reach their seats."

Coming late is the habit of the American world at least, even when taking trains. Being locked out does not remedy this habit, it only evokes a few growls.

Again the management took up the subject through the programme:

"NOTES OF INTEREST

"The hat question is not the only question that arises from time to time to prevent that serene enjoyment of concerts, which is the ideal estate of things hoped for by Management and concert-goers. Perhaps in the Elysian fields, choirs armed with angelic harps, are listened to without distractions furnished by late-comers and early-goers, or by people whose views on the numbers interpreted are as obstreperous as their hats, or the numberless physical annoyances that make for confusion and noise, that seem to be inevitable in concert auditoriums the country over. And this is apropos of the fact that a subscriber has written in to say that 'The general confusion during the last number of the concerts on Friday afternoons is most annoying,' and she continues, 'I am wondering whether a request cannot be put in the programme to stop this nuisance, as has been done with regard to the wearing of hats. This is what one meets with; almost as soon as the last number begins, hats and coats are put on, veils are arranged, and during the playing of the finale people keep leaving, causing a general feeling of unquiet and unrestfulness. This seems to me very discourteous, and is most annoying to those who really want to enjoy the concert from start to finish. I know that sometimes it is necessary for a subscriber to leave early, but may I suggest that the persons who have to leave before the last number, vacate their seats before the Orchestra starts to play.'

"All this seems reasonable enough, but it is a matter entirely in the hands of the concert-goers, who form their own 'court of honor' in these particulars."

However, Philadelphia audiences have improved in concert manners since the olden time. Then the audiences, although considered ill-behaved, were much like European ones; they did throw things at the singers and did not hesitate to express their opinions of the performance. But the city has advanced, as can be seen by the following notice:

"Pistole Reward—To whoever can discover the person who was so very rude as to throw Eggs from the Gallery upon the Stage, last Monday, by which the Cloathes of some Ladies and Gentlemen were spoiled and the performance in some measure interrupted!"*

Now we do not throw things, the performance is only "in some measure interrupted" when we cough and sneeze during concerts and operas and occasionally come in late. Frequent interruptions of a performance by the screams and calls of displeased listeners, to say nothing of constant conversation were the order of the early days of public music.

---

*Sonneck: "Early Concert Life."

Not worse here than elsewhere, but annoying just the same. Now a whisper is hardly ever audible at concerts, and a hiss is called forth only by a modern composition too terrible to allow to pass unnoticed. A hiss every now and again is not an unhealthy sign. It shows that someone is listening; and there are a few coughs but always behind the conductor's back.

Early in the life of the orchestra the public began to write letters of complaint to the management and to the newspapers. The management feels that this is a sign of healthy interest and welcomes these comments. It shows how strong the sense of possession of the orchestra is with its patrons.

Encores have vanished like the missiles of the past. Hats and restlessness are going out of fashion. The audiences of the Philadelphia Orchestra are wonderful groups of people, some of whom have held seats continuously since 1900. Their regular attendance has encouraged the Board of Directors and inspired the conductor and the musicians to artistic achievements. The party of the third part is doing its share toward making the concerts a success.

Chapter IX
The Twenty-fifth Anniversary

Anniversaries are times for reminiscences and a general survey of affairs.

The Corporation known as "The Philadelphia Orchestra Association" to-day consists of four parts:

First, the Association:* comprising the subscribers to the Endowment Funds of $25.00 or more, and the yearly subscribers to tickets for the regular series of concerts; and a Board of Directors elected by them (one-third annually), who in turn elect the officers;

Second, the Philadelphia Orchestra;

Third, the four Women's Committees;

Fourth, the Business Management.

It is hardly necessary to mention the interdependence of this quartette of activities, or to explain how many people have worked to procure an orchestra for Philadelphia.

In 1900–1901 the Philadelphia Orchestra, composed of 85 musicians gave six evening concerts. In 1925–26 this orchestra, composed of 106 musicians, will give performances as per the following schedule:

†Academy of Music, Philadelphia

Regular Series, 29 Friday afternoons, 29 Saturday evenings.	58
Special Series, Monday evenings.	10
Children's Concerts, 2 series.	8
Philadelphia Forum.	3
Philadelphia Award.	1
Out-of-town Concerts:	
New York City.	10
Washington.	5
Baltimore.	3
Pittsburgh, Dayton, Chicago, Cleveland, Toledo, Detroit, Princeton, one each.	7
Total.	105

Record of Performances

Total number of concerts, twenty-five years	2017
Number postponed.	6
Number cancelled (Ottawa, 1924).	1

*By-laws, 1920.
†For full list of performances, see Appendix E.

A more perfect fulfillment of obligations would be hard to find.

The regular series of symphony concerts in Philadelphia has been the primary object and main concern of the Association. Other performances have been included when the Philadelphia demand did not consume all the time of the orchestra. Now a third series is being built up, consisting of ten Monday evening concerts, at which the programmes are identical with those of ten of the regular series. More and more this city is absorbing its own orchestra.

During these twenty-five years much traveling has been done. The first journey was to Reading in 1900. The next year concerts in five Pennsylvania cities were added as well as in Trenton and Wilmington. In 1902-03 the first concerts in Baltimore and Washington were attempted and the first New York appearance was made. Growing bolder with advancing years appearances were made in new cities each year, of which the following are the most important: Boston (1903-04); Baltimore and Washington, five each (1906-07); Pittsburgh, one (1911-12), five pairs (1916-17), New York City, five afternoon concerts (1918-19); Toronto, three concerts (1919-20); New York City, ten concerts (1922-23).

The orchestra has traveled as far east as Portland, Maine; as far west as Detroit and Ypsilanti, Michigan; as far south as Richmond, Virginia, and as far north as Toronto, Canada. During the coming season Chicago will be added to this list.

Traveling has been tinged with adventure. In 1908, when returning from Wilmington, the special train carrying the orchestra was wrecked near Chester. Mr. Pohlig and six musicians were injured, when the cars were derailed and rolled down a steep embankment. Fortunately, there were no serious injuries and all the instruments were unhurt.

Ten years later the orchestra reached Kalamazoo, Mich. with difficulty during a severe blizzard, en route for Grand Rapids, where a concert was to be played. The thermometer fell to 27° below zero in a sixty mile gale. The concert was postponed but later given.

The last experience of winter weather was in Canada in 1924, when the Ottawa concert was cancelled after the audience had waited in perfect good humor for three hours hoping that the train carrying the orchestra could push through the snow.

In the past special trains were almost invariably used. Since railroad transportation has more than doubled, and since the charge for a special train has also been raised, the management wherever possible has availed itself of regular trains, generally running as a second section. Since the party now constitutes upwards of one hundred and twelve people, five twelve-section drawing room cars and one baggage car make up the equipment for night trips. Going to New York, two coaches are attached to an early afternoon train, and a special train home is provided after the performance.

❦ ❦

The labors of the officers and directors have been continuous. The Executive Committee, chosen from the Board in the early days; a sub-committee composed of Dr. Keffer and Mr. McCollin; the Committee of Three, consisting of Mr. Norris, Mr. Wheeler, and the late Mr. Charles A. Braun, who with the president, met daily from 1908 until 1920, shouldered most of the responsibility. Under the new By-Laws the Administration Committee composed of Messrs. Edward W. Bok, James Crosby Brown, Samuel S. Fels, Charles D. Hart, Effingham B. Morris, William Jay Turner, Alexander Van Rensselaer, and Andrew Wheeler, perform the arduous task of meeting every week regularly to dispose of the business of the Association.

In the early days Mr. Henry Whelen, Jr., made it possible to carry on the orchestra under financial difficulties, from 1900 until his death, which, coming so soon after the loss of Fritz Scheel, was a double blow. On May 22nd, 1907, this resolution was passed by the Board of Directors:

"The death of Mr. Henry Whelen, Jr., has deprived this Board of a most capable and efficient officer, and its members, of an esteemed and highly valued friend. To an artistic temperament, he added rare qualities of judgment and discretion inherent in a disciplined mind, and coupled with a sense of duty and habit of industry that continually and cheerfully placed his valuable services at the disposal of the community. The positions of member of the Board of Directors, of the Executive Committee, and of Treasurer of this Association, are but a few of the positions in which he stood in an unselfish relation to his native city, in an effort to discharge what he conceived to be his duty in the development of Music and Art in the community in which he lived.

[157]

"It is also with an acute sense of personal loss that this minute i ordered in the sincere hope that it may beguile those nearest an dearest to him from something of the grief of so great a bereavemen and also serve to perpetuate his memory in a community that ha profited so much from his useful and unselfish citizenship."

* * * * *

Mr. Thomas McKean, for many years Vice-president, wa one of the officers who was always ready to assist in ; financial crisis. Mr. Richard Y. Cook and Mr. Theodore N Ely were especially devoted members of the Board, but al the membership should be included in this category.

The social end, besides many others, has been taken car of by Mr. Van Rensselaer, who has constantly given enter tainments.

❦ ❦

Of the many friends outside of the officers and directors Mr. Philip H. Goepp has worked as hard as any man. From 1901–1902 until 1920–1921 inclusive he was annotator o the programme and well fitted for the task, as he is a musi cian, composer, and author of the series on "Symphonie and their Meaning," authoritative works on this subject He gave his time and his knowledge to the Association, a first without remuneration, so great was his enthusiasn over the continued development of the orchestra. Man days and nights through the years were devoted to the stud of the works performed, and the Association is greatly i his debt.

❦ ❦

During the period of his leadership Mr. Stokowski ha had various honors bestowed upon him. After the secon performance of the Mahler Symphony he was presente with a bronze wreath; on the completion of ten years a conductor in 1922, by the Women's Committees with ; set of twelve silver plates, and with a silver tankard by th Association; the University of Pennsylvania conferred or him the Honorary degree of Doctor of Music in 1920; an in 1922 he was the first recipient of the Philadelphia Awar of Ten Thousand Dollars. His appearances in Europe i: January 1923, when as guest conductor he led orchestras i: France and Italy were greeted with enthusiasm and wit press notices of a laudatory nature.

Although it is a rented building, the Academy of Music is the only dwelling place the orchestra has known, and the auditorium with its architectural beauty and perfect acoustics is a marvelous place for orchestral concerts. Having been built in 1857, its traditions link the past with the present and cast a spell over the music.

The present stage setting, which replaces the gift of the West Philadelphia Women's Committee, is from the design of Mr. Huger Elliott, and was executed as a labor of love by the students of the Pennsylvania Museum and School of Industrial Art for the Association.

❦ ❦

A possession of the Association is the orchestral library that has gradually been accumulated. Beginning with the purchase, for $600.00, of the library of the Philadelphia Symphony Society and augmented in 1911 by Fritz Scheel's collection, and by the constant addition of new works, it is now suited to the needs of the orchestra and valued as a great asset. It contains twelve hundred works with scores, and orchestral parts for one hundred and ten men, besides four hundred and thirty scores without orchestral parts.

❦ ❦

Advantage is often taken of modern musical inventions. For some years much care has been given to the making of Victor Records, which are popular the country over. There is now a list of forty-six, all exceptionally good, and they have brought the orchestra many friends. Radio transmitters are not used at performances. The Board of Directors feels that it is unfair to patrons of the orchestra, who pay for tickets and take the trouble to attend the concerts in person, to broadcast the music throughout the country.

Mr. Stokowski recently secured the rights for the first presentation of the new Hammond Pedal, invented by John Hays Hammond, Jr. The first public performance on the piano with this attachment was at the Philadelphia regular series of concerts, on October 30th and 31st, 1925, when Lester Donahue played the Rachmaninoff Second Concerto. The invention will also be used in Washington, New York City and on the Western tour.

In looking back over the years, details come to mind
Much anxiety used to be felt about Saturday nights, as bad
weather meant a poor audience and knocked the box office
receipts. Now, the audience is anxious for fear of uncom-
fortable delays on the steps during a storm, on account o.
the crowd.

Another detail was the efforts that the women made long
ago to brighten up the appearance of the Saturday evening
house, by asking their friends in the boxes to wear gay
clothes.

The policy of the Philadelphia Orchestra Association has
always been to sell tickets at moderate prices. Tickets for the
best seats for the first regular series of six concerts sold for
$8.00. Students could buy tickets for the amphitheatre for
$1.75 for fourteen rehearsals and $2.00 for fourteen concerts.
The price of tickets has increased seventy per cent and operating expenses have increased five hundred per cent in twenty-
five years, but considering this, the tickets are still moderate. A story is told by Mr. George T. Haley, of the Academy of Music Ticket Office, loyal friend to the orchestra,
of how as a young assistant agent he was in charge of the
window on the first day of the first sale for the Philadelphia Orchestra. He opened promptly at 8.30 a. m.; the first
sale was about ten and the next about four in the afternoon.
Now, his principal business in connection with the orchestra is to placate the people who cannot get the seats they
want or get any seats at all.

The Business Management of the Association has been
since 1915 in the hands of Mr. Arthur Judson, whose ability
and that of the Assistant Manager, Mr. Louis A. Mattson,
is well known. Mr. Judson manages, likewise, the Philharmonic Orchestra of New York and the Cincinnati
Orchestra. Mr. Mattson manages the summer concerts in
Fairmount Park, for which a number of Philadelphia
Orchestra men are engaged. The ease with which a large
amount of business is conducted, and one in which there is
much detail, is due to the organizing talents of Mr. Judson
and to the devotion and long training of the office staff

nder him. The Association is fortunate in having a mana-
er of such rare business acumen, whose talents have devel-
ped as necessity arose; until it is safe to say that there is no
iore ably managed musical organization in the country
han this. To Mr. Mattson falls the task of distributing the
eats, no easy one in 1925, when there are almost none to
ispose of. No mention of the business end of this enterprise
vould be complete without the names of Miss Ruth O'Neill,
Miss Elizabeth M. Russell and Miss Margaret E. Pringle,
ot to forget Mr. Stokowski's private secretary, Miss
McGinty, who eases the thorny business path of an artist.

❧ ❧

Speaking of business, the Endowment Funds of the Asso-
iation were at first in the hands of three trustees but now
re in the care of a Corporate Trustee, the Girard Trust
Company.

But enough of details! Many forces have combined to
nake it possible to maintain an orchestra.

Some years ago Peggy Shippen wrote:

"This remarkable performance (Mahler Symphony), which attracted
music connoisseurs from many cities, and which will remain a lasting
credit to our town, was the result of a combination of forces patiently
brought together by the will, power and genius of one man—Leopold
Stokowski.   * * * * *

"Such triumphs of art scored in this city do more than all the
advertising in the world to place Philadelphia in the lead of the great
American centers. The Mayor has spoken of advertising this city;
these things do this legitimately by adding to its opportunities. The
sooner we realize that it is by honest work and the real thing well
done that we can impose respect for our city and State, the better.

* * * * *

"It is in the last decade or so that those interested have realized
the necessity for 'coming together.' This policy seems to have been
adopted since Alexander Van Rensselaer accepted the presidency of
the Board of Directors. No one could be selected in this entire city
better calculated to bring together the elements indispensable to the
success of such an undertaking. Himself a musician, all his life
identified with musical interests, he is one of the most widely popular
men in this community. * * * * *

"As the audiences grew and became critical, exacting a higher
quality of music, Mr. Van Rensselaer and his board rose to the occasion and met the requirements of growth.

[161]

"The Women's Committee, besides developing the interest in the success of the orchestra, has helped with the Guarantee Fund, which, of course, is the pivot upon which turns the success of the undertaking. Without the backing of money, to pay for the best procurable talent, even the greatest genius is helpless to produce adequately a great work of art.

"It was the combination of Mr. Van Rensselaer's patient and broad policy, of the women's inconspicuous but telling work of years upon the musical intelligence of the community, first under Mrs. A. J. Dallas Dixon's direction and then under that of Miss Frances Wister, that provided the fertile ground upon which the genius of Mr. Stokowski brought out the almost superhuman result of last week.

"The same success will attend similar methods in other fields. The theory of 'splendid isolation' does not apply to our epoch."

❦ ❦

The Philippine Concerts which occurred on March 29th and April 5th, 1900; and which were the forerunners of the Philadelphia Orchestra, were commemorated at the concerts of March 27th and 29th and April 3rd and 4th, 1925, by a notice in the programme and by the playing of certain numbers played at those concerts. They marked the first appearance of Fritz Scheel with an orchestra of professional musicians in Philadelphia.

The Twenty-fifth Anniversary of the first concert on November 16th, 1900, is being celebrated at the concerts of November 13th and 14th, 1925, by simple ceremonies and a repetition of the first programme. It is a long way from the total of seven concerts in 1900, to the one hundred and five concerts arranged for this season. The road has been discouraging and difficult, but the twenty-fifth anniversary is a cause for rejoicing to all lovers of the Philadelphia Orchestra.

Little did the small group of men in 1900 dream that the orchestra they founded would twenty-five years later be known throughout America and Europe.

The "Road One Hundred and Fifty Years Long" has been worth traveling to Philadelphians, to reach the present milestone in the symphonic succession, so far the most important achievement in the city's musical history. If Baedeker were to write a "Guide to Music in America" he would put three stars against the Philadelphia Orchestra.

Chapter X

The Point of the Story

"Time Was unlocks the riddle of Time Is.
That offers choice of glory or of gloom:
The solver makes Time Shall Be surely his."

The point of the story is the music that the Philadelphia Orchestra makes. It would be a tragedy if after twenty-five years anyone could ask "Why?" A tragedy for the officers and directors, for the Women's Committees, and for the reader and writer of this book. For the musicians and for Leopold Stokowski it would be more than a tragedy, the object of life would cease to exist.

Beginning in 1912 the musical record becomes more and more interesting. The leader has poured out his talents for Philadelphia and the feast has been lavish. Programme after programme of the works of the great, interpreted by the brain of Leopold Stokowski have enthralled his audiences. Only a few special selections and occasions can be mentioned, but a perusal of the programmes for thirteen years shows that the average of Philadelphia Orchestra concerts is far above the usual average, for he is a master maker of programmes.

1912–13: Gustav Strube, "Puck"; Herman Sandby, Prelude to Act IV "The Vikings of Helgenland"; Edward Elgar, Symphony No. 1; Guiseppe Martucci, Symphony No. 1; Sigismund Noszkowski, "Die Steppen"; Richard Strauss, "Liesbes Scene" from "Feursnot," "Salome's Tanz"; Henri Rabaud, Symphony No. 2**; Ernest Schelling, "Légende Symphonic."**

1913–14: Hans Erich Pfitzner, "Käthchen von Heilbronn," overture; Fernandez Arbos, "Guajiras,"** violin and orchestra; Florent Schmitt, "Rapsodie Viennoise"**; Albert Roussel, Evocation No. 2 "La Ville Rose"**; Henry Hadley, Symphony, "North, East, South and West"; Erich Korngold, "Schauspiel" Overture; Otto Mueller, member

**First performance in America.

Philadelphia Orchestra, "Dramatic Overture"; Henry A Lang*, Symphony "Fantasies of a Poet"; Beethoven, Ninth Symphony with Chorus.

1914-15: Jan Sibelius, "Finlandia"; Bach, triple concerto piano, violin and flute; Paderewski, Symphony B minor** Special Concerts for the Benefit of the Pension Fund; Mendelssohn, "Lobgesang Symphony" with soloists and sixteen Choral Societies; Wagner Programme. Frederick Stock Symphony C minor; Feruccio Busoni, Indian Fantasy, piano and orchestra**; Sandby, Suite from "The Woman and the Fiddler"; Mrs. H. H. A. Beach, Symphony "Gaelic" Georges Enesco, "Roumanian Rhapsody."

1915-16: Gustav Strube, "Variations on an Original Theme; Camille Zeckwer*, Symphonic Poem, "Sohrab and Rustum" (conducted by composer); Enrique Granados Intermezzo and Epilogue from Goyescas; Gustav Mahler, Eighth Symphony for orchestra soli and chorus;** Strauss "Alpensymphonie."**

1916-17: Frederick A. Stock: Violin Concerto, D minor. Arne Oldberg "June" (conducted by composer); Gustav Mahler, "Das Lied von der Erde,"** symphony for soli voices and orchestra; Max Bruch, Concerto for two pianos written for Rose and Ottilie Sutro (first world performance); Michel Dvorsky, "Chromaticon" piano and orchestra, Josef Hofmann, pianist; Debussy, "The Blessed Damosel" after Rosetti for soprano and Chorus of Women; Schelling, "Impressions," variations for piano and orchestra, composer at the piano; Liszt; Eine Faust Symphonie, orchestra, tenor and bass soli and chorus; Bach, Matthäus Passion, orchestra, soli, Philadelphia Orchestra Chorus, Chorus of Girls from Philadelphia Normal School and Girls' High School.

1917-18: American Programme, Edgar Stillman Kelley Symphony "New England," compositions by Philip H. Goepp, Arthur Foote; Skryabin, "Poème de l'Extase"; Beethoven, Three Equali for four Trombones; Bach, Concerto, three pianos and orchestra, Mme. Olga Samaroff, Bauer, Gabrilowitsch; Sinding, Symphony; Ernest Chausson, "Poème" violin and orchestra, Thaddeus Rich, violin-

*Philadelphian.
**First performance in America.

st; Bloch Programme, concert conducted by composer; Selim Palmgren concerto "The River," piano and orchestra.

1918–19: MacDowell "Indian Suite" dirge in memory of fallen Americans; Dvorsky, "The Haunted Castle"; Debussy "Sirènes," orchestra and women's voices; Lorenziti, Suite for Viole d'Amour, Henri Casadesus, soloist; Rachmaninoff, Air for a Choir of Solo Violins with orchestra; Programme of four American composers, Frederic S. Converse, H. Clough-Leiter, John Alden Carpenter, Cecil Forsyth; Leo Ornstein, piano soli, composer at the piano; Chadwick, "Tam o'Shanter"; Ernest Bloch, Symphony No. 1; Louis Garnier, "Vision" Poème for Orchestra.

1919–20: Beethoven, Choral Fantasy in C minor, piano, orchestra and chorus, Mme. Samaroff, pianist; Malipiero, "Pause del Silenzio"; Loeffler "A Pagan Poem" for Orchestra, with piano, English horn and three trumpets obligato, Bauer pianist; Charles T. Griffes, four compositions for orchestra; Rachmaninoff, Concerto No. 3, piano and orchestra, composer at the piano; Symphony "The Bells"** (after Poe), orchestra solo voices and Philadelphia Orchestra Chorus; Lorenziti, Concerto for Viole d'Amour, double bass and orchestra, Thaddeus Rich and Anton Torello, soloists; Weber, Concertino in F for bassoon and orchestra, Richard Krueger, soloist; André Maquarre, two compositions for orchestra; Mozart Opus 30, arranged as a Concerto for oboe and small orchestra, Marcel Tabuteau, soloist; Beethoven, Ninth Symphony, Philadelphia Orchestra Chorus, marking Ninety-sixth Anniversary of first performance, 1824.

1920–21: Leo Sowerby "Comes Autumn Time"; J. Guy Ropartz, Symphony No. 4; Cyril Scott, concerto piano and orchestra, composer at the piano; John Alden Carpenter "A Pilgrim Vision" to mark Tercentenary of Landing of the Mayflower; Beethoven, Ninth Symphony with Philadelphia Orchestra Chorus; Brahms; double concerto violin and cello, Rich and Penha, soloists; Brahms, "Requiem," soprano and baritone soli, chorus and orchestra; Gilchrist*, Symphonic Poem, unveiling of Gilchrist memorial; Mahler, Symphony No. 2, for orchestra, chorus and solo soprano and contralto.

*Philadelphian.
**First performance in America.

1921–22: Sibelius, Symphony No. 5**; Alfredo Casello "Pages of War" for orchestra; Gregor Fitelberg, Polish Rhapsody**; Bloch, Suite for viola and orchestra; Schoenberg, Five Orchestra Pieces; Vincent d' Indy "Poème de Rivages," d'Indy, guest conductor (first performed on present tour); Bach Passacaglia, orchestrated by Leopold Stokowski (first time); Strawinsky "Sacre du Printemps"**; Manuel de Falla, excerpts from "El Amor Brujo"**; Otto Mueller, Carnival Overture "Schlaraffiada."

1922–23: Debussy "La Cour des Lys"; Ravel, "La Valse Choreographic," Poem for Orchestra; Strawinsky, "Feuerwerk"; Franck Centenary, Symphony D minor. The orchestra was engaged by Dr. Richard Strauss for four New York concerts of his own works exclusively. Dr. Strauss also conducted one in Philadelphia.

1922–1923: Camille Zeckwer, "Jade Butterflies"; Strawinsky, "Trois Poésies de la Lyrique Japonaise"; Enesco Symphony E flat, Roumanian Rhapsody, Enesco, guest conductor; Brahms, concerto for violin, Enesco, violinist January 26th and 27th, 1923, compositions by Milhaud, Poulenc, Auric, Satie; Schelling, "A Victory Ball"; Pick-Mangiagali, "Sortilegi," Symphonic Poem, piano and orchestra; D. G. Mason, Prelude and Fugue, piano and orchestra; Henry Eichheim, Oriental Impressions for Orchestra Schoenberg, "Kammersymphonie".

1923–24: Strawinsky, "Chant du Rossignol"**; Bach concerto for harpsichord; Händel, concerto for harpsichord, Wanda Landowska, soloist; Strawinsky, "Symphonie d'Instruments à Vent"**; Josef Hofmann, compositions for piano and orchestra, East and West, Caliedescope, the Haunted Castle, "Chromaticon" (Dvorsky); Ottorino Respighi, "Sinfonia Drammatica"; Deems Taylor, Suite "Through the Looking Glass"; compositions by Magnard, Jean-Jules-Amable Roger-Ducasse; Hand Krása; Strawinsky, "Renard," burlesque for Chamber Orchestra, two tenors, two basses; Beethoven, Ninth Symphony with Toronto Choir.

1924–25: Nicholas Medtner, piano concerto, composer at piano; Edgar Varese, "Hyperprisms"; Paul Hindemuth, Nusch-Nuschi Dances; Karl Szymsanowski, violin con-

---

**First performance in America.

certo**; Kurt Atterberg, Symphony No. 2; Henry Joslyn, War Dance from Suite, "Native Moments"; Strawinsky programme, Strawinsky guest conductor; Prokokieff, Suite Scythe, "Ala and Lolli"; Arthur Bliss, "Mêlée Fantasque"; Germaine Taillefer, Concerto** for piano and orchestra; Isaac Albeniz, "Fête Dieu à Séville"; Edward Burlingame Hill, Arthur Bliss, compositions for two pianos and orchestra.

It must not be supposed from the above that the usual standard works are not performed. The list is given to show the wide musical range to which Philadelphians are treated. No mention has been made of the many Wagner and Tschaikowsky programmes that have been presented. They have occurred every year and are always a delight.

It is a pleasure to mention the principal players in the orchestra, who are not generally known personally by the audience. It is a case of "by their voices you shall know them," and their voices enthrall the listeners week by week. First comes Dr. Thaddeus Rich, most popular of concertmasters and an assistant conductor of no mean attainments, who is sometimes called to take the conductor's place at the last minute, where he acquits himself with honors. As we look farther there are: David Dubinsky, first second violin; Samuel Lifschey, first viola; Hanns Pick, violoncello; W. M. Kincaid, flute; Marcel Tabuteau, oboe; Daniel Bonade, clarinet; Anton Horner, horn; Walter Guetter, bassoon; Sol. Cohen, trumpet; Gardell Simons, Paul P. Lotz, C. E. Gerhard, trombones; Philip A. Donatelli, tuba; Anton Torello, bass; Vincent Fanelli, Jr., harp; and last but not least, Oscar Schwar, tympani. These players all possess the requisites, which seem to be ability to play and ability to obey, for the response of their wills to the will of the leader is what makes success in an orchestra. One noticeable feature about the musicians is their youth; this is patent to the eye, and to the ear, from the virility of their performance.

To those who do not see farther than the Academy stage, it would be useless to explain that the conductor's activities are not confined to stepping briskly onto the platform and leading concerts. People who have given the matter thought must know that he is working all the year round

**First performance in America.

[167]

for the Philadelphia Orchestra. The rehearsals are very exacting and the players are wonderfully prepared. Conducting a concert means a physical, mental and emotional strain which is only understood by those who have seen the conductor as he comes off the stage. Leading without a score requires perfect concentration. Painstaking effort and patience on the part of Mr. Stokowski bring their reward in the finish of the performance, but it looks so easy! And therein is shown his skill. Next there is the constant search for new works and the mastering of them before rehearsals can begin. Much time is occupied in hearing and selecting players, for no stone is left unturned to find the best artists for each position. The mail is also a subject of importance, as correspondence is kept up with individuals and publishers and then there are letters of complaint or approval, all to be answered. The conductor is a busy man, whose brain never stops working, planning, devising for the orchestra.

Leopold Stokowski's musical gifts are of a nature difficult to describe. What thrills come to one at the remembrance of certain moments, the first hearing of the Bach "Passacaglia," the "Prelude and Liebestod" from Tristan, the symphonies of Brahms, Schubert and Tschaikowsky, Mahler's Eighth, where the chorus "Alles Vergängliches ist nur ein Gleichniss" soars aloft, Beethoven's Seventh, and the Ninth with the Mendelssohn Choir of Toronto. But why mention special moments? The audiences have come to expect every concert to be a "special moment."

Philadelphia is to be congratulated that the orchestra bearing its name is in the hands of Leopold Stokowski, master musician. It is constantly advancing. When one peak on the climb is reached, the clouds roll away and another comes into view. Let no man speak its doom by proclaiming that the summit of Parnassus has been reached by the Philadelphia Orchestra.

❦ ❦

The name of Alexander Van Rensselaer, Esq., appears on the first page of this book. It is fitting that it should also appear on the last, for the president's activities encircle the orchestra. Many records of his deeds appear in the annals of the Association, and many more are engraved in the hearts of his fellow-workers and fellow-townsmen. He is the only person, however, who knows what sacrifices his devotion has entailed. For although a president may appear to enjoy more sunshine than other individuals, he also bears the shock of all the storms. The responsibility of such a post for twenty-five unbroken years is a heavy burden for a man to bear. To say that he has borne it and continued to hold the respect and affection of Philadelphians is the finest tribute that could be paid him.

The story told in this book has been made possible by the president of the Philadelphia Orchestra Association.

In Memoriam

Theodore Thomas
Born October 11, 1835; Died January 4, 1905

"The death of the pioneer of American music, and a veritable Titan of Conductors, Theodore Thomas, brings consternation to the world of music, as this great man stood for all that is pure and noble in his art. An event so calamitous, and peculiarly significant here in Philadelphia, where he was well known and beloved, devolves upon me the sad duty of giving an orchestral expression of our deep grief. While it is true that an all-wise Providence saw fit to remove from the field of action one who had probably reached the apogee of his power and influence, yet keen regret must of necessity be experienced, an emotion best expressed through the medium that the great Thomas made his own—the orchestra. Therefore, I deem it wise to change the programme for the Seventh Concert, selecting such numbers as, in a sense, may be regarded as a mortuary mass. In agreement with this idea, which I am sure my supporters will endorse, I have made the following changes, substituting such numbers that, were the lips now stilled in death able to articulate, they would, I trust, unreservedly approve.

Fritz Scheel
Conductor of the Philadelphia Orchestra."

Philadelphia, January 6, 1905.

Programme

1. Richard Wagner
   Siegfried's Death from "Die Goetterdaemmerung"

2. Wolfgang Amadeus Mozart..............Symphony, G minor

   I. Allegro Molto 4/4   III. Menuetto: Allegro 3/4
   II. Andante 6/8   IV. Finale: Allegro Assai 4/4

3. Jules de Swert........Concerto for Violoncello and Orchestra, No. 2, in C minor, Op. 38

   Allegro moderato—Espressivo, 4/4
   Alfred Saal

4. Richard Strauss........Serenade, Opus 7, Andante, E flat major
   For 2 Flutes, 2 Oboes, 2 Clarinets, 4 Horns,
   2 Bassoons, and Contra Bassoon

5. Ludwig von Beethoven......Overture, "Leonore No. 3," Op. 72

PROGRAMME OF CEREMONIES

FRITZ SCHEEL MEMORIAL

Academy of Music

Wednesday, March Eleventh
Nineteen Hundred and Eight
at Three o'Clock

In Memoriam

FRITZ SCHEEL
BORN LÜBECK, 1852; DIED PHILADELPHIA, 1907

RICHARD WAGNER.............................Vorspiel "Parsifal"

Address
MR. OWEN WISTER

RICHARD STRAUSS.................Tone Poem "Tod und Verklärung"
_____

BEETHOVEN.................Funeral March from Eroica Symphony
DR. S. WEIR MITCHELL
January 9–10, 1914   _____

BEETHOVEN......Slow Movement from Symphony No. 7, in A major
THEODORE N. ELY
November 3–4, 1916   _____

BEETHOVEN......................Eroica Symphony Marcia Funebre
HAROLD ELLIS YARNALL
April 7–8, 1917   _____

MACDOWELL............................"Dirge" from Indian Suite
Tribute to the memory of our soldiers and sailors who
have fallen in the war
November 15–16, 1918   _____

BEETHOVEN......................Eroica Symphony Marche Funèbre
THEODORE ROOSEVELT
January 17–18, 1919   _____

"RESOLUTION PASSED AT MEETING OF BOARD OF DIRECTORS,
NOVEMBER 26th, 1919

"WHEREAS, the Directors of the Philadelphia Orchestra Association
note with deep sorrow the death of Major Henry Lee Higginson,

"And WHEREAS, they recognize that by his death the cause of good
music throughout the country has sustained an irreparable loss,

"And WHEREAS, they recognize their own deep debt of gratitude to
him for his pioneer work in the said cause of music,

[171]

"BE IT RESOLVED that they place on record their very real sense of this great loss and their feeling of sympathy in it not only with the members of his family, but with every officer and member of the Boston Symphony Orchestra Association.

"It is further ordered that the Secretary of the Philadelphia Orchestra Association transmit a copy of this resolution to Mrs. Higginson and to the officers and members of the Boston Symphony Association."

"The Dirge from MacDowell's 'Indian Suite'
will be played

IN MEMORY
of
The Founder of the Boston Symphony Orchestra

MAJOR HENRY LEE HIGGINSON
November 18, 1834—November 14, 1919"

November 28-29, 1919   _____

SCHUBERT........................Unfinished Symphony, Andante
GEORGE W. ELKINS

December 5-6, 1919   _____

WAGNER...........Funeral March from "The Twilight of the Gods"
MRS. ALEXANDER J. CASSATT

January 23-24, 1920

Resolution passed by the Women's Committee, January 20th, 1920.

MRS. ALEXANDER J. CASSATT

"Mrs. Cassatt was associated with the Women's Committee for the Philadelphia Orchestra, as an Honorary Vice-president, at the time of its organization in 1904; in 1909 she was elected to the Board of Managers, and in 1914 became a Vice-president, which position she held until her death on January 9th, 1920. She was Chairman of the Nominating Committee for many years and conducted its affairs with discretion and ability. She was also Chairman of a Committee, which during the winter of 1912 devoted much time and thought to the revision of the By-laws.

"Mrs. Cassatt gave her support to the cause of an orchestra for Philadelphia, however, before the Philadelphia Orchestra was organized as such, and before the Women's Committee had a reason for existing. In the spring of 1900, she organized a committee of women which carried through the two so-called Philippine Concerts and gave Fritz Scheel his first opportunity to appear in Philadelphia as a conductor of an orchestra composed of professional musicians; as a direct result the Philadelphia Orchestra was organized in the fall of that year.

"In spite of failing health and physical suffering, Mrs. Cassatt's interest in the welfare of this Committee and the orchestra never flagged; her wise counsel was freely given, and her gracious presence was always an inspiration. She gave to this Committee the benefit of her wide knowledge of people and affairs, and for this we have a deep sense of gratitude.

"Her last public appearance was at the Philadelphia Orchestra Endowment Fund Campaign Luncheon on November 6th, 1919, on which occasion she presented the gift of one thousand dollars to the Endowment Fund from the Women's Committee as a tribute to its President, Miss Frances A. Wister.

"The influence of her loyalty will remain a rich heritage for the Women's Committee for the Philadelphia Orchestra.

"THEREFORE, BE IT

"RESOLVED, That we, the members of the Women's Committee for the Philadelphia Orchestra, hereby express our affection and respect for Mrs. Cassatt, and our grief and sense of irreparable loss at her death.

"BE IT ALSO RESOLVED, That we record our appreciation of Mrs. Cassatt's interest in the affairs of this Committee, of her work for the Philadelphia Orchestra, and of her distinguished qualities of leadership. We are profoundly touched by the fact that Mrs. Cassatt's last public appearance was in our behalf, and are mindful of the privilege that has been ours in working with her for the cause of music in Philadelphia.

"BE IT ALSO RESOLVED, That this resolution together with the preamble be spread upon the minutes and that copies be sent to Mrs. Cassatt's family as an expression of our deep sympathy in their loss.

Committee on Resolutions

(Signed) FRANCES ANNE WISTER, *Chairman*
ADÈLE G. YARNALL
MRS. SIMON B. FLEISHER
SALLIE HOUSTON HENRY
January 20th, 1920.　　　　　ELIZABETH H. ARNETT"

WAGNER......................Goetterdaemmerung Funeral March
CHARLES A. BRAUN
October 27–28, 1922.　　　　　————————

BEETHOVEN....................Symphony No. 7, Slow Movement
EDWARD G. McCOLLIN
November 30, December 1, 1923.

————————

WAGNER..................Funeral March from Götterdämmerung
WOODROW WILSON
February 8–9, 1924.　　　　　————————

CHOPIN...Funeral March
MRS. ALEXANDER J. DALLAS DIXON
October 16–17, 1925.

[173]

Mrs. Alexander J. Dallas Dixon

"Died September 20, 1925

"Resolution Passed by the Philadelphia Orchestra Association

"The officers and members of the Administration Committee of The Philadelphia Orchestra Association have learned with deep sorrow of the death of Mrs. Alexander J. Dallas Dixon, who had been a member of the Board of Directors of the Orchestra Association since its very beginning, as well as first President of the Women's Committee for The Philadelphia Orchestra. Her charming personality, sweet disposition and wise judgment combined to make her endeared and respected by all her associates.

"In her death we have lost a true and devoted friend of music and a lady with whom it was a pleasure to be associated.'

"The Women's Committee for the Philadelphia Orchestra

"Mrs. Alexander J. Dallas Dixon

"Mrs. Alexander J. Dallas Dixon, the first President of this committee, who died on September 20, 1925, was for several reasons especially dear to our members.

"Captains of ships who take the helm for voyages over uncharted seas, or leaders of expeditions across unknown continents who bring such undertakings to successful ends, receive the honor of their comrades. How much more should we treasure the memory of a pioneer leader, whose enterprise was so skillfully planned that the work for a noble purpose has been able to continue during twenty-one years.

"Long before Mrs. Dixon entered upon the difficult position of President of this committee, however, she was a force in the musical life of the city. As an amateur pianist and singer, and as a member of the Eurydice Chorus and of the Melody Club, she was a well-known and important figure among the devotees of this enchanting art.

"Mrs. Dixon taught the committee many lessons, although some of us were unaware of this fact at the time, and probably she was herself. Behind a delightful simplicity of manner there lay courage, patience, ability, firmness of purpose in an unpopular cause and a shining soul. Therefore, personally and officially, Mrs. Dixon was the greatest ornament that the committee has possessed and the most beloved officer. It is especially distressing to us to lose her from our midst at a time when all friends of the Philadelphia Orchestra are rejoicing in the Twenty-fifth Anniversary of the first concert, which is to be celebrated in November. So devoted a member of the Board of Directors of The Philadelphia Orchestra Association will be much missed on that occasion.

"It may be well said, 'Her ways were ways of pleasantness and her paths were paths of peace,' for, led by her, the Women's Committee for The Philadelphia Orchestra has wended its steps along the same road. Our gratitude will endure while the committee continues to exist.

"A committee composed of the officers has been appointed to present a resolution for action at this special meeting of the Women's Committee for The Philadelphia Orchestra.

RESOLUTION
"MRS. ALEXANDER J. DALLAS DIXON
"First President of the Women's Committee for
The Philadelphia Orchestra—1904–1912

"Mrs. Alexander J. Dallas Dixon was the first President of the Women's Committee for The Philadelphia Orchestra, which was organized at her house on March 11, 1904. Until 1912 she continued as its presiding officer and during these years she held the esteem and affection of the members of the committee and administered its affairs with wisdom, justice and a broad vision.

"Therefore, be it Resolved:

"That we, the officers and members of the Women's Committee, desire to record our deep sense of loss in the death of a beloved former President and late Honorary Vice-President, and to express our appreciation of her fearless initiative, her unfailing good judgment, her gentle but firm character, her wise leadership.

"Be it also Resolved:

"That this resolution be spread upon the minutes and that a copy be sent to her husband.

COMMITTEE
"FRANCES ANNE WISTER, *President*
ADÈLE G. YARNALL, *Vice-president*
SALLIE HOUSTON HENRY, *Vice-president*
HELEN WARREN ALLEN, *Treasurer*
ELIZABETH H. ARNETT, *Corresponding Secretary*
MARGARET S. WOOD, *Recording Secretary*"

October 8, 1925.

APPENDIX

APPENDIX A.

CHARTER
OF
THE PHILADELPHIA ORCHESTRA ASSOCIATION
(Adopted November 1, 1902)

The subscribers hereto, all of whom are citizens of the Commonwealth of Pennsylvania, have associated themselves together for the purpose herein below set forth and being desirous of becoming incorporated agreeably to the provisions of the Act of the General Assembly of the Commonwealth of Pennsylvania, entitled, "An Act to provide for the incorporation and regulation of certain corporations," approved the twenty-ninth day of April in the year of our Lord one thousand eight hundred and seventy-four, and the supplements thereto, do hereby declare, set forth and certify that the following are the purposes, objects, articles and conditions of their said Association for and upon which they desire to be incorporated.

ARTICLE 1.—The name of the corporation shall be The Philadelphia Orchestra Association.

ARTICLE 2.—Its object is to encourage the performance of first-class orchestral music in the City of Philadelphia and for that purpose to establish and maintain The Philadelphia Orchestra.

ARTICLE 3.—The place in which the business of the said corporation is to be transacted is the City of Philadelphia.

ARTICLE 4.—The said corporation is to exist perpetually.

ARTICLE 5.—The said corporation shall have no capital stock.

ARTICLE 6.—The number of Directors of the said corporation shall be twenty-four, and the names and residences of those who are chosen for the first year are as follows:

Name	Residence
GEORGE BURNHAM, JR.	Philadelphia, Pa.
A. J. CASSATT	Philadelphia, Pa.
JOHN H. CONVERSE	Philadelphia, Pa.
ECKLEY B. COXE, JR.	Philadelphia, Pa.
WILLIAM L. ELKINS	Elkins, Pa.
MISS MARY K. GIBSON	Philadelphia, Pa.
CLEMENT A. GRISCOM	Philadelphia, Pa.
MRS. ALFRED C. HARRISON	Philadelphia, Pa.
JOHN H. INGHAM	Philadelphia, Pa.
OLIVER B. JUDSON	Philadelphia, Pa.
EDWARD I. KEFFER	Philadelphia, Pa.
C. HARTMAN KUHN	Philadelphia, Pa.
EDWARD G. McCOLLIN	Philadelphia, Pa.

Name	Residence
THOMAS MCKEAN	Philadelphia, Pa.
CLEMENT B. NEWBOLD	Philadelphia, Pa.
JAMES W. PAUL, JR.	Philadelphia, Pa.
MRS. FRANK H. ROSENGARTEN	Philadelphia, Pa.
RICHARD ROSSMÄSSLER	Philadelphia, Pa.
EDGAR SCOTT	Philadelphia, Pa.
SIMON A. STERN	Philadelphia, Pa.
MISS ANNE THOMSON	Merion, Pa.
ALEXANDER VAN RENSSELAER	Philadelphia, Pa.
HENRY WHELEN, JR.	Philadelphia, Pa.
P. A. B. WIDENER	Ashbourne, Pa.

Witness the hands and seals of the subscribers this first day of November, in the year of our Lord one thousand nine hundred and two (1902):

> A. VAN RENSSELAER (L.S.)
> A. J. CASSATT (L.S.)
> GEO. F. BAER (L.S.)
> HENRY WHELEN, JR. (L.S.)
> JOHN H. CONVERSE (L.S.)
> C. HARTMAN KUHN (L.S.)
> GEO. BURNHAM, JR. (L.S.)
> EDWD. G. MCCOLLIN (L.S.)
> CLEMENT B. NEWBOLD (L.S.)
> JAS. W. PAUL, JR. (L.S.)
> JOHN H. INGHAM (L.S.)
> E. I. KEFFER (L.S.)

State of Pennsylvania

City and County of Philadelphia

Before me, the Recorder of Deeds for the County of Philadelphia, on this twenty-first day of November A. D. 1902, personally appeared Henry Whelen, Jr., John H. Ingham and Edward I. Keffer, three of the subscribers to the foregoing certificate of incorporation and duly acknowledged the same to be their act and deed, and desired that the same might be recorded as such,

Witness my hand and official seal the day and year aforesaid.

> JOS. K. FLESCHER, Deputy Recorder of Deeds (L.S.)

DECREE

In the Court of Common Pleas No. 4, of the County of Philadelphia of December Term 1902, N. 845.

And now this fifth day of January, A. D. 1903, the within Charter and Certificate of Incorporation having been presented to me, a Law Judge of said County, accompanied by due proof of publication of the notice of this application as required by the Act of Assembly and rule of this Court in such case made and provided, I certify that I have examined and perused the said writing, and have found the same to be in proper form and within the purposes named in the first class specified in Section Second of the Act of General Assembly of the Commonwealth of Pennsylvania, entitled "An Act to provide for the Incorporation and Regulation of Certain Corporations," approved April 29th, 1874, and the supplements thereto, and the same appearing to be lawful and not injurious to the community, I do hereby on motion of Edward G. McCollin and John G. Johnson, Esquires, on behalf of the petitioners, order and direct that the said Charter of The Philadelphia Orchestra Association, aforesaid be and is the same hereby approved, and that upon the recording of the same and of this order, the subscribers thereto and their associates shall be a corporation by the name of The Philadelphia Orchestra Association, for the purposes and upon the terms therein stated.

ROBERT N. WILLSON, Judge.

Filed in the office of the Prothonotary of the Court of Common Pleas No. 4 as of December Term 1902 No. 845, on the Fourth day of December A. D. 1902.

C. B. ROBERTS, Deputy Prothonotary.

Recorded in the office for recording Deeds etc. in and for the County of Philadelphia in Charter Book No. 28, page 53 etc.

Witness my hand and seal of office this seventh day of January A. D. 1903.

WM. S. VARE, Recorder of Deeds (L.S.).

APPENDIX B

EXECUTIVE COMMITTEE OF THE PHILADELPHIA ORCHESTRA ELECTED AT THE ORPHEUS CLUB ROOMS, MAY, 1900

HENRY WHELEN, JR.
JOHN C. SIMS
EDWARD G. McCOLLIN
OSCAR A. KNIPE
EDWARD I. KEFFER
OLIVER BOYCE JUDSON
JOHN H. INGHAM, Secretary.

Appendix C

1901–1902
OFFICERS

Alexander Van Rensselaer, President
F. T. Sully Darley, Vice-president
John H. Ingham, Secretary
Henry Whelen, Jr., Treasurer

DIRECTORS

A. J. Cassatt
John H. Converse
Eckley B. Coxe, Jr.
F. T. Sully Darley
William L. Elkins
Miss Mary K. Gibson
Clement A. Griscom
Mrs. Alfred C. Harrison
John H. Ingham
Oliver B. Judson
Edward I. Keffer
Oscar A. Knipe

C. Hartman Kuhn
Edward G. McCollin
Thomas McKean, Jr.
Clement B. Newbold
James W. Paul, Jr.
Mrs. Frank H. Rosengarten
Edgar Scott
Simon A. Stern
Miss Anne Thomson
Alexander Van Rensselaer
Henry Whelen, Jr.
P. A. B. Widener

1902–1903
OFFICERS

Alexander Van Rensselaer, President
Thomas McKean, Vice-president
John H. Ingham, Secretary
Henry Whelen, Jr., Treasurer

DIRECTORS

George Burnham, Jr.
A. J. Cassatt
John H. Converse
Eckley B. Coxe, Jr.
William L. Elkins
Miss Mary K. Gibson
Clement A. Griscom
Mrs. Alfred C. Harrison
John H. Ingham
Oliver B. Judson
Edward I. Keffer
C. Hartman Kuhn

Edward G. McCollin
Thomas McKean
Clement B. Newbold
James W. Paul, Jr.
Mrs. Frank H. Rosengarten
Richard Rossmässler
Edgar Scott
Simon A. Stern
Miss Anne Thomson
Alexander Van Rensselaer
Henry Whelen, Jr.
P. A. B. Widener

DIRECTORS

Mrs. William W. Arnett
George Burnham, Jr.
Alexander J. Cassatt
John H. Converse
Richard Y. Cook
Eckley B. Coxe, Jr.
Mrs. A. J. Dallas Dixon
Miss Mary K. Gibson
Clement A. Griscom
John H. Ingham
Edward I. Keffer
C. Hartman Kuhn

Edward G. McCollin
Thomas McKean
Clement B. Newbold
James W. Paul, Jr.
Mrs. Frank H. Rosengarten
Edgar Scott
Miss Anne Thomson
Alexander Van Rensselaer
Andrew Wheeler, Jr.
Henry Whelen, Jr.
P. A. B. Widener
Miss Frances A. Wister

1906–1907
OFFICERS

Alexander Van Rensselaer, President
Thomas McKean, Vice-president
Andrew Wheeler, Jr., Secretary
Henry Whelen, Jr., Treasurer

DIRECTORS

Mrs. William W. Arnett
George Burnham, Jr.
John H. Converse
Richard Y. Cook
Eckley B. Coxe, Jr.
Mrs. A. J. Dallas Dixon
Miss Mary K. Gibson
Clement A. Griscom
John H. Ingham
Edward I. Keffer
C. Hartman Kuhn
Thomas McKean

Edward G. McCollin
Clement B. Newbold
James W. Paul, Jr.
Mrs. F. H. Rosengarten
Edgar Scott
Miss Anne Thomson
Alexander Van Rensselaer
Andrew Wheeler, Jr.
Henry Whelen, Jr.
P. A. B. Widener
Miss Frances A. Wister

1907–1908
OFFICERS

Alexander Van Rensselaer, President
Thomas McKean, Vice-president
Andrew Wheeler, Jr., Secretary
Arthur E. Newbold, Treasurer

DIRECTORS

Mrs. William W. Arnett
George Burnham, Jr.
John H. Converse
Richard Y. Cook
Eckley B. Coxe, Jr.
Mrs. A. J. Dallas Dixon
Miss Mary K. Gibson
Clement A. Griscom
John H. Ingham
Edward I. Keffer
C. Hartman Kuhn
Edward G. McCollin

Thomas McKean
Arthur E. Newbold
Clement B. Newbold
James W. Paul, Jr.
Mrs. Frank H. Rosengarten
Edgar Scott
E. T. Stotesbury
Miss Anne Thomson
Alexander Van Rensselaer
Andrew Wheeler, Jr.
P. A. B. Widener
Miss Frances A. Wister

[183]

1908–1909

OFFICERS

ALEXANDER VAN RENSSELAER, President
THOMAS MCKEAN, Vice-president
ANDREW WHEELER, JR., Secretary
ARTHUR E. NEWBOLD, Treasurer

DIRECTORS

MRS. WILLIAM W. ARNETT
CHARLES A. BRAUN
GEORGE BURNHAM, JR.
JOHN H. CONVERSE
RICHARD Y. COOK
ECKLEY B. COXE, JR.
MRS. A. J. DALLAS DIXON
MISS MARY K. GIBSON
CLEMENT A. GRISCOM
JOHN H. INGHAM
C. HARTMAN KUHN

THOMAS MCKEAN
ARTHUR E. NEWBOLD
CLEMENT B. NEWBOLD
G. HEIDE NORRIS
MRS. FRANK H. ROSENGARTEN
EDGAR SCOTT
E. T. STOTESBURY
MISS ANNE THOMSON
ALEXANDER VAN RENSSELAER
ANDREW WHEELER, JR.
MISS FRANCES A. WISTER

1909–1910

OFFICERS

ALEXANDER VAN RENSSELAER, President
THOMAS MCKEAN, Vice-president
ANDREW WHEELER, JR., Secretary
ARTHUR E. NEWBOLD, Treasurer

DIRECTORS

MRS. WILLIAM W. ARNETT
CHARLES A. BRAUN
JAMES CROSBY BROWN
GEORGE BURNHAM, JR.
JOHN H. CONVERSE
RICHARD Y. COOK
ECKLEY B. COXE, JR.
MRS. A. J. DALLAS DIXON
THEODORE N. ELY
MISS MARY K. GIBSON
CLEMENT A. GRISCOM
JOHN H. INGHAM

C. HARTMAN KUHN
THOMAS MCKEAN
ARTHUR E. NEWBOLD
CLEMENT B. NEWBOLD
G. HEIDE NORRIS
MRS. FRANK H. ROSENGARTEN
EDGAR SCOTT
E. T. STOTESBURY
MISS ANNE THOMSON
ALEXANDER VAN RENSSELAER
ANDREW WHEELER, JR.
MISS FRANCES A. WISTER

1910–1911

OFFICERS

ALEXANDER VAN RENSSELAER, President
THOMAS MCKEAN, Vice-president
ANDREW WHEELER, Secretary
ARTHUR E. NEWBOLD, Treasurer

[184]

DIRECTORS

Mrs. William W. Arnett
Charles A. Braun
James Crosby Brown
Richard Y. Cook
Eckley B. Coxe, Jr.
Mrs. A. J. Dallas Dixon
Theodore N. Ely
Miss Mary K. Gibson
Clement A. Griscom
John H. Ingham
C. Hartman Kuhn

Thomas McKean
Arthur E. Newbold
Clement B. Newbold
G. Heide Norris
Mrs. Frank H. Rosengarten
Edgar Scott
E. T. Stotesbury
Miss Anne Thomson
Alexander Van Rensselaer
Andrew Wheeler
Miss Frances A. Wister

1911–1912
OFFICERS

Alexander Van Rensselaer, President
Thomas McKean, Vice-president
Andrew Wheeler, Secretary
Arthur E. Newbold, Treasurer

DIRECTORS

Mrs. William W. Arnett
Charles A. Braun
James Crosby Brown
Richard Y. Cook
Eckley B. Coxe, Jr.
Mrs. A. J. Dallas Dixon
Theodore N. Ely
Miss Mary K. Gibson
Clement A. Griscom
John H. Ingham
C. Hartman Kuhn
Thomas McKean

Arthur E. Newbold
Clement B. Newbold
G. Heide Norris
Mrs. Frank H. Rosengarten
Edgar Scott
E. T. Stotesbury
Miss Anne Thomson
Alexander Van Rensselaer
Mrs. L. Howard Weatherly
Andrew Wheeler
J. R. Barton Willing
Miss Frances A. Wister

1912–1913
OFFICERS

Alexander Van Rensselaer, President
Thomas McKean, Vice-president
Andrew Wheeler, Secretary
Arthur E. Newbold, Treasurer

DIRECTORS

Mrs. William W. Arnett
Charles A. Braun
James Crosby Brown
Richard Y. Cook
Eckley B. Coxe, Jr.
Mrs. A. J. Dallas Dixon
Theodore N. Ely
Miss Mary K. Gibson
Clement A. Griscom*
John H. Ingham
C. Hartman Kuhn
Thomas McKean

Arthur E. Newbold
Clement B. Newbold
G. Heide Norris
Mrs. Frank H. Rosengarten
Edgar Scott
E. T. Stotesbury
Alexander Van Rensselaer
Mrs. L. Howard Weatherly
Andrew Wheeler
J. R. Barton Willing
Miss Frances A. Wister

*Died during the season and his place filled by Mrs. Harold E. Yarnall.

[185]

1913–1914
OFFICERS

ALEXANDER VAN RENSSELAER, President
THOMAS MCKEAN, Vice-president
ANDREW WHEELER, Secretary
ARTHUR E. NEWBOLD, Treasurer

DIRECTORS

MRS. WILLIAM W. ARNETT
EDWARD W. BOK
CHARLES A. BRAUN
JOHN F. BRAUN
JAMES CROSBY BROWN
RICHARD Y. COOK
ECKLEY B. COXE, JR.
CYRUS H. K. CURTIS
MRS. A. J. DALLAS DIXON
THEODORE N. ELY
MISS MARY K. GIBSON
JOHN H. INGHAM

C. HARTMAN KUHN
THOMAS MCKEAN
ARTHUR E. NEWBOLD
CLEMENT B. NEWBOLD
G. HEIDE NORRIS
EDGAR SCOTT
E. T. STOTESBURY
ALEXANDER VAN RENSSELAER
MRS. L. HOWARD WEATHERLY
ANDREW WHEELER
MISS FRANCES A. WISTER
MRS. HAROLD E. YARNALL

1914–1915
OFFICERS

ALEXANDER VAN RENSSELAER, President
EDWARD W. BOK, Vice-president
ANDREW WHEELER, Secretary
ARTHUR E. NEWBOLD, Treasurer

DIRECTORS

MRS. WILLIAM W. ARNETT
EDWARD W. BOK
CHARLES A. BRAUN
JOHN F. BRAUN
JAMES CROSBY BROWN
RICHARD Y. COOK
ECKLEY B. COXE, JR.
CYRUS H. K. CURTIS
MRS. A. J. DALLAS DIXON
GEORGE W. ELKINS
THEODORE N. ELY
MISS MARY K. GIBSON

JOHN H. INGHAM
C. HARTMAN KUHN
THOMAS MCKEAN
ARTHUR E. NEWBOLD
G. HEIDE NORRIS
E. T. STOTESBURY
ALEXANDER VAN RENSSELAER
MRS. L. HOWARD WEATHERLY
ANDREW WHEELER
MISS FRANCES A. WISTER
MRS. HAROLD E. YARNALL

1915–1916
OFFICERS

ALEXANDER VAN RENSSELAER, President
E. T. STOTESBURY, Vice-president
ANDREW WHEELER, Secretary
ARTHUR E. NEWBOLD, Treasurer

DIRECTORS

Mrs. William W. Arnett
Edward W. Bok
Charles A. Braun
John F. Braun
James Crosby Brown
Richard Y. Cook
Eckley B. Coxe, Jr.
Cyrus H. K. Curtis
Mrs. A. J. Dallas Dixon
George W. Elkins
Theodore N. Ely
Samuel S. Fels
Miss Mary K. Gibson

Henry McKean Ingersoll
John H. Ingham
C. Hartman Kuhn
Thomas McKean
Arthur E. Newbold
G. Heide Norris
E. T. Stotesbury
Alexander Van Rensselaer
Mrs. L. Howard Weatherly
Andrew Wheeler
Miss Frances A. Wister
Mrs. Harold E. Yarnall

1916–1917

OFFICERS

Alexander Van Rensselaer, President
E. T. Stotesbury, Vice-president
Andrew Wheeler, Secretary
Arthur E. Newbold, Treasurer

DIRECTORS

Mrs. William W. Arnett
Edward W. Bok
Charles A. Braun
John F. Braun
James Crosby Brown
Richard Y. Cook
Cyrus H. K. Curtis
Mrs. A. J. Dallas Dixon
George W. Elkins
Samuel S. Fels
Miss Mary K. Gibson
Charles D. Hart
Henry McKean Ingersoll

John H. Ingham
C. Hartman Kuhn
Arthur E. Newbold
G. Heide Norris
E. T. Stotesbury
Alexander Van Rensselaer
Mrs. L. Howard Weatherly
Andrew Wheeler
Joseph E. Widener
Miss Frances A. Wister
Charlton Yarnall
Mrs. Harold E. Yarnall

1917–1918

OFFICERS

Alexander Van Rensselaer, President
E. T. Stotesbury, Vice-president
Andrew Wheeler, Secretary
Arthur E. Newbold, Treasurer

[187]

DIRECTORS

Mrs. William W. Arnett
Edward W. Bok
Charles A. Braun
John F. Braun
James Crosby Brown
Cyrus H. K. Curtis
George W. Elkins
Samuel S. Fels
Miss Mary K. Gibson
Charles D. Hart
Henry McKean Ingersoll
John H. Ingham

C. Hartman Kuhn
Effingham B. Morris
Arthur E. Newbold
G. Heide Norris
E. T. Stotesbury
Alexander Van Rensselaer
Mrs. L. Howard Weatherl
Andrew Wheeler
Joseph E. Widener
Miss Frances A. Wister
Charlton Yarnall
Mrs. Harold E. Yarnall

1918–1919
OFFICERS

Alexander Van Rensselaer, President
E. T. Stotesbury, Vice-president
Andrew Wheeler, Secretary
Arthur E. Newbold, Treasurer

DIRECTORS

Mrs. William W. Arnett
Edward W. Bok
Charles A. Braun
John F. Braun
James Crosby Brown
Cyrus H. K. Curtis
Mrs. A. J. Dallas Dixon
George W. Elkins
Samuel S. Fels
Charles D. Hart
Henry McKean Ingersoll
John H. Ingham

C. Hartman Kuhn
Effingham B. Morris
G. Heide Norris
E. T. Stotesbury
Miss Anne Thomson
Alexander Van Rensselaer
Mrs. L. Howard Weatherl
Andrew Wheeler
Joseph E. Widener
Miss Frances A. Wister
Charlton Yarnall
Mrs. Harold E. Yarnall

1919–1920
OFFICERS

Alexander Van Rensselaer, President
E. T. Stotesbury, Vice-president*
Andrew Wheeler, Secretary
Arthur E. Newbold, Treasurer

*Resigned during the season.

[188]

DIRECTORS

Mrs. William W. Arnett
Edward W. Bok
Charles A. Braun
John F. Braun
James Crosby Brown
Cyrus H. K. Curtis
Mrs. A. J. Dallas Dixon
George W. Elkins*
Samuel S. Fels
Charles D. Hart
Henry McKean Ingersoll
John H. Ingham

C. Hartman Kuhn
Effingham B. Morris
G. Heide Norris
Miss Anne Thomson
Alexander Van Rensselaer
Mrs. L. Howard Weatherly
Andrew Wheeler
Joseph E. Widener
Miss Frances A. Wister
Charlton Yarnall
Mrs. Harold E. Yarnall

1920–1921
OFFICERS

Alexander Van Rensselaer, President
William Jay Turner, Vice-president
Andrew Wheeler, Secretary
Robert K. Cassatt, Treasurer

DIRECTORS

Mrs. William W. Arnett
Edward W. Bok
Charles A. Braun
John F. Braun
James Crosby Brown
Cyrus H. K. Curtis
Mrs. A. J. Dallas Dixon
William Jay Turner
Samuel S. Fels
Charles D. Hart
Henry McKean Ingersoll
John H. Ingham

C. Hartman Kuhn
Effingham B. Morris
G. Heide Norris
Robert K. Cassatt
Miss Anne Thomson
Alexander Van Rensselaer
Mrs. L. Howard Weatherly
Andrew Wheeler
Joseph E. Widener
Miss Frances A. Wister
Charlton Yarnall
Mrs. Harold E. Yarnall

1921–1922
OFFICERS

Alexander Van Rensselaer, President
William Jay Turner, Vice-president
Andrew Wheeler, Secretary
Robert K. Cassatt, Treasurer

Died during the season and his place taken by William Jay Turner.

[189]

DIRECTORS

1922-1923, 1923-1924, 1924-1925

OFFICERS

DIRECTORS

Appendix D
First Guarantors of the Philadelphia Orchestra
1900–1901

Mr. Horace Allen
Miss Helen Audenried
Mr. Lewis Audenried
Mrs. A. W. Baird
Mr. W. J. Baird
Mr. J. W. Bayard
Mrs. E. F. Beale
Mrs. Louis F. Benson
Mrs. Arthur Biddle
Mrs. George Tucker Bispham
Rev. Cyrus Townsend Brady
Mr. John F. Braun
Miss Frances I. Brock
Dr. Edward Brooks
Miss Harriet Buchanan
Mrs. Edward S. Buckley
Dr. C. E. Cadwalader
Miss F. E. Caldwell
Mrs. Alexander J. Cassatt
Mrs. S. Castner, Jr.
Mr. Frank G. Cauffman
Miss Kate H. Chandler
Mrs. James H. Chapman
Mr. Charles J. Cohen
Mr. John H. Converse
Mrs. Alexander Brown Coxe
Mrs. Chas. E. Coxe
Mr. Eckley B. Coxe, Jr.
Miss Rebecca Coxe
Mr. F. E. Cresson
Mr. David S. Cresswell
Mr. D. E. Crozier
Mr. H. B. Curran
Mr. Chas. W. Dannehauer
Mr. Francis T. S. Darley
Mrs. Samuel G. Dixon
Mr. George B. Dreisler
Mr. Theo. N. Ely
Mr. Chancellor C. English
Mrs. Spencer Ervin
Mrs. Wm. H. Farr
Mr. Chas. H. Fischer

Miss Mary K. Gibson
Mr. W. W. Gilchrist
Mr. Wm. Grew
Miss Mary C. Griffith
Mrs. Clement A. Griscom
Mr. W. Bennett Gough
Mrs. R. Emott Hare
Mrs. J. Campbell Harris
Mr. Austin S. Heckscher
Messrs. C. J. Heppe & Son
Mr. F. D. Howell
Mrs. Warren Ingersoll
Miss M. H. Ingham
Mr. W. H. Joyce
Mrs. O. A. Judson
Mr. O. B. Judson
Dr. Edward I. Keffer
Mr. Philip F. Kelly
Mr. Oscar A. Knipe
Mr. C. Hartman Kuhn
Mrs. Bigelow Lawrence
Miss Nina Lea
Mr. J. Bertram Lippincott
Mrs. E. Lynch
Mr. Edw. G. McCollin
Mrs. H. Pratt McKean
Mr. Thomas McKean
Mr. Frank McLaughlin
Messrs. Henry Miller & Sons
Mr. Joseph M. Mitcheson
Mr. Clement Buckley Newbold
Mrs. Thomas H. Newton
Miss Ethel Parrish
Mrs. Joseph Parrish
Miss M. Parrish
Hon. Clement B. Penrose
Mrs. Eli Kirk Price
Mr. Max Riebenack
Mrs. E. C. Roberts
Mr. W. S. Robinson
Miss Fannie Rosengarten
Mrs. Frank H. Rosengarten

Mr. J. G. Rosengarten
Miss Elsé West Rulon
Miss Emma Schubert
Mr. Edgar Scott
Mrs. Thomas A. Scott
Miss Elizabeth Smith
Mrs. Edward B. Smith
Miss E. K. Smith, Jr.
Mr. S. Decatur Smith
Mrs. A. M. Starr
Mr. Simon A. Stern
Messrs. N. Stetson & Co.
Mrs. Cornelius Stevenson
Mr. W. R. Stobbe
Miss M. D. Tenbrooke
Mr. J. B. Thayer, Jr.
Mr. Geo. C. Thomas
Mr. Henry J. Thouron

Mr. Henry Gordon Thunder
Mr. Alex. Van Rensselaer
Mrs. T. H. Warren
Mr. Henry Waters
Mr. L. R. Welsh
Mr. Andrew Wheeler, Jr.
Miss Gertrude Wheeler
Mr. C. S. Whelen
Mrs. C. S. Whelen
Mr. Henry Whelen, Jr.
Miss Abbie Winnery
Mr. Ellis D. Williams
Mr. Chas. Willing
Mr. David D. Wood
Dr. C. S. Wurts
Mrs. Charlton Yarnall
Mr. Richard Zeckwer
Mr. Harry D. Ziegler

Appendix E

Summary of Concerts Played by The Philadelphia Orchestra
Seasons 1900–1901 to 1924–1925, Inclusive

1—Season 1900–1901:
Six Concerts.................................... 6
Reading, Penna.................................. 1

    Total.................................... 7

2—Season 1901–1902:
Regular Series Concerts..14 }
Public Rehearsals........14 } 28
Allentown, Harrisburg, Lancaster, Reading, York, Penna., Trenton, Wilmington, three (3) each....... 24

    Total.................................... 52

3—Season 1902–1903:
Regular Series Concerts..14 }
Public Rehearsals........14 } 28
Beethoven Cycle................................ 5
Popular Concerts............................... 5
Young People's Educational Series.............. 5
Allentown, Harrisburg, Lancaster, Reading, York, Penna., Wilmington, three (3) each............. 18
Baltimore, Carlisle, Lebanon, Lock Haven, Scranton, Wilkes-Barre, Williamsport, Penna., New York City, Trenton, Washington, one (1) each............... 10

    Total.................................... 71

4—Season 1903–1904:
Regular Series Concerts..14 }
Public Rehearsals........14 } 28
Young People's Educational Lecture Concerts........ 5
People's Concerts.............................. 5
Special Concerts............................... 2
Popular Concert................................ 1
Special (Thibaud) Concert 1
Allentown, Harrisburg, Lancaster, Penna., Wilmington, three (3) each.................................. 12
Boston... 2
Reading, Lebanon, Penna., New York City, one (1) each 3

    Total.................................... 59

[193]

5—Season 1904-1905:
Regular Series Concerts..15 }
Public Rehearsals........15 } 30
People's Concerts..................................... 5
Weingartner Concert, Special...................... 1
Harrisburg, Washington, one (1) each.............. 2
                                                   ──
          Total..................................... 38

6—Season 1905-1906:
Regular Series Concerts..18 }
Public Rehearsals........18 } 36
Lecture Concerts..................................... 4
Baltimore, Washington, Wilmington, three (3) each.. 9
Lancaster, Reading, New York City, two (2) each.... 6
Trenton, Easton, Brooklyn, one (1) each............ 3
                                                   ──
          Total..................................... 58

7—Season 1906-1907:
Regular Series Concerts..20 }
Public Rehearsals........20 } 40
People's Concert, Kensington...................... 1
Baltimore.. 5
Washington... 5
Wilmington... 4
Harrisburg... 3
Trenton.. 2
Easton, Reading, Penna., one (1) each.............. 2
                                                   ──
          Total..................................... 62

8—Season 1907-1908:
Regular Series Concerts, 22 pairs................... 44
"In Memoriam" Concert, Fritz Scheel................ 1
Baltimore.. 5
Washington... 5
Wilmington... 4
Lancaster.. 2
New York City, Trenton, one (1) each............... 2
                                                   ──
          Total..................................... 63

9—Season 1908-1909:
Regular Series Concerts, 22 pairs................... 44
University of Pennsylvania.......................... 2
People's Concerts, Kensington...................... 2
Baltimore.. 5
Washington... 5

Wilmington.. 4
Lancaster.. 2
New York City, Brooklyn, Princeton, one (1) each... 3

    Total.. 67

10—Season 1909–1910:

Regular Series Concerts, 22 pairs.................. 44
Popular Concerts.................................. 10
University of Pennsylvania......................... 6
People's Concerts, Kensington...................... 3
Stetson Concert................................... 1
Baltimore... 5
Washington.. 5
Wilmington.. 4
Princeton... 2

    Total.. 80

11—Season 1910–1911:

Regular Series Concerts, 25 pairs.................. 50
Popular Concerts.................................. 11
National Federation of Music Clubs, Special........ 1
People's Concerts, Kensington...................... 3
University of Pennsylvania......................... 2
Stetson Concert................................... 1
Camden... 5
Wilmington.. 4
Norristown.. 2

    Total.. 79

12— Season 1911–1912:

Regular Series Concerts, 25 pairs.................. 50
Two pairs of Concerts for the Guarantee Fund........ 4
Popular Concerts 6
People's Concerts, Kensington...................... 4
University of Pennsylvania Concerts................. 2
Germantown....................................... 1
Stetson Concert................................... 1
Atlantic City..................................... 2
Camden... 6
Wilmington.. 4
Akron, Cleveland, Easton, Norristown, Pittsburgh,
    Reading, Penna., one (1) each.................. 6

    Total.. 86

13—Season 1912–1913:

Regular Series Concerts, 25 pairs.................... 50
Popular Concerts.................................... 6
People's Concerts, Kensington....................... 3
Germantown... 1
Stetson Concert.................................... 1
University of Pennsylvania.......................... 2
Manuscript Music Society........................... 1
Atlantic City...................................... 2
Camden... 6
Wilmington... 4
Akron, Cleveland, Toledo, Columbus, Detroit, Mich.,
   Pittsburgh, Reading, Penna., Springfield, Mass.,
   Washington, one (1) each 9
                                                    ──
   Total...................................... 85

14—Season 1913–1914:

Regular Series Concerts, 25 pairs.................... 50
Special Concert in Afternoon Series................. 1
Popular Concerts.................................... 6
People's Concerts, Kensington....................... 3
University of Pennsylvania.......................... 2
Stetson Concert.................................... 1
Atlantic City...................................... 4
Princeton.. 2
Washington... 3
Wilmington... 4
Oberlin, Akron, Cleveland, Ann Arbor, Detroit, Bos-
   ton, North Adams, Mass.; Meriden, Middlebury,
   Bridgeport, Waterbury, Norwich, Conn.; New York
   City, Pittsburgh, Easton, Reading, Scranton, one
   (1) each....................................... 17
                                                    ──
   Total...................................... 93

15—Season 1914–1915:

Regular Series Concerts, 25 pairs.................... 50
Special "Pension Fund" Concerts.................... 2
Concert for Young People........................... 1
University of Pennsylvania.......................... 2
Richmond... 3
Washington... 3
Wilmington... 4
Atlantic City...................................... 2
Reading.. 2
Oberlin, Akron, Ann Arbor, Detroit, Baltimore, Buffalo,
   Cleveland, Erie, Indianapolis, New York City,
   Princeton, one (1) each......................... 11
                                                    ──
   Total...................................... 80

[196]

—Season 1915–1916:

Regular Series Concerts, 25 pairs..................... 50
Mahler's Eighth Symphony, extra performances....... 7
Public School ("Public Ledger") Concerts........... 8
Free Sunday Afternoon Concerts.................... 3
University of Pennsylvania........................ 3
Stetson Concert................................. 1
Washington..................................... 5
Wilmington..................................... 4
Atlantic City................................... 2
Baltimore, Bryn Mawr, Buffalo, Oberlin, Cleveland,
    Columbus, Dayton, Detroit, Ypsilanti, Mich.; James-
    town, N. Y., New York City, Norristown, Easton,
    Lancaster, Lebanon, Reading, Penna., Princeton, one
    (1) each.................................... 17
                                                  ——
        Total.................................. 100

—Season 1916–1917:

Regular Series Concerts, 25 pairs..................... 50
Special performance of Bach St. Matthew Passion..... 1
Public School ("Public Ledger") Concerts........... 8
Free Sunday Afternoon Concerts.................... 3
University of Pennsylvania Concerts................ 3
Stetson Concert................................. 1
Five pairs of Concerts in Pittsburgh............... 10
Baltimore...................................... 3
Washington..................................... 5
Wilmington..................................... 5
Atlantic City................................... 2
Albany, Buffalo, Cleveland, Oberlin, Lima, Springfield,
    Columbus, Dayton, Detroit, Ypsilanti, Grand Rapids,
    Jamestown, N. Y., New York City, Portland, Maine,
    Princeton, Lebanon, Reading, Penna., Richmond,
    Va., Wheeling, W. Va., Williamstown, Manchester,
    Mass., one (1) each.......................... 21
                                                  ——
        Total.................................. 112

—Season 1917–1918:

Regular Series Concerts, 25 pairs..................... 50
Reformation Concert, Special 1
Aeolian Concert, Special 1
Red Cross Concert, Special 1
People's Concert at Stetson Auditorium.............. 1
Pittsburgh, 5 pairs.............................. 10
Baltimore...................................... 5
Washington..................................... 5
Wilmington..................................... 5
Oberlin.. 2

Cleveland...
Toronto, Canada.......................................
Camp Dix, N. J., Columbus, Dayton, Detroit, Grand
  Rapids, Kalamazoo, Ypsilanti, Mich., Buffalo, Ro-
  chester, Ithaca, N. Y., New York City, Princeton,
  one (1) each...

TOTAL...................................

19—SEASON 1918–1919:

Regular Series Concerts, 25 pairs....................
French War Relief Benefit...........................
Roosevelt Memorial Concert.........................
Wanamaker Concert...................................
Stetson Auditorium..................................
University of Pennsylvania..........................
Pittsburgh, 5 pairs..................................
Washington..
Baltimore...
Wilmington..
New York City (Afternoon)..........................
New York City, Vacation Association Benefit........
Cleveland...
Toronto...
Oberlin...
Wheeling, W. Va., Pottsville, one (1) each..........
House of Representatives, Harrisburg, Penna.........

TOTAL...................................

20—SEASON 1919–1920:

Concerts, 25 pairs..................................
Endowment Fund Concerts (telephone subscribers)....
Wanamaker, Special.................................
Supervisors of Music, Special......................
Aeolian Concert, Special...........................
Stetson Auditorium.................................
University of Pennsylvania.........................
New York City (Evening)............................
Pittsburgh, 5 pairs................................
Washington...
Baltimore..
Wilmington...
Toronto..
Cleveland..
Harrisburg...
Buffalo, Ithaca, Columbus, Oberlin, Detroit, Pottsville,
  Princeton, one (1) each..........................

TOTAL...................................1

—SEASON 1920–1921:
Regular Series Concerts, 25 pairs................... 50
Monday Evening........................ 3
People's Concert at Stetson Auditorium............ 1
University of Pennsylvania...................... 5
New York City (Series)...................... 8
Froebel League, New York, Special.............. 1
Washington............................. 5
Baltimore.............................. 5
Wilmington............................. 5
Pittsburgh, 5 pairs........................ 10
Harrisburg............................. 5
Toronto............................... 4
Princeton, Pottsville, one (1) each................ 2
     TOTAL...................... 104

—SEASON 1921–1922:
Regular Series Concerts, 25 pairs................... 50
Monday Evening Concerts..................... 3
Children's Concerts......................... 3
Strauss Concert........................... 1
Philadelphia Award......................... 1
Stetson Auditorium......................... 1
University of Pennsylvania.................... 5
New York City (Series)...................... 10
Strauss, New York, Special.................... 4
Washington............................. 5
Baltimore.............................. 5
Pittsburgh, 5 pairs........................ 10
Harrisburg............................. 5
Toronto............................... 4
Princeton, Pottsville, one (1) each................ 2
     TOTAL...................... 109

—SEASON 1922–1923:
Regular Series Concerts, 26 pairs................... 52
Monday Evening Concerts..................... 4
Children's Concerts, 3 pairs................... 6
Wanamaker Concert, Special................... 1
Stanley Theatre, Special..................... 1
"Forum" Concert.......................... 1
("Philadelphia Award") Concert.............. 1
Stetson Auditorium......................... 1
New York City........................... 10
Pittsburgh, 3 pairs........................ 6
Pittsburgh Children's Concerts................. 3
Washington............................. 5
Baltimore.............................. 5
Toronto............................... 4
Harrisburg............................. 3
Princeton, Pottsville, one (1) each................ 2
     TOTAL...................... 105

24—Season 1923-1924:

Regular Series Concerts, 26 pairs...................... 5²
Monday Evening Concerts........................... ⁸
Children's Concerts, 4 pairs........................ ⁸
Philadelphia "Forum," Lecture Concerts............ ⁴
Public School Children............................. ³
Teachers' Convention, Special...................... ¹
Philadelphia Award................................ ¹
Mendelssohn Choir of Toronto, Philadelphia........ ¹
New York City..................................... 1C
Mendelssohn Choir of Toronto, Special, in New York.. 2
Washington....................................... 5
Baltimore... 5
Toronto.. 4
Montreal, Princeton, one (1) each.................. 2
                                                    ——
        TOTAL.................................... 104

25—Season 1924-1925:

Regular Series Concerts, 29 pairs.................. 5⁸
Monday Evening.................................. ⁸
Children's Concerts, 4 pairs .... ⁸
Public School Children........................... ³
Philadelphia "Forum"............................ ³
Philadelphia Award Concert, Special.............. ¹
New York City................................... 1C
Washington...................................... 5
Baltimore....................................... 5
Toronto... 4
Buffalo, Princeton, one (1) each.................. 2
                                                  ——
        TOTAL.................................... 107

APPENDIX F

CONDUCTORS

FRITZ SCHEEL 1900–1907   CARL POHLIG 1907–1912

LEOPOLD STOKOWSKI 1912

PERSONNEL

S. ABAS	Violin	1901–02
PHILIP ABBAS	Cello	1916–17
HARRY ALEINIKOFF	Violin	1915–25
PAUL ALEMANN	Clarinet	1904–25
LOUIS ANGELOTY	Violin	1908–22
P. ANTONELLI	Horn	1920–23
RUFUS M. AREY	Clarinet (Principal)	1923–24
BERNARD ARGIEWICZ	Cello	1917–19
		1924–25
WILLIAM L. ARKLESS	Violin	1900–01
	Viola	1915–18
J. ASCHKE	Piccolo	1901–02
ANTON ASENMACKER	Cello	1917–19
J. AYALA	Trumpet	1916–17
F. V. BADOLLET	Flute	1901–04
HARRY J. BAKER	Battery	1923–24
IRVING J. BANCROFT	Violin	1916–25
PHILIP BANSBACH	Viola	1919–22
W. BARCHEWITZ	Violin	1901–04
CLEMENTE BARONE	Flute and Piccolo	1900–01
	(Principal 1907–10)	1904–10
RICHARD BARONE	Violin	1923–24
HERMAN BASSE	Trumpet (Principal 1904–05,	1904–05
	1914–15)	1914–17
GUS BATTLES	Flute	1906–09
VICTOR BAY	Violin	1922–23
JACOB H. BECK	Trumpet	1900–01
WILLIAM J. BECK	Violin	1906–09
MIRKO BELINSKI	Cello	1904–09
J. F. BELLOIS	Violin	1900–01

JOEL BELOV	Violin	1912–20
		1923–24
SAMUEL BELOV	Viola	1908–20
JOSEPH BENAVENTE	Cello	1917–18
AUGUST BENDER	Trumpet	1901–03
F. BENETER	Violin	1901–02
ISADORE BERV	Horn	1923–25
FREDERICK BETTONEY	Bassoon	1917–20
P. BIANCULLI	Violin	1913–14
HENRY BIELO	Bassoon	1920–22
JULIUS BIELO	Bass	1920–22
ANTONIN BLAHA	Violin	1906–08
		1909–12
MAX BLEYER	Trumpet (Principal 1903–04)	1903–08
MAX BLUMENFELD	Violin	1904–06
H. BOBELL	Violin	1903–04
GUSTAV BOEHM	Violin	1900–01
LOUIS BOEHSE	Bass	1904–07
		1908–25
DANIEL BONADE	Clarinet	1917–22
		1924–25
MILTON BORNSTEIN	Violin	1921–25
ROSARIO BOURDON	Cello	1904–08
DOMENICO BOVE	Violin	1917–23
		1924–25
ISADOR BRANSKY	Viola	1919–20
HORACE BRITT	Cello (Principal)	1907–08
ROGER BRITT	Violin	1914–20
JOSEPH BRODO	Violin	1918–24
LEOPOLD BROECKAERT	Flute	1904–05
H. I. BROWN	Violin	1921–25
J. H. BURKARTMAEIR	Violin	1900–01
NATHAN CAHAN	Bass	1900–24
P. CAHON	Cello	1901–02
L. CAILLIET	Clarinet	1916–25
H. CAMPOWSKY	Violin	1903–17
		1920–23
HERMAN CAROW	Violin	1916–18
HUGO CAROW	Viola	1900–04
		1908–21
S. H. CAUFFMAN	Cello	1901–02
		1903–04
HARRY CHAZIN	Violin	1919–23
S. CHEIFETZ	Viola	1924–25
JOSEF CHUDNOWSKY	Violin	1913–24
JOHN A. CIANCIARULO	Violin	1900–01
		1903–05
GIUSEPPE CIMINO	Horn	1918–19
DAVID COHEN	Violin	1918–25
SOLOMON COHEN	Trumpet	1918–25

Lucius Cole	Violin	1905–19
Frederick W. Cook	Violin	1906–24
Carlton Cooley	Viola	1919–20
William Conrad	Bassoon	1921–22
S. Cortadella	Bass	1923–24
Francesco Cortese	Harp	1900–01
R. Cras	Horn	1919–20
Henri Czaplinski	Violin	1924–25
S. Dabrowski	Violin	1923–25
Benjamin D'Amelio	Violin	1919–24
J. De Boer	Violin	1901–02
George Dechert	Trombone	1901–04
George De Clerck	Viola	1912–19
Victor de Gomez	Cello	1916–19
Frank Delli Gatti	Viola	1920–21
	Violin	1921–23
F. Del Negro	Bassoon	1922–25
Eugene Devaux	Oboe	1910–11
William Diestel	Viola (Principal)	1908–15
Fritz Dieterichs	Clarinet (Principal)	1901–12
Joseph Di Natale	Violin	1917–18
William F. Dodge	Violin	1906–07
Carl Doell	Violin (Concertmaster)	1900–01
P. A. Donatelli	Tuba	1923–25
Frederick Donath	Viola and Celesta	1923–24
Paul Donath	Violin	1903–04
		1907–17
Max Donner	Violin	1907–08
John D'Orio	Horn	1910–18
		1921–25
Alfred Doucet	Oboe (Principal)	1902–13
David Dubinsky	Violin	1900–01
	Viola	1901–02
	Violin (Principal 1912–25)	1908–25
Vladimir Dubinsky	Cello (Principal)	1906–07
A. Dupuis	Oboe	1916–18
W. B. Ebann	Cello (Principal)	1901–02
Sol Eckstein	Bass Clarinet	1900–01
Oscar Eiler	Cello	1912–14
Bruno Einhorn	Cello	1913–17
Benjamin Eisenberg	Violin	1918–19
Maurice Eisenberg	Cello	1917–19
Henri Elkan	Viola	1920–25
S. Elkind	Bass	1921–22
Otto Elst	Trombone (Principal)	1906–16
Rudolph Engel	Viola and Trumpet	1904–25
David Epstein	Viola	1922–25
Leonard Epstein	Viola	1920–24
Meyer B. Epstein	Violin	1923–24
D. H. Ezerman	Cello	1901–02

Pasqual Fabris	Violin	1924-2.
Rudolph Fahsbender	Bass	1920-2.
Julius Falk	Violin	1900-0.
Vincent Fanelli, Jr.	Harp	1913-2.
Carl Fasshauer	Violin	1912-1.
John Fasshauer	Bass	1900-0.
		1907-2.
Henry W. Fehling	Violin (Principal)	1900-0
Harry Feldman	Violin	1923-2.
W. Fenstel	Cello	1900-0.
Emile Ferir	Viola (Principal)	1918-1.
Antonio Ferrara	Violin	1916-2.
		1921-2.
		1924-2.
Luigi Ferrara	Violin	1917-1.
		1919-2.
Paul Fillsack	Violin and Clarinet	1901-2.
John Fisnar	Bassoon	1922-2.
John A. Fischer	Flute and Piccolo	1909-2.
R. Fischer	Cello	1902-0.
Clarence Fogg	Viola	1900-0.
		1903-0.
		1906-0.
Emil Flogmann	Cello	1919-2.
		1921-2.
C. Franke	Violin	1901-0.
George O. Frey	Tuba	1921-2.
	Trombone and Euphonium	1923-2.
Nathan Frey	Viola	1921-2.
A. Friese	Battery	1901-0.
Max Froelich	Cello	1918-2.
John Fruncillo	Viola	1900-0.
Paul Fuchs	Bassoon	1902-0.
Mario Garaffoni	Bass	1924-2.
Edgar A. Gastel	Violin	1900-0.
Erwin Gastel	Cello	1900-0.
Fred Geib	Tuba	1904-0.
Edward W. Geffert	Trombone	1917-2.
Victor Geoffrion	Bass	1922-2.
C. E. Gerhard	Trombone	1900-0.
		1904-0.
		1921-2.
A. Ginsburg	Violin	1924-2.
Angelo Giurato	Violin	1900-0.
Harry Glantz	Trumpet	1915-1.
Beaumont Glass	Violin	1910-1.
Joseph Glassman	Bass	1917-1.
Abram Goldfuss	Violin	1918-2.
Jerome Goldstein	Violin	1917-2.
A. Gorodetzky	Violin	1920-2.

CHARLES GREBE	Cello	1900–01
		1903–04
		1908–17
FRED P. GREIMS	Cello	1900–01
H. GREIMS	Viola	1901–02
HERMAN GREVESMÜHL	Violin	1902–03
WILLIAM S. GREENBERG	Viola	1923–25
GEORGES GRISËZ	Clarinet (Principal)	1922–23
JOHANN GROLLE	Violin	1902–05
		1907–11
R. GROSSMAN	Cello	1901–02
HARRY F. GROVER	Viola	1918–19
WILLIAM GRUNER	Bassoon (Principal 1906–07)	1906–17
WALTER GUETTER	Bassoon	1922–25
B. GUSIKOFF	Cello	1920–25
ISADORE GUSIKOFF	Cello	1921–25
WILLIAM H. GUSSEN	Violin	1900–01
WILLIAM H. GUYON	Flute and Piccolo	1907–09
CARL HAFERBURG	Viola	1901–02
		1903–05
L. M. HAFERBURG	Viola	1902–03
EMIL HAHL	Viola	1902–19
RAYMOND J. HALL	Cello	1920–23
ERICH HALTENORTH	Violin	1901–02
	Viola	1904–24
H. HALTENORTH	Violin	1903–04
CHARLES F. HAMER	Cello	1919–20
SIDNEY HAMER	Cello	1918–22
PAUL HANDKE	Trumpet (Principal 1902–03)	1901–03
F. H. HARTMANN	Trombone	1900–01
H. HARTMAN	Bass	1900–01
A. HASE	Bass	1904–06
		1920–25
ALBERT HASE	Bass	1901–04
OTTO HAUBENREISSER	Violin	1905–09
GUSTAV HEIM	Trumpet (Principal)	1905–07
A. HEINE	Violin	1903–04
HERMAN HELLER	Violin	1900–02
JOHN HELLBERG	Bassoon	1900–01
P. HENKELMAN	Oboe and English Horn	1901–25
OTTO HENNEBERG	Horn	1905–25
RUDOLPH HENNIG	Cello (Principal)	1900–01
DAYTON M. HENRY	Violin	1918–25
A. HEYNEN	Bassoon	1901–02
HANS HIMMER	Cello	1904–14
H. J. HORNBERGER	Violin	1900–04
ANTON HORNER	Horn (Principal)	1902–25
JOSEPH HORNER	Horn	1900–01
		1902–25
ERNEST HUBER	Bass	1919–20

A. Huster	Violin	1901–02
L. Hutinet	Trombone	1916–17
Roland Huxley	Violin	1906–08
John G. Ingle	Violin	1900–01
William Jaeger	Trumpet	1900–01
Joseph A. Jakob	Horn	1909–10
Sol E. Jarrow	Viola	1905–06
Lewis C. Jocher	Bass	1900–01
		1907–13
Clarence Jordan	Violin	1924–25
Ernest Kaehler	Violin	1900–01
		.1907–13
Maurice Kaplan	Viola	1920–25
Alfred Kastner	Harp	1901–02
		1903–04
Joseph E. Kearney	Viola	1903–04
Oscar Keller	Clarinet	1902–04
Geoerge William Keyser	Viola	1908–19
Carl Kihlman	Violin	1903–19
W. M. Kincaid	Flute (Principal)	1920–25
Hans Kindler	Cello (Principal 1916–20)	1914–20
Samuel Kliachko	Cello	1920–22
Karl Klupp	Horn	1901–04
Carl Kneisel	Cello	1908–17
		1919–22
F. H. Knorr	Bass	1900–01
Henry Koch	Horn	1900–01
A. Koehler	Trumpet	1903–04
H. Koenig	Violin	1903–04
Jan Koert	Violin	1900–02
	Viola (Principal)	1902–08
Benjamin Kohon	Bassoon (Principal)	1912–15
A. Korb	Violin	1901–06
Elkan Kosman	Violin (Concertmaster)	1901–02
Fabien Koussevitzky	Bass	1923–25
Boris Koutzen	Violin	1924–25
Hugo Kreisler	Cello	1906–07
Emil Kresse	Violin, Tympani and Battery	1901–02
		1904–25
George Kresse	Violin	1901–03
		1906–07
Christian Kriens	Viola	1902–04
Richard Krueger	Bassoon (Principal)	1901–06
		1907–08
		1909–12
		1915–22
E. Kruger	Violin	1903–05
Otto Kruger	Violin	1905–17
Paul Krummeich	Violin	1903–07
William Kruse, Jr.	Bassoon	1920–21

Alexis Kudisch	Violin	1918–19
Julius G. Kumme	Viola	1900–01
Max Lachmuth	Oboe and English Horn	1900–01
Joseph La Monaca	Flute	1910–25
F. M. Lapetina	Viola	1900–01
Francis J. Lapitino	Harp	1911–13
Emile Latisch	Bass	1910–17
Vincent Lazarro, Jr.	Bass	1921–25
H. C. Le Barbier	Trumpet (Principal)	1909–14
Morris Lein	Trumpet	1923–25
J. W. F. Leman	Viola	1908–18
Miln Lemisch	Viola	1900–01
Alfred Lennartz	Cello	1902–16
B. F. Leventhal	Viola	1911–23
Harry Levy	Violin	1918–19
Robert Lindemann	Clarinet (Principal)	1913–17
A. Lipkin	Violin	1922–25
George Livoti	Violin	1923–24
Gustave A. Loeben	Viola and Celesta	1919–25
Alfred Lorenz	Violin	1901–02
		1903–17
	Viola (Principal)	1917–18
	Violin	1918–25
Franz Lorenz	Cello	1909–17
Paul P. Lotz	Trombone	1900–01
		1909–25
H. Lucas	Viola	1901–02
Arthur Luck	Bass	1914–18
C. Stanley Mackey	Tuba	1900–04
		1905–15
Robert Mädler	Bass	1902–07
E. Maestre	Cello	1922–24
E. Malach	Bass	1918–19
Theodore Mansfelt	Cello	1904–05
André Maquarre	Flute (Principal)	1918–20
Daniel Maquarre	Flute (Principal)	1910–18
Attillio Marchetti	Oboe (Principal)	1913–15
John Marquardt	Violin (Concertmaster)	1902–03
Mrs. John Marquardt	Harp	1902–03
Herman Martonne	Violin	1917–20
Gustav Mayer	Battery	1916–23
Henry Mayer, Jr.	Battery	1907–23
Albert Meichelt	Trumpet	1902–04
Nicola Melatti	Violin	1922–24
Emilio Meriz	Violin	1917–18
Herbert G. Mertz	Violin	1919–20
J. Messias	Cello	1901–02
Harry W. Meyer	Violin	1904–15
John A. Meyer	Violin	1900–01
Paul Meyer	Violin	1914–21

HENRY J. MICHAUX	Viola (Principal 1915–17)	1915–25
CHARLES S. MILLER	Violin	1918–19
ROBERT MINSEL	Horn (Principal 1901–02)	1901–04
OSKAR MODESS	Bassoon (Principal)	1900–01
BERNHARD MOLLENHAUER	Violin	1900–01
JOHN W. MOLLOY	Violin	1920–25
ALBERT R. MORET	Violin	1902–20
FRANK S. MORTON	Violin	1906–07
HERMAN MUELLER	Viola and Bassoon	1910–17
	Bassoon	1917–25
MATTHEW J. MUELLER	Violin	1922–25
OTTO MUELLER	Violin	1907–14
		1921–24
C. H. MULLER	Bass	1900–01
G. MUNSCH	Clarinet	1901–02
CHARLTON LEWIS MURPHY	Violin	1900–01
EDWARD MURRAY	Viola	1924–25
LUDWIG NAST	Cello	1902–04
GENNARO M. NAVA	Viola	1922–23
F. A. NICOLETTA	Harp	1923–25
DAVID NOWINSKI	Violin	1906–17
BRAM OBERSTEIN	Cello	1923–24
W. OESTERREICH	Flute and Piccolo	1903–04
MAX OLANOFF	Violin	1918–19
GUSTAV OLK	Viola	1903–04
HUGO OLK	Violin (Principal)	1902–04
SAMUEL OLLSTEIN	Violin	1920–22
GUSTAV PAEPKE	Violin	1902–05
		1922–23
MATYAS PAULI	Bass	1918–23
L. PELLEGRINI	Violin	1919–20
MICHEL PENHA	Cello (Principal)	1920–25
WILLIAM PFANNKUCHEN	Bassoon	1906–07
WALTER PFEIFFER	Violin	1910–19
EARL PFOUTS	Violin (Principal part of season 1911–12)	1911–18
PAUL PIESCHEL	Bassoon (Principal)	1908–09
STEPHEN PILLISCHER	Violin	1924–25
PAUL PITKOWSKY	Violin	1921–25
PAUL PLANERT	Bass	1901–05
BENJAMIN PODEMSKI	Battery	1923–25
ALEXANDER POPOFF	Violin	1923–25
P. POPPERL	Violin	1901–02
M. POTTAG	Horn	1901–02
MILTON PRINZ	Cello	1924–25
KARL QUERENGAESSER	Bass	1901–15
PAUL RAHMIG	Bass (Principal 1901–14)	1901–17
		1919–20
		1924–25
EDWARD RAHO	Oboe	1913–25

Lewis Raho	Oboe	1918–24
Howard F. Rattay	Violin	1905–06
Harold W. Rehrig	Trumpet	1923–25
Joseph Reiter	Horn (Principal)	1900–01
A. Rensch	Oboe	1901–02
Kalman Reve	Violin	1923–24
J. Rhodes	Viola	1901–02
L. M. Rice	Viola	1902–03
Thaddeus Rich	Violin (Concertmaster)	1906–25
Albert Riese	Horn	1904–09
		1910–25
Herman Rietzel	Oboe	1911–13
Albert Ritter	Tympani	1902–03
A. Ritzke	Clarinet	1900–01
August H. Rodemann	Flute (Principal)	1902–07
C. H. Rodenkirchen	Trumpet (Principal 1907–09)	1907–09
		1911–15
Edmond Roelofsma	Clarinet	1902–20
B. Roeschmann	Violin	1900–01
		1903–04
Jean Rogister	Viola	1923–24
Sam Rosen	Viola	1919–20
		1921–25
M. Roth	Violin	1924–25
E. Rozanel	Trumpet	1917–18
R. Rykmans	Bass	1901–02
Alfred Saal	Cello (Principal)	1904–06
Herman Sandby	Cello (Principal)	1902–04
		1908–16
Adolph Sauder	Oboe	1900–01
Herbert F. Saylor	Violin	1904–05
Fritz Schaefer	Viola	1904–05
Julius Scheel	Violin (Principal)	1901–12
Paul Scheele	Viola	1904–15
Reinhold Schewe	Violin	1900–01
		1907–16
K. Schinner	Horn	1901–02
William Schlechtweg	Trombone	1904–15
Hans Schlegel	Flute and Piccolo	1916–25
Alexander Schmidt	Violin	1908–12
Emil Schmidt	Viola	1900–01
Emil F. Schmidt	Violin	1900–01
		1903–04
		1908–23
George Schmidt	Viola	1902–11
Henry Schmidt	Violin	1920–25
Richard Schmidt	Viola (Principal)	1900–01
William A. Schmidt	Cello	1903–04
		1911–12
		1914–25

CHARLES M. SCHMITZ	Cello	1900–01
PHILIPP SCHMITZ	Cello	1903–13
		1919–25
CHARLES F. SCHOENTHAL	Flute (Principal 1900–01)	1900–01
		1909–10
GEROLD SCHON	Cello	1918–20
JOHN G. SCHON	Bassoon	1916–20
GEORGE SCHOTT	Cello	1912–18
FRED SCHRADER	Trombone (Principal)	1904–06
B. SCHREIBMANN	Trumpet	1921–23
B. SCHUCH	Violin	1901–02
EDMUND SCHUËCKER	Harp	1904–09
JOSEPH SCHUËCKER	Harp	1909–11
MAX SCHULZ	Violin	1902–05
RICHARD SCHURIG	Bass (Principal)	1900–02
OSCAR SCHWAR	Tympani	1903–25
MICHEL SCIAPIRO	Violin	1914–15
MAX SELINSKI	Violin	1907–14
FRANK SELTZER	Trumpet	1907–11
ERNEST SERPENTINI	Oboe	1924–25
JULES J. SERPENTINI	Clarinet	1920–25
DAVID SHAIEVITCH	Flute	1905–06
J. BYRON SHANNON	Bass	1920–24
MARCUS SHERBOW	Violin	1900–04
JOSEPH SHERMAN	Violin	1923–25
S. SIANI	Bass	1924–25
ADRIAN SIEGEL	Cello	1922–25
BERNARD SIEGERT	Cello	1920–21
ISRAEL SIEKIERKA	Violin	1924–25
HARRY SILBERMAN	Violin	1917–18
EMILE SIMON	Cello	1907–14
GARDELL SIMONS	Trombone	1915–25
JACOB SIMKIN	Violin	1920–23
		1924–25
J. C. SMALL	Piccolo	1900–01
JOSEF SMIT	Cello	1924–25
ISADOR SOKOLOFF	Cello	1914–18
MAX SOTTNEK	Violin	1909–13
WILLY SPECKIN	Bass	1903–04
		1905–10
ALFRED SPEIL	Violin	1901–03
S. SPOOR	Violin	1919–20
GUSTAV STANGE	Trombone	1902–04
L. STARZINSKY	Viola	1901–02
		1903–10
ROBERT STEIN	Cello	1902–03
BRUNO STEINKE	Cello	1919–20
BRUNO STEYER	Viola	1924–25
KARL STIEGELMAYER	Oboe	1901–10
WALTER H. STOBBE	Battery	1900–01

WILLIAM R. STOBBE	Tympani	1900–01
A. F. STOCKBRIDGE	Violin	1906–07
LEON STOLL	Viola	1900–01
WILLIAM STOLL, JR.	Violin	1900–01
ALFONS STORCH	Violin	1904–06
P. STRAHLENDORF	Violin and Bass Clarinet	1901–02
K. STREUBER	Bass	1901–02
EDWARD A. STRINGER	Violin	1900–01
JACOB STROBLE	Violin	1900–01
JULIUS STURM	Cello	1902–04
MICHAEL SVEDROFSKY	Violin (Concertmaster)	1904–06
MARCEL TABUTEAU	Oboe (Principal)	1915–25
EDUARD TAK	Violin	1905–06
MORRIS TARTAS	Viola	1919–20
ALEXANDER J. THIEDE	Violin	1920–25
ANDREW THOMAS	Tuba	1915–21
HANS TIEDGE	Violin and Battery	1902–17
ANTON TORELLO	Bass (Principal)	1914–25
LUDWIG TREIN	Cello	1900–02
		1903–04
		1907–11
R. UNGER	Cello	1901–02
G. UNGLADA	Violin	1908–12
EMIL URBASH	Flute and Piccolo	1902–03
JAMES VALERIO	Battery	1924–25
F. W. VAN AMBURGH	Clarinet	1912–13
HEDDA VAN DEN BEEMT	Violin (Principal 1906–07)	1901–07
		1911–20
	Celesta	1920–24
AUGUST VAN LEUWEN	Flute	1901–02
ISRAEL S. VAN SCIVER	Battery	1900–01
ALBERT VAN STRATUM	Violin	1905–06
AMÉDÉE VERGNAUD	Viola	1924–25
ROMAIN VERNEY	Viola (Principal)	1920–25
A. VILLANI	Bass	1922–23
ADOLPH VOGEL	Cello	1921–25
J. VOGEL	Trombone	1901–02
HENRY F. VOLMER	Viola	1900–01
LOUIS VOLMER	Cello	1900–01
ERNST WAGNER	Trombone	1901–04
FREDERICK E. WAGNER	Trumpet (Principal 1900–01)	1900–01
		1917–21
JOSEF WALDMAN	Violin	1912–16
ROBERT WALTER	Violin	1903–06
HENRY WARNER	Violin	1900–02
EMIL WASCHEK	Viola	1905–06
FRANK S. WATSON	Cello	1918–25
NELSON J. WATSON	Bass	1923–24
HERMAN WEINBERG	Violin	1919–25
KARL WEINELT	Horn	1904–05

H. Weissenborn	Clarinet	1900–01
William Welker	Violin	1900–01
Daniel R. Wells	Viola	1900–02
William M. Wells	Cello	1900–04
M. F. Wenning	Violin and Bassoon	1901–03
Charles R. Wenzel	Cello	1904–06
Florenz Werner	Violin	1901–03
L. Wertheim	Viola (Principal)	1901–02
Carl Whitaker	Bass	1900–01
G. Wicking	Violin	1902–03
Heinrich Wiemann	Bass	1924–25
Ernest S. Williams	Trumpet	1917–23
Benjamin H. Winterstein	Violin	1916–18
Florian Wittman	Viola	1922–23
H. Wittmann	Bass	1900–01
John K. Witzemann	Violin	1900–17
M. Wollenberg	Bass	1906–07
John Wulf	Bass	1907–19
G. Zapp	Violin	1901–02
Karl W. Zeise	Cello	1922–24
Leon Zeitzew	Violin	1920–21
Alexander Zenker	Violin	1916–25
Paul Zierold	Cello	1905–07
L. Ziporkin	Bass	1917–19
Albert Zoellner	Horn	1900–01

NOTE—This list includes only those men who completed a season's work.

Philadelphia Orchestra Chorus*
December 1920
First Sopranos

Mrs. G. W. Anderson '19
Mrs. Annabel I. Bell '19
Miss Mildred S. Benners '20
Miss Helen G. Blakely '19
Mrs. Mildred S. Cascaden '19
Miss Blanche E. Cascaden '19
Miss Mildred Castor '20
Miss Diana A. Cauffman '19
Mrs. M. Christie '15
Mrs. P. Benson Collard '19
Miss Gertrude Ely '15
Mrs. H. B. Ewing '15
Mrs. Pearl M. Gilday '20
Mrs. Robert C. Glenn '19
Miss Winfrey Glenn '19
Mrs. Harold Greene '20
Miss Naomi V. Grobe '20
Mrs. Harold H. Happold '20
Miss Agnes M. Higbee '16

Miss Clara L. Holden '15
Miss H. G. Hullstrung '20
Mrs. Gertrude M. Jones '20
Mrs. A. H. Koehl '20
Mrs. H. C. Kressly '19
Mrs. Milton Kutz '19
Miss Etta C. LeVine '20
Miss Helen B. Lewis '15
Mrs. Howard McMorris '20
Miss Irma F. Maldonado '20
Miss Sophia Maleson '19
Miss Grace E. Mahorter '20
Miss M. Eliz. Morrison '19
Miss Clara A. Nagel '19
Miss Anna L. Neil '15
Miss Ida H. Oetter '16
Miss Dorothy E. Pierce '19
Miss Elizabeth Powers '20
Miss Marian M. Riddle '19

*NOTE—Figures following names denote year of admission.

Miss Ethel K. Ridge '20
Miss Alva Sergeant '14
Mrs. Albert E. Seymour '20
Mrs. Mable T. Shick '20
Mrs. Philip Sterling '20
Miss Emma L. Stratton '19
Mrs. M. L. Sutton '20

Mrs. Lilian S. Toudy '20
Miss Volita Wells '19
Mrs. M. N. Williamson '20
Miss Freeda Wolley '19
Miss Josephine E. Zwick '19
Miss A. Elise Hartman '19
Miss Margaret S. Lewis '15

Second Sopranos

Mrs. Gilbert P. Albrecht '15
Miss Faye Atkinson '19
Miss Caroline Austin '20
Miss Helen M. Batten '14
Miss Amella E. Bein '14
Miss Mildred E. Cascaden '20
Mrs. Grace Colgan '20
Miss Marion W. Eisenhart '20
Miss Theo R. Eldredge '19
Mrs. Ruth F. Eliasson '19
Miss Mary Dale Hackett '14
Miss Elsie M. Hauck '19
Miss Marie L. Henry '20
Miss Geordie P. Joline '15
Mrs. Albert G. Kleefeld '15
Miss Kath. W. McCollin '16
Miss Edith M. Miller '20

Miss Jean P. Mumford '19
Mrs. R. S. B. Perry '19
Miss Helen C. Philips '19
Miss Joanna L. Potter '14
Miss Emma M. Rea '19
Miss Elsie G. Rodgers '15
Miss E. A. Rossmassler '15
Miss Bernice Russell '19
Miss Louise P. Schwarz '14
Miss C. Evelyn Smith '15
Miss Marguerite D. Smith '19
Miss Phoebe Hart Smith '19
Miss Helen R. Snyder '19
Miss Milava Stankowitch '14
Mrs. John B. Thayer, 3rd '16
Mrs. Anna M. Wilt '19
Miss Helen B. Wineland '15

First Altos

Miss Olive I. Berry '14
Miss Ada Bess '20
Miss J. R. Bonniwell '19
Miss Joyce Bowers '19
Miss Helen I. Chambers '19
Miss Frances B. Codling '20
Miss May Coldran '20
Miss Anna E. Ellwanger '15
Miss Adele L. Fox '16
Miss Anne Geyer '19
Miss Creda Glenn '19
Miss K. Marie Good '15
Miss Margaret Greaves '20
Miss Flora E. Gruning '20
Miss Marion W. Gushee '20
Miss Marguerite E. Ingram '15

Miss Clara A. Jewell '19
Miss Elizabeth K. Jones '15
Miss Eliza Kannegieser '15
Miss Helen R. Kern '19
Miss Mildred E. Locke '15
Miss Morton J. Meyers '14
Miss Margaret Montgomery '19
Miss Sarieta M. Renton '15
Mrs. E. M. Reynolds '20
Miss Clara L. Ristine '15
Mrs. R. J. Robinson '19
Miss Caroline L. Rothman '20
Miss Pauline C. Rumpp '15
Mrs. Leopold Seyffert '16
Miss Lydia P. Wise '15
Miss Olive Wolf '16

Mrs. David J. Wright '20

Second Altos

Miss Marie M. Barr '14
Mrs. Joseph M. Beckett '19
Miss Edith M. Boyd '14

Miss Florence H. Burk '19
Miss Ada V. Clouden '14
Miss Anna Cohn '15

Note—Figures following names denote year of admission.

Miss Susie J. Dailey '15
Miss F. Edna Davis '15
Miss F. Carolyn Deaver '19
Miss M. P. Euchelberger '19
Mrs. Charles W. Foust '15
Miss Irene F. Goenner '16
Miss Alma L. Kellmer '20
Miss Roberta Laird '15
Mrs. John H. McCracken '14
Mrs. Ida A. McGirr '20
Mrs. Harry A. Mackey '15

Mrs. Maurice Markley '16
Miss Annetta R. Masland '20
Miss Georgia P. Palmer '15
Miss Mary M. Pearson '19
Mrs. William Pollock '19
Miss Ray Rawlings '20
Miss Ethel H. Stewart '14
Miss Helen A. Straughn '15
Miss Alma M. Tegge '19
Miss Jane Whitehead '19
Miss E. May Williamson '14

First Tenors

Mr. Gilbert P. Albrecht '14
Mr. A. W. Allen '20
Mr. Donald G. Baird '20
Mr. Henry W. Clavier, Jr. '15
Mr. Alan C. Cunningham '15
Mr. Robert Dewar '20
Mr. Charles E. Frew '15
Mr. Josephus J. Frost '15
Mr. Alfred H. Gonzales '15
Mr. Arthur G. Graham, Jr. '19
Mr. Henry K. Hollinger '20

Mr. J. Mitchell Hooper '19
Mr. Chas. A. Hunsberger '14
Mr. William Jamison '15
Mr. Adolph Mehnen '15
Mr. Samuel Albert Nook '20
Mr. George D. Phillips '20
Mr. Benjamin W. Price '15
Mr. Harold C. Rawley '14
Mr. Albert E. Seymour '14
Mr. Geo. H. Staniforth '15
Mr. Elmer E. Traub '15

Mr. J. Henry Warren '19

Second Tenors

Mr. John E. Abnett, Jr. '19
Mr. Adolf Balod '20
Mr. Jos. K. Bartholomew '15
Mr. Edwin S. Bartlett '14
Dr. Charles A. Behney '20
Mr. John W. Culp '20
Mr. Edw. W. Dietsch '20
Mr. C. Seymour Evans '15
Mr. L. J. Finnan, Jr. '16
Mr. Wm. D. Hamill '15

Mr. Wm. Lloyd Harding '19
Mr. Eugene Muller '16
Mr. Thomas Nelson, Jr. '20
Mr. Adam H. Patterson '19
Mr. William Pollock '15
Mr. J. R. Satterthwaite '19
Mr. Reese R. Smith '20
Mr. Alexander Stewart '20
Mr. Allan F. Titus '20
Mr. George R. Tyson '19

First Bassos

Mr. H. Carl Albrecht '14
Mr. Charles A. Bjorklund '19
Mr. George P. Boggs '20
Mr. Raymond T. Bohn '20
Mr. Albert W. Braeuninger '15
Mr. John A. Brook '20
Mr. Henry T. Denby '20
Mr. Bertram F. Everit '15
Mr. Wm. H. Faville '19
Mr. R. H. Fleming '14

Mr. George S. Gengenbach '
Mr. Robert C. Glenn '15
Mr. Jas. B. Greenwood '20
Mr. J. Courtland Hamer '15
Mr. Raymond E. Hess '20
Mr. W. Chester Hill '20
Mr. Edward E. Hipscher '20
Mr. Alvah H. Koehl '20
Mr. Frederick Landstreet '1
Mr. Eugene Maes '19

NOTE—Figures following names denote year of admission.

[214]

Mr. William Millham '15
Mr. Hugh R. Parrish '19
Mr. Francis H. Rockett '20
Mr. Wm. J. Searle, Jr. '20
Mr. Howard F. Story '20

Mr. Richard M. Sutton '19
Mr. Arthur Synnestvedt '15
Mr. Frank B. Titus '20
Mr. Edward L. Wallace '20
Mr. Bernard G. Wise, Jr. '20

Mr. William Zimmermann '19

Second Bassos

Mr. Jas. H. W. Althouse '15
Mr. John H. Arnett '20
Mr. Harry Broese '15
Mr. Clinton M. Christine '15
Mr. A. P. Chute '14
Mr. Stephen T. Conway '20
Mr. W. R. Crawford '20
Mr. F. H. Eaton '20
Mr. C. L. Farraday '15
Mr. Frank A. Hartranft '14
Mr. William C. Hess '20
Mr. Harry K. Kirk '16

Dr. Eugene K. Krause '16
Mr. Wm. McGowan, Jr. '20
Mr. Ray Miller '20
Mr. Carl F. Rumpp '19
Mr. Oliver F. Saylor '19
Mr. Dennis Sosnowski '19
Mr. Milton B. Stallman '16
Mr. Hubert Synnestvedt '16
Mr. Geo. B. Whidden '14
Mr. Frank J. Williams '20
Mr. Frank D. Witherbee '19
Mr. J. C. Wrenshall, Jr. '19

Note—Figures following names denote year of admission.

Managers of the Philadelphia Orchestra
1900–1925

Oliver Boyce Judson, 1901–02
George P. Eckels, 1902–03
John Mahnken, 1903–04, 1904–05
Ernest J. Lanigan, 1905–06
Charles Augustus Davis, 1906–07 to 1909–10
Harvey M. Watts, 1911–12, 1912–13
Ralph Edmunds, 1913–14, 1914–15
Arthur Judson, 1915–16
Horace Churchman, 1910–11, Controller

Office Staff
1925

Arthur Judson, 1915
Louis A. Mattson, 1907
Elizabeth M. Russell, 1917
Margaret E. Pringle, 1916
Mary A. McGinty, 1917
Ruth M. O'Neill, 1910

Appendix G

Assistant Conductors
Guest Conductors
Organizations That Have Appeared With the Philadelphia
Orchestra
Soloists Who Have Appeared With the Philadelphia Orchestra

Assistant Conductors

A. H. Rodemann, 1907: Philadelphia, February 15–16, conducte
regular concerts during Scheel's illness.

Thaddeus Rich, 1914: Assistant Conductor, Kensington, Philade
phia, April 8; November 5–6, 1915, entire programme with exceptio
Schoenberg's Kammer-symphonie; November 9, 1915, Stetson conce
Norristown, January 11, 1916; Philadelphia regular concerts, Janua
28–29, 1916; Philadelphia Girls' High School, January 31, 1916; La
caster, Pa., February 1, 1916; Easton, Pa., February 17, 1916; Readin
Pa., February 22, 1916; University of Pennsylvania, February 24, 191
Boys' Central High School, March 7, 1916; Germantown High Schoo
March 30, 1916; Frankford High School, April 13, 1916; Stetson Co
cert, January 9, 1917; Atlantic City, N. J., January 22, 1917; Readin
Pa., February 20, 1917; University of Pennsylvania, February 21, 191
Stetson Concert, November 7, 1917; Pittsburgh, Pa., February 11, 191
Oberlin, Ohio, February 13, 1918; Philadelphia, December 28, 191
Toronto, February 22, 1919; Philadelphia, March 21–22, 28–29, Apr
12–15–16, 1919; Stetson, March 25, 1919; Wilmington, March 24, 191
Stetson, November 15, 1921; University of Pennsylvania, January 1
1922; Philadelphia regular concerts, January 20–21, 1922; University c
Pennsylvania, February 8, 1922; University of Pennsylvania, March
1922; University of Pennsylvania, March 22, 1922; Pittsburgh, Nover
ber 10, 1922, January 13, 1923, and March 23, 1923, conducted Chi
dren's concerts; Stetson, November 14, 1922; Harrisburg, March 2
1923; Pittsburgh, March 23, 1923; Philadelphia regular concerts, Ja
uary 19–20, 1923; Philadelphia regular concerts, January 11–12, 192
Princeton, March 18, 1924; Philadelphia regular concerts, January 2
24, 1925; Princeton, March 2, 1925.

Guest Conductors

Ernest Bloch, 1918: Philadelphia, January 25–26, conducted pr
gramme of his own works.

Leandro Campanari, 1907: Philadelphia, February 22–23, Marc
1–2; Harrisburg, February 19; Trenton, February 21; Reading, Februar
25; Washington, February 26; Baltimore, February 27, during Scheel'
illness.

Alfredo Casella, 1921: Philadelphia, October 28–29, conducted hi
own "Pages of War."

ALPHONSE CATHERINE, 1919: Philadelphia, January 31–February 1, conducted entire programme.

FRANK GUERNSEY CAUFFMAN, 1909: Philadelphia, March 5–6, conducted his own "Legende."

GEORGE W. CHADWICK, 1911: Philadelphia, March 29, conducted his own Suite Symphonique at National Federation of Musical Clubs Concert.

VINCENT D'INDY, 1922: Philadelphia, January 6–7; Princeton, January 9; Washington, January 10; Baltimore, January 11; Harrisburg, January 12; Pittsburgh, January 13–14, conducted entire programme.

GEORGES ENESCO, 1923: New York, January 2; Philadelphia, January 5–6; Washington, January 9; Baltimore, January 10; Harrisburg, January 11; Pittsburgh, January 12–13; Pottsville, January 17, conducted entire programme.

OSSIP GABRILOWITSCH, 1920: Philadelphia, April 3–5, conducted entire programme.

PHILIP H. GOEPP, 1909: Philadelphia, March 5–6, conducted his own Academic March; February 1, 1911, conducted his own Wedding March; April 2, 1913, conducted his own Wedding March, one number by Wm. Gerstley and one by H. Pfitzner—all Philadelphia.

SAMUEL GARDNER, 1919: Philadelphia, October 24–25, conducted his own "New Russia."

HENRY HADLEY, 1910: Philadelphia, November 25–26, conducted his own "Culprit Fay"; New York, March 9, 1920, conducted his own overture, "Othello."

VICTOR HERBERT, 1912: Philadelphia, February 16–17, conducted the prelude to Act III of his own "Natoma."

HENRY ALBERT LANG, 1911: Philadelphia, March 1, conducted his own Fantastic Dances (Popular Concert); Philadelphia, April 2, 1913, conducted his "Fantasies of a Poet" (Manuscript Music Society Concert).

WASSILI LEPS, 1908: Philadelphia, February 21–22, conducted entire Programme on account Pohlig's injuries from railroad accident; also Philadelphia, March 13–14, 1908, and March 5–6, 1909, conducted his own "In the Garden of the Gods"; Philadelphia, February 15, 1911 (Popular Concert), conducted Clarence Bawden's "Ballade" for Piano; Wilmington, February 5, 1912, conducted entire Wagner programme; Philadelphia, April 2, 1913 (Manuscript Music Society Concert), conducted his own aria for soprano and orchestra, "Nirvana."

WILLEM MENGELBERG, 1921: Philadelphia, March 18–19, conducted entire programme.

DARIUS MILHAUD, 1923: Philadelphia, January 26–27, conducted entire programme.

OTTO MUELLER, 1913: Philadelphia, April 2, conducted his own Symphonic poem "Atlantis," at Manuscript Music Society Concert.

HORATIO PARKER, 1911: Philadelphia, March 29, conducted his own aria "Crépuscule," at National Federation of Musical Clubs Concert.

SERGEI RACHMANINOFF, 1909: Philadelphia, November 26–27, conducted his own Symphony in E minor and Moussorgsky's fantasy, "Une nuit sur le mont chauve"; also played group piano soli.

HERMAN SANDBY, 1915: Philadelphia, February 19–20, conducted his own orchestral suite, "The Woman and the Fiddler."

[217]

CYRIL SCOTT, 1920: Philadelphia, November 5–6, conducted his own "Two Passacaglias for Orchestra."

FREDERICK STOCK, 1924: Philadelphia, January 18–19–21; Washington, January 22; Baltimore, January 23, conducted entire programme.

RICHARD STRAUSS, 1904: Philadelphia, March 4–5; Boston, March 7–8; conducted "Tod und Verklärung," "Till Eulenspiegel," also a group of his own songs; Philadelphia, November 30, 1921; New York, October 31, 1921; November 15, 1921, December 13, 1921, December 27, 1921; Philadelphia, December 23–24, 1921, conducted entire programme.

IGOR STRAWINSKY, 1925: Philadelphia, January 30–31, conducted entire programme of own works.

GUSTAV STRUBE, 1915: Philadelphia, December 31-January 1, 1916, conducted his own "Variations on an Original Theme."

HEDDA VAN DEN BEEMT, 1913: Philadelphia, Manuscript Music Society Concert, April 2, conducted his own "Introduction and Scene" for orchestra, "Aucassin et Nicolette"; Philadelphia, April 3–4, 1914, conducted same composition.

WILLEM VAN HOOGSTRATEN, 1925: Philadelphia, January 16–17–19; Washington, January 20; Baltimore, January 21, conducted entire programme.

LOUIS VON GAERTNER, 1910: Philadelphia, December 22–23, conducted his own Tone Poem, "Macbeth."

FELIX WEINGARTNER, 1905: Philadelphia, February 16, conducted entire programme—special concert.

CAMILLE ZECKWER, 1916: Philadelphia, February 4–5, conducted his own "Sohrab and Rustum."

ORGANIZATIONS WHICH HAVE APPEARED WITH
THE PHILADELPHIA ORCHESTRA

BACH CHOIR OF BALTIMORE (1907), Baltimore.

EURYDICE CHORUS OF PHILADELPHIA (1908, 1912).

FORTNIGHTLY CLUB OF PHILADELPHIA (1908, 1916).

BEN GREET PLAYERS (1909).

JUNGER MAENNERCHOR SINGING SOCIETY OF PHILADELPHIA (1914).

MENDELSSOHN CHOIR OF TORONTO (1924), Philadelphia.

MENDELSSOHN CLUB OF PHILADELPHIA (1903, 1904, 1907, 1911, 1913, 1914, 1916, 1919).

PHILADELPHIA ORCHESTRA CHORUS (1916, 1917, 1919, 1920, 1921).

PITTSBURGH CHORUS, trained by Charles Heinroth (1921), Pittsburgh.

SCHOLA CANTORUM OF NEW YORK (1919), New York.

Organizations participating in the Lobgesang Symphony:

CANTAVES CHORUS, EURYDICE CHORUS, FELLOWSHIP CLUB, FORTNIGHTLY CLUB, GERMANTOWN CHORAL SOCIETY, HAYDN CLUB, JUNGER MANNERCHOR, LYRIC CLUB, MATINEE MUSICAL CLUB, MENDELSSOHN CLUB, ORPHEUS CLUB, PHILADELPHIA CHORAL SOCIETY, STRAWBRIDGE AND CLOTHIER CHORAL SOCIETY, TREBLE CLEF CLUB, VOCAL ART SOCIETY, WANAMAKER CHORAL SOCIETY.

Outside organizations participating in the performance of Bach's "St. Matthew Passion":

GIRLS' NORMAL SCHOOL and GIRLS' HIGH SCHOOL CHORUSES.

Philip Abbas	Cellist	1917
Mabelle Addison	Contralto	1914, 1915
Frances Alda	Soprano	1914
Perley Dunn Aldrich	Baritone	1910
Merle Alcock	Contralto	1921
Paul Alemann	Bass Clarinet	1923
Ethel Altemus	Pianist	1907, 1911, 1916
Paul Althouse	Tenor	1916
Horace Alwyne	Pianist	1924
Pasquale Amato	Baritone	1910
Rufus M. Arey	Clarinetist	1924
Robert Armbruster	Pianist	1912, 1916
Pepito Arriola	Pianist	1910
Adele Aus Der Ohe	Pianist	1903
Cecile Ayres	Pianist	1914
Wilhelm Bachaus	Pianist	1912, 1914, 1923
Della Baker	Soprano	1920
Inez Barbour	Soprano	1916, 1921
John Barclay	Baritone	1921, 1922, 1924
Louise Barnolt	Contralto	1911
Mary Barrett	Soprano	1915, 1918, 1919
Vera Barstow	Violinist	1916
Georgia Richardson Baskerville	Pianist	1915
Harold Bauer	Pianist	1902, 1908, 1914, 1916, 1917, 1918, 1919, 1920, 1922
Edna Harwood Baugher	Soprano	1912
Clarence Bawden	Pianist	1910, 1911
Dan Beddoe	Tenor	1915
Wassily Besekirsky	Violinist	1915, 1916
Louis Bailly	Viola	1921
David Bispham	Baritone	1903, 1904, 1911, 1921
Lillian Blauvelt	Soprano	1900, 1903, 1904
Fannie Bloomfield Zeisler	Pianist	1902, 1903, 1904, 1907, 1908, 1915, 1916
Edith Wells Bly	Pianist	1910, 1916
Giuseppe Boghetti	Tenor	1915
Edward Bonhote	Baritone	1910
Elizabeth Bonner	Contralto	1919, 1923
Leonard Borwick	Pianist	1914
Rosario Bourdon	Cellist	1907
Domenico Bove	Violinist	1916
Sophie Braslau	Contralto	1915
John F. Braun	Tenor	1902, 1908, 1911, 1914, 1915
Robert Braun	Pianist	1915
Elizabeth Pritchard Brey	Soprano	1922
Bertha Brinker	Soprano	1912
Horace Britt	Cellist	1907, 1908
Viola Brodbeck	Soprano	1913, 1915

EDDY BROWN	Violinist	1918, 1920
HELEN BUCHANAN	Soprano	1914, 1915, 1919
RICHARD BUHLIG	Pianist	1907, 1908
MRS. JOSEPH BUNTING	Soprano	1904
ALOYS BURGSTALLER	Tenor	1903
TOM BURKE	Tenor	1922
RICHARD BURMEISTER	Pianist	1902
FERRUCCIO BUSONI	Pianist	1911, 1915
MME. CHARLES CAHIER	Contralto	1922
GIUSEPPE CAMPANARI	Baritone	1905, 1908
TERESA CARRENO	Pianist 1901, 1908, 1909, 1913, 1914	
PABLO CASALS	Cellist	1915, 1918, 1920
ANNA CASE	Soprano	1911, 1917
MARIE CASLOVA	Violinist	1916
ALFREDO CASELLA	Pianist	1921, 1923
CECILE CHAMINADE	Pianist	1908
KITTY CHEATHAM	Interpreter of Children's Songs	1913, 1914
WALTER CLAPPERTON	Basso	1922
JULIA CLAUSSEN	Mezzo-Soprano	1918
ACHILLE COCOZZA	Violinist	1910
DAVID COHEN	Violinist	1917
SOL COHEN	Trumpet	1923, 1925
FRANK M. CONLY	Basso	1911
HORATIO CONNELL	Bass-Baritone	1912, 1914, 1917
LUTHER CONRADI	Pianist	1908
EMILIA CONTI	Soprano	1914
ELSA LYONS COOK	Soprano	1915, 1917, 1919
CARLTON COOLEY	Violinist	1921
	Winner of Stokowski Medal	
ALBERT CORNFELD	Violinist	1915
ALFRED CORTOT	Pianist 1918, 1920, 1922, 1925	
CHARLES M. COURBOIN	Organist	1922
MARCELLA CRAFT	Soprano	1916
JULIA CULP	Lieder Singer	1914, 1916
CLAUDE CUNNINGHAM	Baritone	1906
ROYAL DADMUN	Baritone	1920, 1921
EUGENE D'ALBERT	Pianist	1905
MARGUERITE D'ALVAREZ	Contralto	1922
MURRAY DAVEY	Basso	1912
REBECCA DAVIDSON	Pianist	1917
ELEANORE DE CISNEROS	Mezzo-Soprano	1908
EMILIO DE GOGORZA	Baritone	1907, 1915, 1916
JOSE DELAQUERRIERE	Tenor	1924
F. DEL NEGRO	Bassoon	1923, 1924
MARY HISSEM DE MOSS	Soprano	1908
VLADIMIR DE PACHMANN	Pianist	1904, 1907, 1911
SUSANNA DERCUM	Contralto	1915, 1916
EMMY DESTINN	Soprano	1915
MINA DOLORES	Soprano	1923

P. Donatelli	Tuba	1923
Alfred Doucet	Oboe	1910
Nicholas Douty	Tenor	1905, 1907, 1914, 1918
Vladimir Dubinsky	Cellist	1907
Marcel Dupre	Organist	1922
Claire Dux	Soprano	1922
W. B. Ebann	Cellist	1902
Mischa Elman	Violinist	1909, 1912, 1913, 1914, 1915, 1916, 1917
Myrtle Elvyn	Pianist	1914
Georges Enesco	Violinist	1923, 1924
Edwin Evans	Baritone	1915, 1919
Mildred Faas	Soprano	1914, 1915, 1919
Jules Falk	Violinist	1910
Vincent Fanelli, Jr.	Harpist	1914, 1923
Frank L. Farrell	Pianist	1914
Geraldine Farrar	Soprano	1919
Maude Fay	Soprano	1916
Idette Feinman	Pianist	1917, 1922
Mrs. Logan Feland	Soprano	1913
Emile Ferir	Viola	1918
Alice Fidler	Contralto	1918, 1919, 1920
Adelaide Fischer	Soprano	1916
John A. Fischer	Flutist	1922, 1923, 1925
Carl Flesch	Violinist	1914, 1923, 1925
Felix Fox	Pianist	1903
Mary Woodfield Fox	Pianist	1911
Cornelius Franke	Violinist	1902
Olive Fremstad	Soprano	1917, 1918
Carl Friedberg	Pianist	1917
Blanche Friedmann	Soprano	1911
Mme. Povla Frijsh	Soprano	1918, 1919
Rudolf Friml	Pianist	1905
Clarence Fuhrman	Pianist	1915
Ossip Gabrilowitsch	Pianist	1900, 1902, 1907, 1915, 1916, 1917, 1918, 1919, 1920, 1923
Johanna Gadski	Soprano	1905, 1906, 1907, 1908, 1915
Rudolph Ganz	Pianist	1913, 1920
Samuel Gardner	Violinist	1919
Mabel Garrison	Soprano	1916, 1917, 1924
Edith L. Gastel	Soprano	1912
Lucy Gates	Soprano	1916
Eva Gauthier	Mezzo-Soprano	1922
Elena Gerhardt	Soprano Lieder Singer	1913, 1915, 1916, 1917, 1921, 1922
Jean Gerardy	Cellist	1901, 1905, 1922
Jeanne Gerville-Réache	Contralto	1912, 1913
Dinh Gilly	Baritone	1913
Frank Gittelson	Violinist	1914, 1916
Thelma Given	Violinist	1920

ALMA GLÜCK	Soprano	1910, 1911, 1914, 1915, 1916
LEOPOLD GODOWSKY	Pianist	1912, 1916
DOROTHY GOLDSMITH	Pianist	1912, 1917
EFFIE LELAND GOLZ	Violinist	1915
KATHARINE GOODSON	Pianist	1908, 1909, 1913, 1914, 1920
PERCY GRAINGER	Pianist	1916
MRS. WILLIAM HOUSTON GREENE	Soprano	1911, 1913
CHARLES GREGOROWITSCH	Violinist	1901
HERMANN GREVESMUHL	Violinist	1903
DAVID GRIFFIN	Baritone	1915
BONARIOS GRIMSON	Violinist	1913
GEORGES GRISEZ	Clarinet	1923
MAUD GROVE	Contralto	1910
WALTER GUETTER	Bassoon	1923, 1925
HENRY GURNEY	Tenor	1915
ARTHUR HACKETT	Tenor	1920, 1923
EMILY STOKES HAGAR	Soprano	1915
MARGUERITE HALL	Contralto	1904
MARIE HALL	Violinist	1905
MARK HAMBOURG	Pianist	1902, 1907
RACHEL HAMILTON	Soprano	1917
VAHRAH HANBURY	Soprano	1920
ELSIE STEWART HAND	Pianist	1903
HAROLD HANSEN	Tenor	1924
THEODORE HARRISON	Baritone	1914, 1915
ARTHUR HARTMANN	Violinist	1906
SUE HARVARD	Soprano	1913
HUGO HEERMANN	Violinist	1905
JASCHA HEIFETZ	Violinist	1918
ALEXANDER HEINEMANN	Baritone and Lieder Singer	1912
ANTON HEKKING	Cellist	1907
OTTO HENNEBERG	Horn	1923
RUDOLPH HENNIG	Cellist	1901
MYRA HESS	Pianist	1922
FLORENCE HINKLE	Soprano	1910, 1911, 1912, 1913, 1914, 1915, 1916, 1917, 1920, 1921, 1922
ALLEN C. HINCKLEY	Basso	1909
JOSEF HOFMANN	Pianist	1901, 1902, 1904, 1907, 1913, 1915, 1917, 1918, 1919, 1922, 1923, 1924
LOUISE HOMER	Contralto	1905, 1908, 1913, 1914
HORACE R. HOOD	Baritone	1913
ANTON HORNER	Horn	1923
JOSEPH HORNER	Horn	1923
HENRY HOTZ	Basso	1918
MAE HOTZ	Soprano	1917, 1919
BRONISLAW HUBERMAN	Violinist	1922, 1923
CAROLINE HUDSON-ALEXANDER	Soprano	1914
ESTELLE HUGHES	Soprano	1919, 1920

Winner of Stokowski Medal

Elsa Alves Hunter	Soprano	1920
Ernest Hutcheson	Pianist 1906, 1908, 1910, 1915, 1921	
Maria Ivogun	Soprano	1922
Sascha Jacobinoff	Violinist	1917, 1918
Rafael Joseffy	Pianist	1904
Clara Yocum Joyce	Contralto	1913
Franceska Kaspar-Lawson	Soprano 1908, 1909, 1911, 1912	
Albert Kastner	Harpist	1901
Emily Stuart Kellogg	Contralto	1907
Grace Kerns	Soprano	1913
Margaret Keyes	Contralto 1911, 1914, 1916, 1917	
W. M. Kincaid	Flutist 1922, 1923, 1924, 1925	
Hans Kindler	Cellist 1915, 1916, 1917, 1918, 1919, 1921, 1922, 1923, 1924, 1925	
Karl Klein	Violinist	1907
Charles E. Knauss	Pianist 1905, 1906, 1907, 1911, 1913	
Paul Kochanski	Violinist 1921, 1923, 1924	
Tilly Koenen	Contralto and Lieder Singer	1910, 1916
Augusta Kohnle	Contralto	1913
Benjamin Kohon	Bassoon	1914
Nina Koshetz	Soprano 1922, 1923, 1924	
Elkan Kosman	Violinist 1901, 1902	
Fritz Kreisler	Violinist 1901, 1902, 1905, 1907, 1908, 1910, 1913, 1915, 1917, 1920, 1921	
Richard Krueger	Bassoon	1920
Joseph La Monaca	Flutist	1925
Frederic Lamond	Pianist	1924
Wanda Landowska	Pianist and Harpsichordist	1923, 1924
Edward Lane	Pianist	1922

Winner of Stokowski Medal

Marie Stone Langston	Mezzo-Soprano 1911, 1913, 1914	
Edward Lankow	Baritone	1920
Francis Lapitino	Harpist	1911, 1912
Earle Laros	Pianist	1914, 1916
Florence Larrabee	Pianist	1915
Hulda Lashanska	Soprano	1921, 1924
Roberta Lee	Soprano	1919
Maurits Leefson	Pianist	1907
Alfred Lennartz	Cellist and Organist	1915
Wassili Leps	Pianist	1908, 1910, 1911, 1912
Emilie Fricke Lesher	Pianist	1922
Mischa Levitzki	Pianist	1921
Josef Lhevinne	Pianist	1907, 1909
Josef and Rosina Lhevinne	Pianists	1922
James Liebling	Cellist	1914
Albert Lindquest	Tenor	1917

HUBERT LINSCOTT	Basso	1924
S. H. LIPSCHUETZ	Basso	1912, 1913
CARLO LITEN	Dramatic Reader	1918
ALFRED LORENZ	Violinist	1904
WALDEMAR LUTSCHG	Pianist	1905
MADELEINE McGUIGAN	Violinist	1915, 1916, 1917
J. CAMPBELL McINNES	Baritone	1920
MARGARET McMULLIN	Soprano	1919
GUY MAIER	Pianist	
	(with Lee Pattison)	1924, 1925
ANDRÉ MAQUARRE	Flutist	1919, 1920, 1921
DANIEL MAQUARRE	Flutist	1911, 1912, 1913, 1914,
		1915, 1916, 1918
MARVINE MAAZEL	Pianist	1920
EDWARD MACDOWELL	Pianist	1901
WILL C. MACFARLANE	Organist	1917
C. STANLEY MACKEY	Tuba	1914
FRANCIS MACMILLEN	Violinist	1911
HELEN MACNAMEE-BENTZ	Soprano	1911, 1913, 1914, 1915
CHARLOTTE MACONDA	Soprano	1903
JOHN MARQUARDT	Violinist	1903
MRS. JOHN MARQUARDT	Harpist	1903
HELENA MARSH	Contralto	1923
HENRI MARTEAU	Violinist	1906
FREDERIC MARTIN	Basso	1907
GURNEY MATTOX	Violinist	1915
MARGARET MATZENAUER	Contralto	1917, 1918, 1919,
		1920, 1921
GEORGE MEADER	Tenor	1921
NICHOLAS MEDTNER	Pianist	1924
ELSA MEISKEY	Soprano	1917
KATHRYN MEISLE	Contralto	1918
YOLANDA MERÖ	Pianist	1911, 1913, 1916,
		1921, 1924
CAROLINE MIHR-HARDY	Soprano	1904, 1905
GWILYN MILES	Baritone	1901
LETITIA RADCLIFFE MILLER	Pianist	1916
SELDEN MILLER	Pianist and Organist	1905, 1906
MARGARET ASHMEAD MITCHELL	Soprano	1915
BENNO MOISEIWITSCH	Pianist	1919, 1923
GRISHA MONASEVITCH	Violinist	1924
	Winner of Stokowski Medal	
RUTH MONTAGUE	Mezzo-Soprano	1923
	Winner of Stokowski Medal	
EDWARD MUMMA MORRIS	Pianist	1914, 1915
LAMBERT MURPHY	Tenor	1916, 1917, 1920
MARGUERITE NAMARA-TOYE	Soprano	1912
HAROLD NASON	Pianist	1907
AGNES THOMSON NEELY	Soprano	1906
OTTO NEITZEL	Pianist	1906, 1907
ANNA NEWHOFF	Pianist	1920

Frank A. Nicoletta	Harpist	1923
Mitja Nikisch	Pianist	1924
Elsie North	Soprano	1911
Guiomar Novaes	Pianist	1917, 1921
Margarete Ober	Soprano	1915
Hugo Olk	Violinist	1902, 1903
Sigrid Onegin	Contralto	1922
Leo Ornstein	Pianist	1919, 1921, 1925
Anna Otten	Violinist	1902
Ignace Jan Paderewski	Pianist	1914
William H. Pagdin	Tenor	1908
Kathleen Parlow	Violinist	1911, 1916, 1921
Lee Pattison	Pianist	
	(with Guy Maier)	1924, 1925
Frederick Patton	Basso	1920
Michel Penha	Cellist 1920, 1921, 1922, 1923, 1924	
Louis Persinger	Violinist	1912
Alexander Petschnikoff	Violinist	1906, 1908
May Peterson	Soprano	1916, 1921
Fernand Pollain	Violoncellist	1918
Mildred Potter	Contralto	1915
John Powell	Pianist	1917, 1923
Maud Powell	Violinist	1914, 1916
Michael Press	Violinist	1924
Raoul Pugno	Pianist	1903, 1906
Robert Quait	Tenor	1920
Agnes Clune Quinlan	Pianist	1910
Sergei Rachmaninoff	Pianist 1909, 1919, 1920, 1921	
Paul Rahmig	Double Bass	1914
Harold Randolph	Pianist 1906, 1909, 1910, 1913, 1915	
Alfred Reisenauer	Pianist	1905
Gertrude Rennyson	Soprano	1911, 1914
Thaddeus Rich	Violinist 1906, 1907, 1908, 1909,	
1910, 1911, 1912, 1913, 1914, 1915, 1916, 1917, 1918, 1919, 1920,		
	1921, 1922, 1923, 1924, 1925	
Albert Riese	Horn	1923
Mrs. Albert M. Rihl	Soprano	1904
Emma Roberts	Mezzo-Soprano	1915, 1920
Christian Rodenkirchen	Trumpet	1914
Max Rosen	Violinist	1918
Moriz Rosenthal	Pianist	1906, 1907
Arthur Rubinstein	Pianist	1906, 1922
Cornelius Rübner	Pianist	1908, 1910
Zipporah Rosenberg	Soprano	1912, 1913
Elsa Ruegger	Violoncellist	1903, 1906
Ella Rumsey	Contralto	1920
Alfred Saal	Violoncellist	1905, 1906
Camille Saint-Saens	Pianist	1906
Carlos Salzedo	Harpist	1918, 1919
Carlos Salzedo	Pianist	1924

OLGA SAMAROFF	Pianist	1905, 1906, 1907, 1909
1914, 1915, 1916, 1917, 1918, 1919, 1920, 1921, 1922, 192		
HERMAN SANDBY	Violoncellist	1902, 1904, 1908
1909, 1910, 1911, 1912, 1913, 1914, 1915, 191		
EMIL SAUER	Pianist	190
EMILE SAURET	Violinist	190
ERNEST SCHELLING	Pianist	1905, 1913, 1915, 1917, 192
HANS SCHLEGEL	Flutist	192
EMIL F. SCHMIDT	Violinist	192
E. ROBERT SCHMITZ	Pianist	192
ALEXANDER SCHMULLER	Violinist	1921, 192
ARTUR SCHNABEL	Pianist	192
ALWIN SCHROEDER	Violoncellist	1905, 1908, 190
EDMUND SCHUËCKER	Harpist	190
MAX SCHULTZ	Violinist	190
ERNESTINE SCHUMANN-HEINK	Contralto	1902, 1904, 1906, 1907
1911, 1912, 1914, 191		
OSCAR SCHWAR	Tympanist	192
CYRIL SCOTT	Pianist	192
HENRI SCOTT	Basso	191
OSCAR SEAGLE	Baritone	191
VIVIENNE SEGAL	Soprano	191
MRS. F. A. SEIBERLING	Contralto	191
TOSCHA SEIDEL	Violinist	1918, 191
JOHANNES SEMBACH	Tenor	1915, 1916, 191
MARCELLA SEMBRICH	Soprano	1902, 191
ARRIGO SERATO	Violinist	192
JULES J. SERPENTINI	Clarinet	192
IRMA SEYDEL	Violinist	191
ARTHUR SHATTUCK	Pianist	191
OSCAR SHUMSKY	Violinist	192
ALEXANDER SILOTI	Pianist	1922, 192
BRUCE SIMONDS	Pianist	192
GARDELL SIMONS	Trombone	192
MARGARET SITTIG	Violinist	192
JEAN SKROBISCH	Tenor	191
MRS. FARRINGTON SMITH	Soprano	191
DAVID SOKOLOVE	Pianist	192
ALBERT SPALDING	Violinist	1915, 191
AUGUST SPANUTH	Pianist	190
JANET SPENCER	Contralto	190
THEODORE SPIERING	Violinist	191
MAUD SPROULE	Contralto	190
HELEN STANLEY	Soprano	192
EVELYN STARR	Violinist	191
GERTRUDE MAY STEIN	Soprano	190
FRIEDA STENDER	Soprano	190
S. TUDOR STRANG	Organist	1910, 191
G. RUSSELL STRAUSS	Baritone	190
PAULINE STRAUSS-DE AHNA	Soprano	1904
HENRY SUCH	Violinist	191

Rose and Ottilie Sutro	Pianists	1916
Michael Svedrofsky	Violinist	1905, 1906
Noah H. Swayne, 2d	Basso	1911
Marguerite Sylva	Soprano	1911
Marcel Tabuteau	Oboe	1915, 1917, 1920, 1921, 1923, 1924
Pasquale Tallarico	Pianist	1911, 1913
Emil Telmanyi	Violinist	1921
Maggie Teyte	Soprano	1919, 1920
Jacques Thibaud	Violinist	1903, 1904, 1917, 1918, 1919, 1920, 1921, 1922
Dorothea Thullen	Soprano	1913
Henry Gordon Thunder	Organist	1916
William Sylvano Thunder	Organ and Harmonium	1915, 1916, 1917, 1920, 1921
Anton Torello	Double Bass	1914, 1917, 1920, 1921
Ruth Townsend	Mezzo-Soprano	1915
Evalyn Tyson	Pianist	1919
Aline Van Barentzen	Pianist	1916, 1917
Marcia Van Dresser	Soprano	1918, 1919
Ellison Van Hoose	Baritone	1903, 1912
Henri Varillat	Baritone	1912
Ferenc Vecsey	Violinist	1921
Romain Verney	Viola	1921, 1922, 1923
Paul Volkmann	Tenor	1904, 1908
Constantin Von Sternberg	Pianist	1903, 1905, 1910, 1916
Julian Walker	Basso	1904
Helen Ware	Violinist	1913, 1914
Alma Weisshaar	Soprano	1912
Hunter Welsh	Pianist	1914
Florenz Werner	Violinist	1902
Reinald Werrenrath	Baritone	1916, 1917, 1920, 1921
Clarence Whitehill	Baritone	1911, 1916
Charlotte Demuth Williams	Violinist	1921
Ernest Williams	Trumpet	1921
Evan Williams	Tenor	1913
Arthur Howell Wilson	Pianist	1910, 1911
Flora Wilson	Soprano	1910
Rosalie Wirthlin	Contralto	1917
Herbert Witherspoon	Basso	1915, 1917
John K. Witzemann	Violinist	1902, 1903, 1904, 1906, 1910, 1913, 1915, 1916
Ludwig Wüllner	Reader and Liedersinger	1908, 1910
Eugene Ysaye	Violinist	1904, 1913
Camille Zeckwer	Pianist	1904, 1913, 1914
Marie Zeckwer-Holt	Soprano	1907, 1908, 1910, 1917
Efrem Zimbalist	Violinist	1912, 1914, 1916, 1918, 1919, 1921
Marie Kunkel Zimmerman	Soprano	1902, 1905, 1906, 1907
Augusta Zuckermann	Pianist	1902

APPENDIX H

THADDEUS RICH, *Assistant Conductor and Concertmaster*

Dr. Thaddeus Rich, who has been the concertmaster of the Philadelphia Orchestra since 1906, was born in Indianapolis. He began to play the violin in 1893, and when he was twelve years old showed such remarkable talent that he was sent to Leipsig, where he entered the Leipsig Conservatory, graduating with honors at the age of fifteen. In 1901 he accepted a position as first violinist with the famous Gewandhaus Orchestra under Arthur Nikisch, and two years later he went to Berlin as concertmaster of the Charlottenburg Opera. Here he studied violin with Joachim and composition with Pfitzner. In 1905 he returned to America, and Fritz Scheel, who was then conductor of the orchestra, heard him play and immediately engaged him as concertmaster. At his performances in Philadelphia he has played nearly every modern and classic concerto of value in violin literature.

HANS KINDLER, *First Violoncellist—1916–20*

Hans Kindler was born in Rotterdam, Holland, and was educated in in the High School and University of that city. When he was nine years old he began to play the 'cello, and later he attended the Rotterdam Conservatory, where he studied under Mossel, Jean Gerardy, and Casals. He was for two years solo cellist with the Deutsches Opernhaus, Berlin-Charlottenburg, and during his residence in Berlin he taught the 'cello at the Scharwenka Conservatory. Mr. Kindler has appeared with the principal orchestras in Berlin, Amsterdam, Birmingham, and Hanover, under such famous conductors as Mengelberg, Kunwald, Schönberg, Landon Ronald, etc. He has also played in joint recitals with Julia Culp, Xaver Scharwenka, and Ferruccio Busoni, who dedicated to him a transcription of a Chromatic Fantasy by Bach. He has also played for the Queen of Holland and for the Prince and Princess of Wied in Berlin.

DAVID DUBINSKY: *First second Violinist*, was born in Odessa, Russia, educated in Philadelphia. Began his musical education at the age of eleven. Studied the violin under Schradieck and Sauret. Original member of Philadelphia Orchestra. Four seasons in Pittsburg Orchestra under Emil Paur, serving as principal second violin. Played in Cincinnati Orchestra in May Festivals of 1906 and 1914 Boston Festival Orchestra. *Engaged for Philadelphia in 1908.*

ROMAIN JOSEPH VERNEY: *First Viola*, was born in Paris, France, graduated with honors from the Paris Conservatory, where he studied under

heophile Laforge, at the age of eighteen. Was one of the principals at
ie Opera Comique and played in the Concerts Colonne. Came to this
ountry in 1906 to be first viola with the New York Symphony Orches-
a, where he remained for five years, and from there went to the
hicago Grand Opera Company. *Engaged for Philadelphia Orchestra 1920.*

WILLIAM MORRIS KINCAID: *First Flute*, was born in Minneapolis,
lucated at Punahan, Honolulu, also Columbia University. While liv-
ig in Hawaiian Islands began to study the piano at the age of seven,
ute at the age of eight, and after moving to the United States, the
rgan. He studied the flute at Institute of Musical Art with George
arrère, from which he graduated in the regular and artist course. He
layed with New York Symphony Orchestra for five years. Soloist at
oncerts in and around New York and on tour with New York Sym-
hony and New York Chamber Music Society. *Engaged for Philadelphia*
rchestra in 1921.

MARCEL TABUTEAU: *First Oboe*, was born at Compiègne (Oise), France.
ie began his musical studies at the age of six, with his brother-in-law,
well-known violinist. At the age of thirteen he became a pupil at
aris Conservatory under Georges Hillet, the famous master of the
rench Oboe School, where he studied five years. In 1904 was awarded
ie first prize at Paris Conservatory. His teacher advised him to come
o this country and recommended him to Walter Damrosch, with whom
e played for several seasons, and in 1908 was engaged by Toscanini at
ie Metropolitan Opera House. *Engaged for Philadelphia Orchestra in 1915.*

ANTON HORNER: *First Horn*, was born in Gossengrun, Bohemia. He
egan to play the violin at the age of eight under his father's instruc-
on, who was a professional musician; began to learn the horn at thir-
en, entered Leipsig Conservatory at fourteen where he studied for
ver three years, violin under Hans Becker, and horn under Frederick
umbert. Three years with Pittsburgh Orchestra. (Also plays violin.)
ngaged for Philadelphia Orchestra in 1902.

RICHARD KRÜGER: *First Bassoon*, was born in Berlin, Germany. Re-
eived private instruction in violin and piano from the age of twelve to
ourteen; then four years at the Parlow Conservatory of Music, Berlin,
eing a pupil of Otto Schoenberg in the study of the bassoon. Played
ith Symphony Orchestra at Aix-la-Chapelle and Cologne, and under
ie direction of Richard Strauss, Felix Weingartner, Felix Mottl and
ritz Steinbach, also with Theodore Thomas Orchestra in Chicago.
Also plays piano and violin.) *Engaged for Philadelphia Orchestra 1901.*

ANTONIO TORELLO: *First Double Bass*, was born at San Sadurni de
oya, Province of Barcelona, Spain. Received his musical education at
ie Municipal School of Music at Barcelona. Began to play bass at the
ge of ten, played in an orchestra and at fourteen was playing solos.
layed in the following orchestras: Associacion Musical de Barcelona,
oston Opera Orchestra, Boston Festival Orchestra, has been heard as

soloist in Spain, Portugal and Madeira Island, and in the United Stat
during the Boston Festival Orchestra tour in 1911, all through the Ne
England States, Pittsburgh, Denver, Cleveland, etc. Came to America
1909. *Engaged for Philadelphia Orchestra in 1914.*

DANIEL BONADE: *First Clarinet,* was born in Geneva, Switzerlan
Studied the clarinet under M. Lefèbre (solo clarinet at Paris Oper
in 1904, and won first prize at Paris Conservatory in 1913. Played
Paris in Sechiari Symphony Orchestra and in Monteux Symphon
Orchestra (Paris). *Engaged for Philadelphia Orchestra in 1917.*

SOLOMON COHEN: *First Trumpet,* was born in New York City. Beg
studying trumpet in 1912 under Mr. Shlossberg of the New York Ph
harmonic; then studied harmony under Hedda van dem Beemt. *Engag
for Philadelphia Orchestra 1918.*

J. WALTER GUETTER: *First Bassoon,* was born in Philadelphia. Studi
violin from nine to fourteen years of age; at fourteen began study
bassoon and piano. From 1910 to 1914 studied at Klindworth Scha
wenka Conservatory of Music, Berlin, under Adolf Guetter, princip
bassoonist of former Royal Opera. With Chicago Symphony Orchest
from 1915–22. Appeared as soloist with local Orchestra at St. Markne
kirchen, Saxony, in 1914; in Chamber Music Concerts in Chicago a
Philadelphia; with Philadelphia Orchestra at Children's Concerts
1923. *Engaged for Philadelphia Orchestra in 1922.*

MICHEL PENHA: *First Cellist,* 1920–1925, was born in Amsterda
Holland. He began his general musical education at Amsterdam Co
servatory, and studied under Professors Mossel, Hugo Becker and Josef
Salmen. Toured as soloist in Europe, Indies, South America and Unit
States. *Engaged for Philadelphia Orchestra in 1920.*

WILLIAM OSCAR SCHWAR: *Tympanist,* was born in Bautzen, Saxon
Germany. Began to play the violin at the age of ten. Studied tympa
under Mr. Heinemann, first tympani player at the Royal Opera a
teacher at Royal Conservatory at Dresden, Germany. Was a member
the Royal Opera at St. Petersburg, and has played in all the leadir
cities of Germany and European countries under the following music
directors and in the cities here cited: Felix Mottl, Karlsruhe; Treckle
Dresden; Sauer, Coblentz, Frischen, Hanover. Shortly after joining t
Philadelphia Orchestra he made a sensation by his wonderful playing
the overture "Romeo and Juliet" by Tschaikowsky. When he had fi
ished, the entire orchestra applauded him with great enthusiasm, a
action which is seldom accorded a member of an orchestra in rehears
by his colleagues. (Also plays snare drum, bells and xylophone.) E
gaged for Philadelphia Orchestra in 1903.

GARDELL SIMONS: *Trombone,* was born at Allegan, Michigan. He beg
the study of the trombone at the age of nine and a few years later cor
menced a systematic course of study in Chicago. Since it was difficult
that time to get instruction of a high order from Trombonists he reli
mostly upon singers and instrumentalists of repute for his instruction

reathing, phrasing, articulation and expression, and at length became
ne of the originators of the Modern School of trombone playing; also
tudied harmony and composition to some extent. Played first trom-
one with Philharmonic Orchestra, New York City, Arens "People's
ymphony," Volpe Symphony and others. Wide experience as soloist
/ith concert bands and concert companies, etc., and plays mostly his
wn compositions or violin music adapted by himself to the trombone.
ngaged for Philadelphia Orchestra 1915.

DANIEL MAQUARRE: *First Flute*, 1910–1918, was born in Brussels.
Vhen five years old he began the study of music in Paris, and in 1893,
ntered the National Conservatory of Paris to study flute and harmony;
n 1896 he won the first prize for the flute. Toured in the United States
s soloist with Mme. Emma Nevada in 1901, and was for two years
oloist with Longy Club, of Boston. In 1902 became member of the Bos-
on Symphony Orchestra, where he remained for seven seasons; also one
eason with New York Philharmonic. Organized the D. Maquarre
nsemble of Instruments in fall of 1913 in Philadelphia. *Engaged for
Philadelphia Orchestra 1910.*

ANDRÉ MAQUARRE: *First Flute*, 1918–1920, was born in Brussels.
3egan his musical studies at the age of eight at the Paris Conservatory,
vith Solfegio and Piano under Martini, also studied Harmony with
_andon, Flute with Henry Altes and Composition with Massenet.
*layed in several orchestras in Paris, also Opera. Joined the Boston
ymphony Orchestra in 1898 as solo flute, and from 1906–1917 was con-
'uctor of the Boston Symphony Orchestra during the period of the
*Pop" Concerts season at Symphony Hall. Wide soloist experience in
ymphony orchestras, chamber music organizations, also obligato with
ingers, such as Melba, Gilibert and others. Founded the Maquarre
extet in Boston in 1901. Composed three operas and a number of orches-
ral pieces in Symphonic form, an overture played by the Boston Sym-
•hony Orchestra; and chamber music for wind choir and songs. *Engaged
or Philadelphia Orchestra 1918.*

PETER HENKELMAN, *First English Horn and Oboe*, was born in Heusden,
Holland. Attended school in Holland, and at the age of seven began
o study the violin. A few years later he began the study of the piano,
nd at the age of thirteen entered the Royal Conservatory at The
Hague, where he started to study the oboe and English horn, as well
s continuing his studies of the violin, piano and theory. He has
•layed with the City Symphony Orchestra at Haarlem and Utrecht,
he Winderstein Orchestra of Leipzig, the Symphony Orchestra of
3udapest, the City Orchestra of Heidelberg, as well as with the
Concertgebouw of Amsterdam. *Engaged for the Philadelphia Orchestra 1901.*

APPENDIX I

AURIC—Nocturne (January 26–27, 1923)

BLISS—Mêlée Fantasque (February 27–28, 1925)

BRAUNFELS—Fantastic Variations (October 14–15, 1921)

CARPENTER—"A Pilgrim Vision" (November 26–27, 1920)

CONVERSE—"The Mystic Trumpeter" (March 3–4, 1905)

DE FALLA—Excerpts from "El Amor Brujo" (April 15–17, 1922)

D'INDY—Symphony No. 2, in B flat (December 30–31, 1904)

D'INDY—"Wallenstein" (December 19–20, 1902)

DVORAK—Heldenlied (December 27–28, 1901)

FITELBERG—Polish Rhapsody (November 4–5, 1921)

GLAZOUNOW—Scènes de Ballet (February 24–25, 1905)

GRANADOS—Intermezzo and Epiloque from "Goyescas" (March 10–1
1916)

HAUSEGGER—Symphonic Poem, "Wieland der Schmied" (October 17–1
1913)

MAHLER—Symphony No. 8 (March 2, 1916)

MAHLER—Das Lied von der Erde (December 16, 1916)

DANIEL GREGORY MASON—Symphony No. 1, in C minor (Februar
18–19, 1916)

PURCELL—Trumpet Prelude (December 26–27, 1924)

RABAUD—Symphony No. 2, in E minor (October 24–25, 1913)

RACHMANINOFF—Symphony No. 3, "The Bells" (February 6–7, 1920)

RIMSKY-KORSAKOW—Excerpts from "Kitesch" (Solitude and The
Battle), (October 26–27, 1923)

SCHELLING—A Victory Ball (February 23–24, 1923)

SKRYABIN—Symphony No. 3, "Le Divin Poème" (November 19–20,
1915)

SIBELIUS—Symphony No. 5, in E flat (October 21–22, 1921)

RICHARD STRAUSS—Alpensymphonie (April 28–29, 1916)

STRAWINSKY—Le Chant du Rossignol (October 19–20, 1923)

STRAWINSKY—Symphonies d'Instruments à Vent, à la mémoire de Claud
Achille Debussy (November 23–24, 1923)

STRAWINSKY—Sacre du Printemps (March 3–4, 1922)

MAX BRUCH—Concerto for two Pianos and Orchestra (December 29-30, 1916) First World Performance.

MEDTNER—Concerto in C minor for Piano and Orchestra (October 31–November 1, 1924)

ORNSTEIN—Second Concerto for Piano and Orchestra (February 13–14, 1925)

SZYMANOWSKI—Concerto for Violin and Orchestra (November 28-29, 1924)

TAILLEFERRE—Concerto for Piano and Orchestra (March 20-21, 1925)

Performances of the Ninth Symphony of Beethoven:

March 26, 1903; January 1-2, 1904; February 7-8, 1907; February 27, 1907 (Baltimore); March 13-14, 1914; May 7-8, 1920; December 3-4, 1920; April 8, 1921 (Pittsburgh); February 21, 1924 (Toronto); March 4, 1924 (New York); March 6, 1924 (Philadelphia with Mendelssohn Choir of Toronto)

APPENDIX J

PHILADELPHIA ORCHESTRA
MR. FRITZ SCHEEL, Conductor

FIRST CONCERT
Friday, November 16, 1900, at 8.15 P. M.

PROGRAMME

CARL GOLDMARK.....................Overture, "In Spring," Op. 36

LUDWIG VAN BEETHOVEN.........Symphony No. 5, C. minor, Op. 67
    I. Allegro con brio.............................2–4
    II. Andante con moto..........................3–8
    III. Allegro.................................3–4
    IV. Allegro.................................4–4

Intermission of ten minutes

PETER ILITSCH TSCHAIKOWSKY .... Concert for Pianoforte, No. 1,
B. flat minor, Op. 23
    I. Allegro, non troppo e molto maestoso.........3–4
    II. Andantino simplice..........................6–8
    III. Allegro con fuoco..........................3–4

KARL MARIA VON WEBER........."Invitation to the Dance," Op. 65
Orchestration by Felix Weingartner

RICHARD WAGNER...............Entry of the Gods into "Walhalla"
MR. OSSIP GABRILOWITSCH, Soloist

SECOND CONCERT
Friday, December 14, 1900, at 8.15 P. M.

PROGRAMME

LUDWIG VAN BEETHOVEN..................Overture Leonore, No. 3

JOHANNES BRAHMS................Symphony No. 2, D major, Op. 73
    I. Allegro non troppo
    II. Adagio non troppo
    III. Allegretto grazioso (Quasi Andantino)
    IV. Allegro con spirito

AMBROISE THOMAS........................."Mad Scene" (Hamlet)

Intermission of ten minutes

PETER I. TSCHAIKOWSKY.................Serenade for Strings, Op. 48
    Andantino non troppo—Allegro Moderato
    Moderato, Tempo di Valse—Larghetto
    Elegiaco—Andante, Allegro con spirito

Songs

    "Spring Has Come" (Hiawatha), Tyler
    "Skylark," Händel
    "An April Birthday," Ronalds

BEDRICH SMETANA............................"Vltava" (Moldau)
    From Symphonic Poem "My Fatherland"
      MME. LILLIAN BLAUVELT, Soloist
      SELDEN MILLER, Accompanist

THIRD CONCERT
Friday, January 18, 1901, at 8.15 P. M.
PROGRAMME

RICHARD WAGNER.............................A Faust Overture
LUDWIG VAN BEETHOVEN..................Symphony No. 4, Op. 60
    I. Adagio—Allegro Vivace
    II. Adagio
    III. Allegro Vivace
    IV. Allegro ma non troppo
                Intermission

H. VIEUXTEMPS............................Concerto No. 2, Op. 19
    I. Allegro
    II. Andante
    III. Rondo—Allegro

ENGELBERT HUMPERDINCK......................Moorish Rhapsody
    I. Tarifa (Sunset Elegy)
    II. Tanger (A Night in a Moorish Cafe)
    III. Tetuan (A Ride in the Desert)
      MR. FRITZ KREISLER, Soloist

FOURTH CONCERT
Friday, February 8, 1901, at 8 P. M.
PROGRAMME

WILLIAM W. GILCHRIST............................Symphony in C
    I. Introduction, Vivace Impetuoso. Allegro Molto
    II. Adagio, Andante Moderato
    III. Scherzo, Vivace
    IV. Finale, Molto Allegro

EDWARD MACDOWELL.................Concerto for Piano No. 2
    I. Larghetto. Poco piu Mosso e con Passione
    II. Presto Giocoso
    III. Largo. Molto Allegro

CARL MARIA VON WEBER......................Overture "Oberon"
EDWARD GRIEG.................Berceuse for Strings, from Op. 68
HEINRICH HOFFMANN.................Elves and Giants, from Op. 22
ANTON DVORAK......................Slavonic Dances III and VII
      EDWARD MACDOWELL, Soloist

FIFTH CONCERT
Wednesday, March 6, 1901, at 8.15 P. M.
PROGRAMME
CARL GOLDMARK.....................Overture "Sakuntala," Op. 1

AUGUST LINDNER............... Concerto for Violoncello, E minor
    a. Serenade—Andante
    b. Tarantelle—Allegro Vivace

PETER TSCHAIKOWSKY.............Symphony "Pathétique," Op. 7
    I. Adagio—Allegro non troppo
    II. Allegro con Gracio
    III. Allegro Molto Vivace
    IV. Finale—Adagio Lamentoso

FRANZ LISZT......................................Les Prélude
    MR. RUDOLPH HENNIG, Soloist

SIXTH CONCERT
Friday, April 19, 1901, at 8.15 P. M.
PROGRAMME
JOACHIM RAFF.............................Symphony "Im Walde"
    I. Allegro
    II. Largo—Allegro Assai
    III. Allegro

EDUARD GRIEG.......................Concerto for Piano in A fla
    I. Allegro Moderato
    II. Adagio
    III. Allegro Moderato

PETER TSCHAIKOWSKY........Overture—Fantasie, "Romeo and Juliet
    MME. TERESA CARREÑO, Soloist

Appendix K

DIRECTORS

Mrs. Frank Aydelotte
Mrs. J. Claude Bedford
Mrs. William H. Biester
Mrs. Samuel Dyer Clyde
Mrs. Morton P. Dickeson
Mrs. William Easby
Mrs. Albert Fox
Mrs. Harold C. Goddard
Mrs. Edward F. Hitchcock
Mrs. Benjamin R. Hoffman
Mrs. Edward K. Innes
Mrs. Robert F. Irwin
Mrs. Willis D. Jameson
Mrs. E. R. Keller
Mrs. N. B. Kelly

Mrs. S. Leonard Kent, Jr.
Mrs. Gibson McIlvaine
Mrs. Robert L. McLean
Mrs. John A. Miller
Mrs. T. Haldean Moore
Mrs. Charles Musser
Mrs. George Bispham Page
Mrs. A. A. Parker
Miss Edith Peters
Mrs. Richard Peters, Jr.
Mrs. J. Frederick Petry
Mrs. J. Lord Rigby
Mrs. John David Shattuck
Mrs. Channing Way
Mrs. Henry M. Wirz

COMMITTEES OUT-OF-TOWN

The Delaware Committee (1907–1908)
(Wilmington)
for
The Philadelphia Orchestra
Formed May, 1905

Mrs. Lewis C. Vandegrift, President
Mrs. Joseph Swift, Vice-president
Mrs. William Betts, Secretary
Miss Annie T. Flinn, Treasurer
Mrs. Otho Nowland, Chairman Guarantee Fund
Mrs. Ellwood C. Jackson, Chairman Auxiliary Committee
Mrs. A. H. Berlin, Chairman Press Committee

Mrs. John Bancroft
Mrs. John B. Bird
Miss Martha Bradfield
Mrs. Daniel M. Bates
Mrs. T. Leslie Carpenter
Mrs. Allan J. Colby
Mrs. W. F. Curtis
Mrs. William K. du Pont
Mrs. Harlan Gause
Mrs. Charles E. Griffith
Mrs. Norman Huxley

Mrs. Alfred R. Jones
Mrs. A. E. Kruse
Miss Kurtz
Miss Lore
Mrs. D. J. Reinhardt
Mrs. J. E. Smith
Mrs. Harry J. Stoeckle
Mrs. Calvin Swayne
Mrs. William F. Sellers
Mrs. Henry B. Thompson
Mrs. James P. Winchester

The Washington Committee (1907–1908)
for
The Philadelphia Orchestra
Formed May, 1906

Miss Aileen Bell, Acting Chairman

(The names of a large Committee and a list of Patronesses are unavailable.)

THE BALTIMORE COMMITTEE (1907–1908)
for THE PHILADELPHIA ORCHESTRA
Formed May, 1906
LAWRASON RIGGS, ESQ., President
HIS EMINENCE CARDINAL GIBBONS
HIS EXCELLENCY GOVERNOR EDWIN WARFIELD
RIGHT REVEREND BISHOP WILLIAM PARET, D.D.

Vice-presidents

HON. CHARLES J. BONAPARTE
BERNARD N. BAKER, ESQ.
FRANK FRICK, ESQ.
J. SWAN FRICK, ESQ.
GAUN M. HUTTON, ESQ.
DR. HENRY BARTON JACOBS
SIGNOR PIETRO MINETTI
PHILIP OGDEN, ESQ.
WILSON PATTERSON, ESQ.
DR. THOMAS L. SHEARER
R. MANSON SMITH, ESQ.
JOHN MARSHALL THOMAS, ESQ.
EDWIN L. TURNBULL, ESQ.
JERE H. WHEELWRIGHT, ESQ.
J. B. NOEL WYATT, ESQ.

MRS. BERNARD N. BAKER
MRS. CHARLES J. BONAPARTE
MRS. DAVID L. BARTLETT
MRS. WILLIAM ELLICOTT
MRS. T. HARRISON GARRETT
MRS. JOHN GILL
MRS. GAUN M. HUTTON
MRS. HENRY BARTON JACOBS
MRS. HOWARD MUNNIKHUYSEN
MRS. WILLIAM PARET
MRS. WILSON PATTERSON
MRS. NELSON PERIN
MRS. R. MANSON SMITH
MRS. JAMES MADISON THOMPSON
MRS. EDWIN WARFIELD
MRS. JERE WHEELWRIGHT

MISS SHEARER, Chairman

HONORARY MANAGERS

MRS. W. S. BELDING
MRS. JOHN S. BERRY
MISS OCTAVIA BATES
MRS. FREDERICK M. COLSTON
MRS. J. S. ELLARD
MRS. CHARLES M. FRANKLIN
MRS. RICHARD GRIFFITH
MRS. PAUL HAUPT
MRS. DAVID HUTZLER
MRS. GRIER HERSH
MRS. CHARLES KEIDEL
MRS. C. MANIGAULT MORRIS
MISS MARY L. PARKER
MRS. FREDERICK B. STIEFF
MRS. WILLIAM S. THAYER
MRS. SIDNEY TURNER
REV. F. WARD DENYS
MILES FARROW, ESQ.
DR. CHARLES M. FRANKLIN
EDWIN FRANK, ESQ.
MAURICE GREGG, ESQ.
DR. B. MERRILL HOPKINSON
EDWIN SCHENCK, ESQ.
CHARLES WEBER, JR., ESQ.

ACTIVE MANAGERS

MISS BLOODGOOD
MISS BESSIE CAMPBELL CLARK
MRS. ISAAC DIXON
MRS. J. HAMSLEY JOHNSON
MRS. ERNEST KNABE
MISS LURMAN
MRS. EDWARD H. MCKEON
MRS. S. C. ROWLAND
MRS. SIGMUND SONNEBORN
MRS. OSCAR A. TURNER
MRS. CLARENCE WATSON
MRS. ROBERT W. WOOD
MRS. GEORGE L. ZELL
FREDERICK M. COLSTON, ESQ.
CHARLES E. DOHME, ESQ.
FREDERICK H. GOTTLIEB, ESQ.
DR. JOHN HEMMETER
REV. OLIVER HUCKEL
ERNEST JENKINS, ESQ.
ROBERT OLIVER LEHR, ESQ.
THEODORE MARBURG, ESQ.
REV. JOHN TIMOTHY STONE

THE WOMEN'S COMMITTEE FOR THE PHILADELPHIA ORCHESTRA
invites you to be present at a meeting in the interest of

THE PHILADELPHIA ORCHESTRA
to be held at the

ARUNDELL CLUB
1000 North Charles Street, Baltimore,
on
Thursday afternoon, December fourteenth (1905)
at half after three o'clock

Under the patronage of
MRS. JOSIAH LAW BLACKWELL
MRS. ALEXANDER BROWN
MRS. GEORGE DALLAS DIXON
MRS. S. NAUDAIN DUER
MRS. WILLIAM M. ELLICOTT
MRS. GEORGE T. GIBSON
MRS. DANIEL C. GILMAN
MRS. JOHN P. POE
MRS. HAROLD RANDOLPH
MISS MARY BUTLER SHEARER
MRS. W. PLUNKETT STEWART
MRS. JESSE TYSON
MRS. GEORGE L. ZELL

Music by
MRS. THOMAS S. KIRKBRIDE, JR., Pianist
and
MR. JOHN WITZEMANN, Violinist
and MR. ALFRED SAAL, Violoncellist
Members of the Philadelphia Orchestra

APPENDIX L

ANNOUNCEMENT OF CHILDREN'S CONCERTS
THE PHILADELPHIA ORCHESTRA ASSOCIATION

Founded 1900

Maintaining and Operating

THE PHILADELPHIA ORCHESTRA

104 Musicians

LEOPOLD STOKOWSKI, Conductor

Special Announcement

Children's Concerts Season 1921–1922

Wednesday Afternoons at Four

December 14th, 1921   February 1st, 1922
March 8th, 1922

Academy of Music

In Answer to a Long-Felt Need

The Philadelphia Orchestra Association announces a
Series of Three Children's Concerts
for the coming season under the auspices of:

THE MATINEE MUSICAL CLUB	THE CITIZEN'S COMMITTEE
Mrs. Frederick W. Abbott, Chairman	Mrs. Frederick Rosengarten Chairman
Mrs. Edwin B. Garrigues	Mrs. Robert Von Moschzisker
Mrs. Helen Pulaski Innes	Mrs. John Hampton Barnes

The Board of Education
Dr. Edwin C. Broome, Superintendent of Schools, Philadelphia
Dr. Enoch W. Pearson, Director of Music in the Public Schools
Dr. Hollis Dann, Director of Music, State Dept. of Education
The Women's Committee for the Philadelphia Orchestra
The Germantown & Chestnut Hill Women's Committee for The
  Philadelphia Orchestra.
The West Philadelphia Women's Committee for The Philadel-
  phia Orchestra
The Media, Chester & West Chester Women's Committee for
  The Philadelphia Orchestra
The Civic Club of Philadelphia
The New Century Club

The Philomusian Club
The Pennsylvania Federation of Music Clubs
The Philadelphia Association of Settlements

These Concerts will be conducted by Mr. Stokowski, who has arranged a series of programmes lasting one hour, during which short talks will be given about the instruments, as well as about the selections played.

The Concerts are for Children, and no adult will be admitted unless accompanied by one or more children.

COMMITTEE ON CHILDREN'S CONCERTS

MISS FRANCES A. WISTER, Chairman

MR. EDWARD W. BOK   DR. CHARLES D. HART

SCHEDULE OF PRICES (No Tax)	Series of Three Concerts
Parquet and Balcony Boxes, seating six...................	$18.00
Parquet and Balcony Boxes, seating four.................	12.00
Parquet, Parquet Circle and Balcony Seats................	2.25
Family Circle...	1.50
Amphitheatre...	.75

Appendix M

The musical life of this city has reached a stage in its development that must make it apparent to all who are interested in the advancement of matters of art and education that if we are to continue the progress of the past few years and take our place as a city of any musical importance, the next and most necessary step is the founding of a Permanent Philadelphia Orchestra. Such an undertaking is one that requires serious consideration, and the co-operation not only of our music-loving public but of all citizens who are interested in our civic progress.

In order to establish an orchestra such as would be a distinct credit to the city, it is necessary to have a paid-up fund of not less than $250,000.

The following Committee, before issuing this circular, have given the matter great consideration, carefully looked into various organizations in other cities, and feel confident that if they meet with liberal response Philadelphia will have in a few years an orchestra second to none in America. When Boston, Chicago, Cincinnati, Buffalo, Pittsburgh, and other cities, not nearly so large or so wealthy, have established permanent orchestras, it is surely time that we should interest ourselves and unite in aiding to form an organization in keeping with our size and importance. This will not be possible with less than the sum before mentioned, which they trust you will aid them in securing upon the following terms and conditions:

1. Subscribers shall not be bound by their subscriptions unless the sum of $200,000 shall have been subscribed.

2. The fund shall be used only for the purpose of establishing and maintaining a permanent Philadelphia Orchestra, and it shall be applied for that purpose by the following Trustees:

or their successors. The discretion of such Trustees shall be absolute as regards the administration of the fund, and they shall have power to fill any vacancy occurring in their number, they having agreed to abide by the conditions herein stated.

The Trustees shall invest $200,000 of the fund, using only the interest thereof and the additional $50,000 shall be used for current expenses of the first few years, when the expenses will be heavier and the deficit greater.

3. The orchestra shall be composed, first, of the best musicians resident in Philadelphia; then, of the best musicians obtainable either in this country or abroad. In order to insure the success of the enterprise, it is absolutely necessary that the highest standard be maintained, that the reputation of the orchestra can be established in other cities beside our own, for it is not possible for an orchestra to become self-supporting that cannot command engagements outside the city to which it belongs.

4. The Board of Trustees, when it considers that the completion of the fund is assured, shall select the leader upon the careful and unbiased consideration of the merits and records of all candidates submitted to it. Such candidates, however, to be only men of the highest reputation either in Europe or America, and the leader one whose name will add to the prestige of the orchestra both here and in other cities.

5. The selection and placing of the musicians shall be made by the leader, subject to conditions in paragraph three.

6. As the subscribers contribute to the fund solely for the benevolent purpose of advancing the cause of music in Philadelphia and release all control over said fund, they shall not be considered as partners with each other, or with the Trustees in the conduct or management of said orchestra.

7. The Board of Trustees shall never exceed nine in number.

8. Subscribers to the permanent fund shall have choice of seats in advance of the general public for all Symphony Concerts.

The Committee earnestly requests all who are interested and who will aid them by subscribing to the Fund, to kindly give the matter their prompt attention, and send in any subscription or communication as soon as possible, for if the Orchestra is to be established by next season, it is necessary to push matters without delay.

Mr. and Mrs. W. W. Arnett

Mr. Francis R. Abbott

Mr. and Mrs. Samuel T. Bodine

Mr. Richard S. Brock

Mr. James M. Beck

Mrs. William Bucknell

Mr. and Mrs. James M. Bennett

Mr. Henry C. Blair

Mr. David Bispham

Miss Emma M. Boyles

Dr. Edward Brooks

Blasius & Sons

Mr. Charles A. Braun

Mrs. M. M. Baltz

Mr. Samuel Castner, Jr.

Mr. Richard Y. Cook

Mrs. Edward H. Coates

Mrs. J. Gardner Cassatt

Mrs. Edward Coles

Mrs. William T. Carter

Mr. Harrison K. Caner

Mr. and Mrs. W. W. Curtin

Miss Mary M. Cohen

Mr. and Mrs. J. deW. Cookman

Dr. Hugh A. Clarke

Mr. Gilbert Raynolds Combs

Mr. and Mrs. Frederick S. Dickson

Mr. F. T. Sully Darley

Mr. Frederick Douredoure

Mr. and Mrs. Stephen P. Darlington

Mr. Nicholas Douty

Mr. William L. Elkins

Mr. Carl Edelheim

Mr. Chancellor C. English

Mr. Henry Erben

Mrs. Charles Este

Mrs. George Harrison Fisher

Mr. and Mrs. Caleb Fox

Mr. and Mrs. George C. Fletcher

Mr. Charles N. Fahnestock

Mr. Charles Fearon

Miss Elizabeth Wilson Fisher

Mr. and Mrs. W. W. Gibbs

Mr. and Mrs. Wm. B. Gough

Mrs. J. Ernest Goodman

Mr. W. W. Gilchrist

Mrs. Charles W. Henry

Mr. and Mrs. Byerly Hart

Mr. Edward I. H. Howell

Miss Margaret Harvey

Mr. Ellis Clarke Hammann

Mr. Alfred Curtin Hirsh

Mr. Max Heinrich

Mr. Samuel B. Huey

Mr. James Hay

Mr. H. H. Hallowell

Mr. John H. Ingham

Mrs. Charles E. Ingersoll

Mr. Henry McKean Ingersoll

Miss Hilda Justice

Mr. J. George Klemm

Dr. Edward Iungerich Keffer

Mr. and Mrs. J. L. Ketterlinus

Mr. and Mrs. George B. Kester

Miss Florence Keen

Mr. Edward Knapp

Mr. and Mrs. Arthur Lea

Mr. August B. Loeb

Mr. Algernon Sidney Logan

Mr. and Mrs. Thomas McKean

Mrs. Henry Pratt McKean

Mr. Edward Garrett McCollin

Mr. James C. Miller

Mr. Selden Miller

Miss Alice Lewis Murphy

Miss Agnes Morrison

Mr. and Mrs. Harrison S. Morris

Mr. Charles T. Murphy

Mr. Frederick R. Meigs

Mrs. Markoe

Miss Helen L. Murphy

Mrs. J. P. Mumford

Miss Mary Wanamaker Mille

Miss Adelaide Madeira

Mr. Edmond Morris

Mr. G. Heide Norris

Mr. Charles E. Pugh

Miss Marie Virginia Peck

Mr. Charles R. Peck

Mrs. Frank Pleasanton

Mrs. John Worrell Pepper

Mr. Frederick Peakes

Mr. Enoch Pearson

Mr. Joseph Rosengarten

Mrs. Frank H. Rosengarten

Dr. J. M. Reeves

Mr. and Mrs. Richard Rossmaessl

Mrs. Harry B. Rosengarten

Dr. Henry C. Register
Miss Elsé West Rulon
Mrs. Thomas A. Scott
Mr. Justus C. Strawbridge
Mr. N. A. Stout
Mr. Monroe Smith
Mr. and Mrs. John Hasletine Shinn
Mr. A. M. Sheppard
Mr. Calvin Mason Smith
J. Stetson & Co.
Mr. Constantin von Sternberg
Mr. Frank Thomson
Mr. George C. Thomas
Mrs. Charles Newbold Thorpe
Miss Kate Tilge

Mrs. Eliza D. Turner
Mr. S. S. Thompson
Mr. and Mrs. W. H. Tenbrook
Mr. Louis C. Whitney
Mr. and Mrs. Owen Wister
Dr. George Woodward
Mr. Massah M. Warner
Mr. Clarence Wolf
Miss Woolman
Mr. Albert B. Weimer
Mrs. Wm. Rotch Wister
Mr. Andrew Wheeler, Jr.
Mr. E. Burgess Warren
Mr. P. A. B. Widener
Mr. Richard Zeckwer

The following members of the Board of the Musical Fund Society:

Mr. Wm. F. Biddle
Mr. O. C. Bosbyshell
Mr. John H. Carr
Mr. H. G. Clay
Dr. Richard J. Dunglison
Mr. Jas. W. Hazlehurst
Mr. Wm. H. Hollis

Mr. Geo. P. Kimball
Dr. Alfred C. Lambdin
Mr. Edw. G. McCollin
Mr. R. P. Robins
Mr. Charles M. Schmitz
Mr. Charles P. Turner
Mr. C. Wetherill

Manuscript Society of Philadelphia
W. W. Gilchrist, President

The Symphony Society of Philadelphia
Dr. E. I. Keffer, President

A Philadelphia newspaper 1899:

"How to Get an Orchestra"

"It need not be difficult in Philadelphia to form as fine an orchestra as anybody is willing and able to pay for. A permanent orchestra is a very costly institution. It involves the permanent employment of anywhere from fifty to a hundred good musicians, at salaries sufficient to secure their constant and exclusive services as orchestra players throughout the active portion of the year. A simple calculation will show that the expense of this mounts quickly by tens of thousands.

"Even in a great city, with a very large public interested in orchestral music, it is scarcely possible to meet this expense by the receipts from local concerts. There is a limit to the number of concerts that can be prepared or that can find hearers in one place, so that a large fixed orchestra can hardly earn its living—unless in some great place of popular resort, like the Crystal Palace at London or the Trocadero at Paris. Boston, an exceptionally self-reliant metropolis, provides two full audiences a week for the symphony concerts in Music Hall for

[247]

twenty-four weeks in the year, but it is known that this does not meet the expense of the orchestra. Experience furnishes no evidence of any such hunger for orchestral music among the general public of Philadelphia as would justify a reliance on its financial support for an orchestra of the class of that which private generosity has maintained at Boston and that has established a standard with which, as a business enterprise, it would be necessary to compete.

"Clearly, therefore, such an enterprise, if undertaken here, must be undertaken either in a missionary spirit by those who regard music as an elevating influence in the community, or for their own gratification, by those who wish for greater musical opportunities for themselves. In either case, or both, the promoters must expect to pay the piper. And this being the case, we should say that those who pay have an entire right to choose their piper—to organize their orchestra in their own way and put it in charge of whom they please.

"The discussion that has been going on recently upon this subject has run wide of the mark. It is not a question of the best way to organize an orchestra, but simply whether there is anybody ready to put up the money to have an orchestra at all. If there is not, the whole discussion is futile; if there is, we cannot see that the details concern anybody else. The rest of us can pay for our tickets and find fault, or we can let it alone, as we have done with so many excellent orchestra concerts, past and present. Something beside the purely musical appeal is required to attract an audience, very few of whom can know the actual difference between one band and another, except in size and in some of the more meretricious technical effects, and if this can be supplied by personal social or fashionable interest and influence, there is that much gained.

"It is an old rule in Philadelphia, that when anybody undertakes to do anything, everybody else proposes a different way. This has always prevented the natural development of a local orchestra, and always will do so as long as the matter is open to public contention. The first essential to the establishment of a high-class orchestra is capital. If that is provided, the rest can be obtained, and those who provide it have the right to determine how to spend it, and the right also to command appreciation and support. Without this we can dispute till the cows come home with no more result than at any other time in the past forty years, during which time everybody has been agreed that Philadelphia should have such an orchestra, but no two agreed as to who should conduct it, or how it should be maintained."

Public Ledger, March 4, 1899:

"A Philadelphia Orchestra"

"The movement which has long been on foot to establish a permanent symphony orchestra in this city, one which should from its inception challenge favorable comparison with any other orchestra in the United States, and one in which all who take an interest in music might feel a justifiable pride, has now taken such definite shape that its accomplishment is practically assured.

"A perusal of the prospectus of the Philadelphia Permanent Orchestra which was issued yesterday by the committee who have piloted the undertaking into its present haven, and which will be found published in full on another page, shows that a paid-up fund of $250,000 is necessary for the work in hand. All who are interested in the civic progress of the city, and those in particular who are interested in music, are invited to contribute to the fund.

"The details of the scheme speak for themselves, but the pith of the understanding is that $200,000 of the fund shall be permanently invested and the interest used for the advancement of the orchestra, while the $50,000 cash balance is to be devoted to the current expenses of the first few years. Preference is to be given to musicians resident in Philadelphia, and the Board of Trustees is to select the leader from conductors of acknowledged reputation at home or abroad.

"That such an institution will be of great and permanent value to the city, there can be no possible doubt. A symphony orchestra of the calibre proposed is as essential to the musical taste of the rising generation as a well endowed public library is to their literary education. Without an acknowledged standard to judge by, musical taste and musical judgment become chaotic, and degenerate by feeding without discrimination on what is inferior.

"That such an organization will draw full houses, those who have seen the Academy packed to the ceiling at every concert given by the Boston Symphony Orchestra will not doubt, and the fact that Philadelphia has enabled a grand opera company of the first magnitude to give an extended season here with a large margin of profit for the past two years, is another demonstration of the existence of a large musical public. It must be admitted that the musical public of Philadelphia is peculiar in some respects; it has a rooted antipathy to mediocrity and an invincible dislike of being managed from New York. But the public know what they want. They have long wanted an orchestra—a real orchestra—of their own. Various obstacles have cropped up from time to time in the way, but the last one—the war with Spain—no longer exists; the way has been cleared and the time is ripe for the accomplishment of its desire.

"The names of the committee who will direct the affairs of the orchestra are substantial guarantees of an able, impartial and business-like administration of its affairs, and the names of those who have endorsed it financially, a list that will be doubled and trebled in a few days, are certain indications that the orchestra will shortly be an accomplished fact."

Appendix N

First Circular Announcing The Philadelphia Orchestra Mailed in September, 1900, to About 4000 People

THE PHILADELPHIA ORCHESTRA
85 Performers
Mr. Fritz Scheel, Conductor

A series of six Symphony Concerts will be given at the Academy of Music during the season of 1900–1901, on the following dates: Friday evening, November 16; Friday evening, December 14; Friday evening, January 18; Friday evening, February 8; Wednesday evening, March 6; Friday evening, April 19.

Soloists of the first rank will assist at the concerts, and names will be announced as soon as pending engagements have been made.

The prices of season tickets, with reserved seats to the six concerts, are: Boxes with six seats $75; boxes with four seats $50; other seats $8, $6 and $4; proscenium boxes on application.

Sale of seats to holders of Patronesses' Cards will begin at Miss Harris's office, No. 1115 Chestnut Street, on Wednesday morning, October 10, at 9 o'clock.

The series announced above is the outgrowth of two Symphony Concerts given last winter for the benefit of sufferers by the Philippine War. The committee in charge was the auxiliary to the committee of ladies who supervised the Philippine concerts, and it is intended that the management of the series of the coming season shall be generally the same. To cover expenses of the concerts a guarantee fund has been subscribed, the amount of which is sufficient to meet the requirements of the present undertaking; but it is hoped that our people will give the concerts such liberal support as to prevent a deficit at the end of the season.

* * * * *

The Philippine concerts proved the availability of many of our resident musicians for work of the highest grade, and the committee has undertaken the task of organizing this series of concerts because it believes that with a sufficient number of rehearsals, under capable direction, our home players will be able to render great orchestral compositions efficiently and acceptably.

Mr. Scheel will insist upon frequent and thorough rehearsals of the music; and no labor nor expense will be spared to make the work of preparation complete and the musical results wholly satisfactory.

The committee feels, however, that without a widely spread interest among the people of Philadelphia, its chief object would not be realized. That object is largely to promote the musical culture of the city, and to improve its status as a center of musical effort. Therefore, an appeal is

ade to every Philadelphian who understands what this undertaking
may mean to the city's future musical life for active interest and
o-operation.

Most useful help can be given to the movement by making its object
nown to friends and acquaintances; all personal effort will be an effec-
ive aid to the committee's work.

Whether or not the receipts equal the expenses of the concerts, it is
he hope of the committee that this movement for music in Philadelphia
vill receive hearty encouragement and support from every one who has
pride in the city's artistic life.

Committee:

HENRY WHELEN, JR.
JOHN C. SIMS
EDWARD G. McCOLLIN
OSCAR A. KNIPE
DR. EDWARD I. KEFFER
OLIVER BOYCE JUDSON
JOHN H. INGHAM, Secretary,
508 Chestnut Street

CIRCULAR LETTER MAILED TO PATRONESSES WHO HAD NOT
PURCHASED TICKETS ABOUT TEN DAYS BEFORE SALE
TO PUBLIC, OCTOBER, 1900:

THE PHILADELPHIA ORCHESTRA
85 Performers
MR. FRITZ SCHEEL, Conductor

The Management of the Philadelphia Orchestra wishes to inform
hose interested in the concerts that the sale of season tickets has pro-
gressed most favorably. Of the forty-nine boxes forty-one have been
old, and about thirteen hundred seats have been taken. There now
emain unsold but 140 seats in the Parquet, 103 in the Parquet Circle
nd 76 in the Balcony. Prompt application at Heppe's Piano Rooms,
1115 Chestnut Street, will be necessary to secure choice places. Should
hese seats be disposed of, there will, of course, be no sale of reserved
eats for single concerts.

Such wide-spread support is the best proof that the public of Phila-
elphia has undoubted faith, not only in the musical ability of Mr.
cheel and his men, but also in the value of this effort to advance the
ause of orchestral music in our community. The attitude of the musical
rofession toward the project is clearly set forth in the enclosed circular.

Committee:

HENRY WHELEN, JR.
JOHN C. SIMS
EDWARD G. McCOLLIN
OSCAR A. KNIPE
DR. EDWARD I. KEFFER
OLIVER BOYCE JUDSON
JOHN H. INGHAM.

THE PHILADELPHIA ORCHESTRA
MR. FRITZ SCHEEL, Conductor

Believing that the public would be glad to hear what the Music
Profession in Philadelphia thinks of this undertaking, the committee i
charge has written to a few of the leading musicians, asking for the
views. Extracts from their replies are given below.

The intelligent and keen critical standpoint from which their life
training enables them to judge, gives weight to their words, and th
complete unanimity of opinion which they express is noteworthy.

From Mr. Thomas a'Becket, President, Pennsylvania State Musi
Teachers' Association:

"Without a doubt the best man who has taken up residence in Phil
delphia during the past forty years. This opinion is shared by the old
of our orchestral musicians; also by men who have recently playe
under his conducting. It has been fully demonstrated, first, that M
Scheel has wonderful ability in handling musicians—amateur as well
professional—and drawing from them their best work; second, th
there is in Philadelphia—which I have maintained for twenty-fiv
years—the nucleus for a good orchestra. The great need has been th
proper man to bring together conflicting elements. (The movemen
has, indeed, my heartiest support."

From Dr. Hugh A. Clarke, Professor of Music, University of Pennsy
vania:

"I believe Mr. Scheel to be a leader of first-rate ability in ever
respect. His work during the past winter gives ample evidence of h
high standing as a musician and a conductor. The movement for th
establishment of an orchestra in Philadelphia has my most cordial su
port, as I am convinced that it has now taken the right shape and is
the hands of the right people."

From Mr. W. W. Gilchrist, Principal of the Central Conservatory
Music, Leader of the Mendelssohn Club, Leader of the Harrisbur
Oratorio Society, etc.:

"Those in whose judgment I have confidence speak very highly of him
The movement has my cordial support."

From Dr. Alfred C. Lambdin, Musical Editor, of "The Philadelph
Times."

"To the broad musical knowledge, the imaginative perception, th
technical accomplishment that makes up the interpretive artist of hig
rank, he seems to add those peculiar personal qualities, the power
expressing his musical ideas through the medium of others, that diffe
entiate the real 'conductor.' The value of such a man in any music

community is measured only by his opportunity. The great value of Mr. Scheel's work this winter has been in the fresh and full artistic authority, which he has brought to bear upon our disorganized musical forces here. The two concerts at the Academy abundantly demonstrated what can be done under such leadership and how it can be done. The movement, therefore, to continue that work, and develop it on the lines already laid down, commands my most cordial support."

From Mr. D. D. Wood, Organist of St. Stephen's Church, Instructor at Philadelphia Musical Academy, Teacher of Harmony, Counterpoint, etc.:

"Mr. Scheel is possessed of all those rare qualifications which go to make up a great leader.

"He is most excellent musician of large and varied experience, an earnest and conscientious worker, a man of great personal magnetism, and thoroughly capable of making the very best of the means at his disposal. As a conductor he deserves a place in the very first rank.

"The work accomplished by Mr. Scheel during the past winter has been eminently successful, and deserves the cordial recognition of all true lovers of musical art, and of all who are interested in the progress of that art in our city.

"I am in hearty sympathy with the movement set forth in your circular."